SUMMER

SUMMER

A SPIRITUAL BIOGRAPHY
OF THE SEASON

EDITED BY GARY SCHMIDT
AND SUSAN M. FELCH

ILLUSTRATIONS BY BARRY MOSER

Walking Together, Finding the Way®
SKYLIGHT PATHS®
PUBLISHING
Nashville, Tennessee

Library of Congress Cataloging-in-Publication Data
Summer : a spiritual biography of the season / edited by Gary Schmidt and Susan M. Felch ; illustrations by Barry Moser.
p. cm.
Includes bibliographical references (p.   ).
ISBN 1-59473-083-0 (hardcover)
ISBN 978-1-68336-577-8 (pbk)
1. Summer—Religious aspects—Meditations. 2. Summer—Literary collections. 3. Cookery. I. Schmidt, Gary D. II. Felch, Susan M., 1951–
BL65.N35S93 2005
204'.32—dc22   2005006338
10   9   8   7   6   5   4   3   2

Manufactured in the United States of America
Cover Design: Tim Holtz
Cover Photo: © Juan Olvido, reprinted courtesy of istockphoto.com

SkyLight Paths is creating a place where people of different spiritual traditions come together for challenge and inspiration, a place where we can help each other understand the mystery that lies at the heart of our existence.

SkyLight Paths sees both believers and seekers as a community that increasingly transcends traditional boundaries of religion and denomination—people wanting to learn from each other, walking together, finding the way.

SkyLight Paths, "Walking Together, Finding the Way" and colophon are trademarks of LongHill Partners, Inc., registered in the U.S. Patent and Trademark Office.
Walking Together, Finding the Way
Published by SkyLight Paths Publishing
An Imprint of Turner Publishing Company
4507 Charlotte Avenue, Suite 100
Nashville, TN 37209
Tel (615) 255-2665
www.skylightpaths.com

For Jerry and Jan Fondse,
with thanks for halcyon days
—G. S.

For Harry Weimer,
who cultivated my earliest summers
—S. M. F.

CONTENTS

PART THREE: Family and Community

PART FOUR: Nature and Grace

PREFACE

It would be just right to think that on a summer morning, one of the monks of the Abbey of Reading, perhaps coming out of the church at dawn following prayers, heard the chorus of birds that was welcoming the new day. It may have been that he could smell the freshness of the River Kennet to the south and perhaps, farther away, the Thames flowing eastward to London town. Perhaps beyond the cloister he looked out to the green fields divided by long rows, and from the farms across the river, he heard the sounds of the young lambs and calves, strong now on their legs. And it would be just right to think that this young monk went to the scriptorium, chose a scrap of parchment, dipped his pen in ink, and wrote the lines that became the most famous English lyric of the Middle Ages.

> *Summer is a-coming in,*
> *Loudly sing cuckoo,*
> *Groweth seed and bloweth mead,*
> *And springeth woods anew.*
> *Sing cuckoo.*
> *Ewe now bleateth after lamb,*
> *Loweth after calf the cow,*

Bullock starteth,
Buck now farteth,
Merry sing cuckoo.
Cuckoo, cuckoo,
Well singest thou, cuckoo,
Nor cease thee never now.

Whether this monk crafted this lyric on a summer morn around 1240, or whether he wrote down a song that he had heard, he was recording a verse that celebrated the joys of summer. It is a verse filled with the vibrancy of newness, of life that was starting up again after a long winter and spring, of a world filled with all sorts of creatures in the wild and on the farm. And the sense of their presence filled him with joy and song.

Five centuries earlier, and on the other side of the globe in China, the poet Li Bai also sat down on a summer day and, perhaps more meditatively, surveyed the world around him—a moment recorded in his poem "In the Mountains on a Summer Day."

Gently I stir a white feather fan,
With open shirt sitting in a green wood.
I take off my cap and hang it on a jutting stone;
A wind from the pine-trees trickles on my bare head.

Li Bai's lyric is quiet and reflective, filled too with the pleasure of the sensual, but visual and tactile. The stirring wind, the smell of the pines, the fresh green of the woods—all of these evoke a joy in the summer world that the medieval poet would have shared, though the two poets are separated by time and culture and geography.

When we think of summer, we often think in images: the beach, the shimmers of heat on the subway, the backyard cookout, camp, an ice cream truck jingling through the neighborhood, a playground basketball game, a Fourth of July parade, blooming gardens, the sea, tennis rackets and badminton rackets and baseball gloves and bocce balls, chess in the park, picnics, green and dark thunderstorms, traffic heading out of the city to the Jersey shore, outdoor concerts from a bandstand, popsicles, a sailboat bobbing cheerily on blue waves, a fire hydrant opened and spraying cold water on blistering asphalt and squealing kids. Our impulses on a summer day are much like those of the medieval poet and Li Bai, responding to the warmth and sunlight of this season when everything is growing, when the sun seems close, when the routines of our lives are able to be disrupted by quiet days up in the mountains, our caps hanging on jutted stones—or by more active vacations away from the normal and expected. Summer is celebratory, and in a way, we hope it never ends: "Well singest thou, cuckoo, / Nor cease thee never now."

But of course, it does end—though we hardly notice its progression toward that end. Unlike, say, spring, which begins with its feet in winter slush and ends with its hands up in the air among sunbeams and the scent of lilacs, summer seems to us to remain still. It may end too quickly with the return of autumnal duties and responsibilities, but it seems to *end*, to cease abruptly—not to progress toward that ending. Time in the summer does not seem to move; instead, time *collects*, or perhaps it might be better said to *pool*. One of the spiritual lessons of summer is just that: to allow time to pool. To halt in our headlong rush. To be fully in a particular time. To stop long enough to see what lies around us, rather than to be always merely glimpsing. To sit still on a mountain while the wind sifts through pine needles and trickles down upon us.

In the Christian liturgical year, summer comes in Ordinary Time. Lent, Holy Week, and Pentecost Sunday fifty days later are over. Advent is a very long time away. Between them stretch a length of days that are to be "counted"—"ordinary" in fact comes from "ordinal" and is not meant to suggest that the time is "ordinary" or simply "commonplace," a gray area we pass through between the high sacred holidays of Easter and Christmas. The liturgical calendar insists, in fact, that each day is meaningful and worthy of being counted. It calls us to the summer sense that days matter—even the long and lazy days of summer, or even the heated stay-where-it's-cool days of summer, or even the frenzied holiday days of summer, or even the frustratingly routine days of summer when all the world seems on vacation and you, you alone remain behind to carry on. Every day matters, says summer. Look around you.

How does it matter? The writers in this anthology suggest the kinds of time that summer pools. There is the time for delight and play (stickball on the street, the first cold plunge into the pool), the time for cultivating the world around us (the gardener turning up the soil, the writer turning the dictionary pages), the time for community (the family reunion, the company picnic), the time to more closely love the world of natural things (the trip to the zoo, setting out the annuals), and the time for retreat (the cottage on the lake, the beloved annual vacation trip, the cool spot in the basement). Each of these pools of time carries its own summer lessons; each of them teaches us to pay attention somewhat differently, and in somewhat different directions.

In Sonnet 12, Shakespeare warned the young man that time passes quickly; before we know it, we see "summer's green all girded up in sheaves / Borne on the bier with white and bristly beard." It is an observation that verges on the cliché: "The summer has gone by so quickly," we say. The passing of time may be another spiritual lesson of the season, but with that awareness should come too a sense that our experience in the pools of summer time can change us. We may come to those autumnal routines and responsibilities refreshed, invigorated, ready to see, in Shakespeare's words, "the violet past prime," "sable curls all silvered o'er with white," and "lofty trees ... barren of leaves, / Which erst from heat did canopy the herd."

This is the theme of the Welsh poet William Henry Davies, whose "When on a Summer's Morn" echoes the sentiments of both Li Bai and the medieval poet and suggests that those summer sentiments leave him renewed.

When on a summer's morn I wake,
And open my two eyes,
Out to the clear, born-singing rills
My bird-like spirit flies.
To hear the Blackbird, Cuckoo, Thrush,
Or any bird in song;
And common leaves that hum all day,
Without a throat or tongue.
And when Time strikes the hour for sleep,
Back in my room alone,
My heart has many a sweet bird's song—
And one that's all my own.

Dr. Lehman's Dandelion Wine

Ingredients:

- 4 quarts dandelion flowers
- 4 quarts boiling water
- 4 pounds sugar
- 1 lemon
- 2 oranges

Pour boiling water over the flowers. Let stand 24 hours. Then boil 20 minutes. Put the rind of the lemon and orange in when boiling. Strain through colander. Add the pulp of the lemon and orange sliced in when it is lukewarm. Add a tablespoon of yeast and let stand a week. Than strain it through cheesecloth and put it up. Keep a month before using. If you put it in a jar, do not tighten the lid all at once. (Don't seal too soon, or you will over-pressure the bottles.)

Add yeast when cold, either directly or float it on toast. Let stand for 3 weeks then sieve through cheesecloth. Bottle, but don't cork tightly for at least two months. Should stand for six months before using. If you don't want to wait six months, try quick dandelion wine. Pour one cup white wine over 1 Tbsp. chopped dandelion leaves and let sit for one hour.

PART ONE

Play and Leisure

INTRODUCTION

The number of muscular motions in a golf swing, we are told, is one hundred and twenty-eight. One hundred and twenty-eight! And it doesn't matter whether the swing is good or bad. There are still one hundred and twenty-eight different muscular motions going on. The thought is almost appalling, and to dwell on it must lead to paralysis at the tee. One hundred and twenty-eight! You can get ninety percent of the muscular motions right and still have twelve or thirteen motions completely and awfully wrong. In one swing! Which may explain a lot.

So why do we do it, on a summer afternoon, when the sky is so blue and the grass is so green? Why try to perfect something that is so obviously not perfectible in this mortal world? Or why go to the tennis court to organize feet and knees and twisted torso and arm to hit the backhand that, more often than not, sails long? Or why stand at home plate to coordinate hand and eye in such a way that one might hit a sphere with a polished lunk of wood? Or send disks across waxed cement surfaces to score seven or eight or ten points—unless your black disk is pushed off its square by a loathsome red disk? Or throw a ball down a long alley to get it close, close, close to another ball—but not touch it? Or stand with a flat bat at a wicket and ... well, do whatever one does while standing with a flat bat at a wicket.

Why do we play when the stakes seem so worthless? (And it will not do here to take the high moral plain and say that we play so that we can stay in shape. If this were so, then we might all just as well affirm Winston Churchill's suggestion that golf is a good walk spoiled.)

Summer offers suggestions about our play. In the cycle of seasons, we tend to think of winter as the time when life slows down, when trees are bare and animals move to dormancy and all the frenzied activity of life comes to an end until springtime. But our human and societal experience does not always affirm this, particularly as we have organized our lives apart from the land. For most of us, it is summer that creates the spaces that allow us to live leisurely—if only for a time. We take two or three weeks and head to a vacation spot. Or we craft a long weekend and head to the lake shore or the ocean. Or we spend a Saturday morning watching a holiday parade, and then perhaps Saturday afternoon downtown in the cool darkness of the natural history museum. In the early evening, we go out to the front porch and watch the world go by, or lean back with the newspaper. Later, we go to the bookstore to buy—not *Madame Bovary,* but a beach read.

Even, for many of us, the chores that take up our time in summer seem the chores of leisure. We cut the grass, weed and edge the garden, climb up to the gutters along the eaves and clean them out, hose down the car, prune back the lilacs that have lost their blossoms by now. These are not the chores of spring cleaning or winter survival. There is a pace and quality to them that suggests that, in fact, we could do all this tomorrow or the day after. We are somehow at leisure in a warm world. It is a point that the shepherd Hobbinoll echoes in Edmund Spenser's *The Shepheardes Calendar* (first published in 1579), when he advises the luckless and loveless Colin Cloute to look around him at the summer world that is his field of employment:

> *Lo Colin, here the place, whose pleasaunt syte*
> *From other shades hath wean'd my wandring mynde.*
> *Tell me, what wants me here, to worke delyte?*
> *The simple ayre, the gentle warbling wynde,*

So calme, so coole, as no where else I fynde:
The grassye ground with daintye Daysies dight,
The Bramble bush, where Byrds of every kynde
To the waters fall their tunes attemper right.

Taken from the "June" section of the poem, this passage cele-
brates a world that in one sense is merely the scene for Hobbinoll's
rather unproductive employment. But at the same time in this summery country, he lacks nothing "to worke delyte." He is at leisure.

What is striking here is that nothing in Hobbinoll suggests that
this is a waste of time, that he should be doing something else, that
this is inappropriate, and we would all instead be better off working
to produce tangible matter. Summer sides unrepentantly with Hobbinoll to insist that play and leisure have their place, and are not to
be disdained or soiled with a stain of guilt. The Psalms themselves
declare the pleasures of leisure, in which we may sing songs and play
music in moments when we are not in our work routines (unless
one is a professional musician). Summer provides the time for our
play—that portion of our human experience so vitally necessary to
our sanity, which must allow us to step back for a moment from our
self-importance and our drivenness to provide a larger perspective.

What that larger perspective gives us is a sense of scale. In the
end, it does not matter whether we win a round of golf. Spiritually
speaking, winning may be more dangerous than losing. For unless
we are intemperately consumed with the drive for competition, in
the end, we play golf and tennis and softball and shuffleboard and
cricket for the pleasure of one another's company, for the joy of
community, for the mutuality of the moment. Who would rather
not be with the friend who, having sliced a ball four times in a row
into unreachable high grass, laughs and laughs and laughs at the
sport of it, rather than with the friend who, having hit a decent shot
after all, grouses about how he should have been able to hit it a lot
farther, and shatters his driver against a tree? It is play, insists summer. It is delight; it is merriment. It is a pause in the action, a
moment to let this thought come: maybe I am not so critical to the

world after all, a humbling time when we might dare to believe that stopping and looking round us might be more important than driving toward the distant horizon.

The pieces in this section begin with the near-magic of summer vacation, and move to a close with a mother and child on a beach, and what amounts to an expression of gratitude and thanks that itself sounds like a magical invocation. Along the way are pieces that sharply and acutely recall for us moments and images and experiences that we may have participated in—directly or obliquely— because of the leisures of summer. Beach houses and unexpected accidents, longer times with one's mother, trips of exploration, a pause during a hike through the summery woods and an awareness of their wildness, a rainstorm, an awareness of the tenacity of relationships—these pieces find such things in those leisure moments that the summertime provides. Here, summer says, is refreshment and engagement—which is, after all, why we play.

A Prayer

God of creation, God of the seasons,
bless your creatures with seasons of delight.

Lord of the Sabbath,
you who have established the rhythms of life,
establish in us also the rhythms for human
     prospering;
grant us the good sense to enjoy Sabbath rest in
     this season.

Grant us, moreover, wisdom to know that there
     is a time to play,
a time to cease from our labors,
a time to sense majesty in a blue sky,
     richness in green grass,
     love in faithful friends,
     and joy in our being.

Grant us, then, blue skies this summer, and
   green grass;
grant us faithful friends and the time, strength,
   and spirit for play.
Grant us the wit to know the goodness of this
   creation,
which, blind, defiant, or ungrateful, we despoil.

Send our roots rain; send our hearts ease,
so that we may show in our lives
that we can live rightly in this season of our
   lives
and see it as if for the first time,
in wonder, in awe, and in a spirit of thanksgiving.

Amen.

—James Vanden Bosch

Ray Bradbury

From Dandelion Wine

Some of the most powerful memories of summer come out of our childhood, when we wake up on a June morning and suddenly remember that school is out and that summer stretches in front of us as endlessly as the infinities of space. Everything is different. The old routines are gone. The relentless school bus isn't coming. The bells will be silent in silent hallways. And all the world is leafy green, and will be green, forever and ever.

Of course, it won't always be this way, and even as children we know, if someone were to ask, that summer must, must come to an end. But that isn't how it feels on that first morning when even the smells are different, and we get up as early as we did for the mid-winter trek to school, just so that we won't miss anything.

> *This is summer vacation—the keen sense that the world has shifted into new patterns of delight, and game and joy, and the gloriously embraced illusion that those patterns will not end.*

This is summer vacation—the keen sense that the world has shifted into new patterns of delight, and game and joy, and the gloriously embraced illusion that those patterns will not end.

This is the sense of summer that fantasy writer Ray Bradbury creates in the opening to *Dandelion Wine* as Douglas Spaulding wakes up on that first morning of summer vacation and creates the new patterns in his town. He is twelve already, on the very cusp of adolescence; this is his last summer of childhood. But the magic of his imagination is still powerful, and if the hint that the magic is coming to an end makes this passage poignant—for childhood, like summer, embraces the illusion of permanence—it is nonetheless evocative: Though we too slam open the doors and step into a new season, we remember the illusion and look around us, half-wondering if it might be true after all.

From *Dandelion Wine*

It was a quiet morning, the town covered over with darkness and at ease in bed. Summer gathered in the weather, the wind had the proper touch, the breathing of the world was long and warm and slow. You had only to rise, lean from your window, and know that this indeed was the first real time of freedom and living, this was the first morning of summer.

Douglas Spaulding, twelve, freshly wakened, let summer idle him on its early-morning stream. Lying in this third-story cupola bedroom, he felt the tall power it gave him, riding high in the June wind, the grandest tower in town. At night, when the trees washed together, he flashed his gaze like a beacon from this lighthouse in all directions over swarming seas of elm and oak and maple. Now ...

"Boy," whispered Douglas.

A whole summer ahead to cross off the calendar, day by day. Like the goddess Siva in the travel books, he saw his hands jump everywhere, pluck sour apples, peaches, and midnight plums. He would be clothed in trees and bushes and rivers. He would freeze, gladly, in the hoarfrosted ice-house door. He would bake, happily, with ten thousand chickens in Grandma's kitchen.

But now—a familiar task awaited him.

One night each week he was allowed to leave his father, his mother, and his younger brother Tom asleep in their small house next door and run here, up the dark spiral stairs to his grandparents' cupola, and in this sorcerer's tower sleep with thunders and visions, to wake before the crystal jingle of milk bottles and perform his ritual magic.

He stood at the open window in the dark, took a deep breath and exhaled.

The street lights, like candles on a black cake, went out. He exhaled again and again and the stars began to vanish.

Douglas smiled. He pointed a finger.

There, and there. Now over here, and here ...

Yellow squares were cut in the dim morning earth as house lights winked slowly on. A sprinkle of windows came suddenly alight miles off in dawn country.

"Everyone yawn. Everyone up."

The great house stirred below.

"Grandpa, get your teeth from the water glass!" He waited a decent interval. "Grandma and Great-grandma, fry hot cakes!"

The warm scent of fried batter rose in the drafty halls to stir the boarders, the aunts, the uncles, the visiting cousins, in their rooms.

"Street where all the Old People live, wake up! Miss Helen Loomis, Colonel Freeleigh, Miss Bentley! Cough, get up, take pills, move around! Mr. Jonas, hitch up your horse, get your junk wagon out and around!"

The bleak mansions across the town ravine opened baleful dragon eyes. Soon, in the morning avenues below, two old women would glide their electric Green Machine, waving at all the dogs. "Mr. Tridden, run to the carbarn!" Soon, scattering hot blue sparks above it, the town trolley would sail the rivering brick streets.

"Ready John Huff, Charlie Woodman?" whispered Douglas to the Street of Children. "Ready!" to the baseballs sponged deep in wet lawns, to rope swings hung empty in trees.

"Mom, Dad, Tom, wake up."

Clock alarms tinkled faintly. The courthouse clock boomed. Birds leaped from trees like a net thrown by his hand, singing. Douglas, conducting an orchestra, pointed to the eastern sky.

The sun began to rise.

He folded his arms and smiled a magician's smile. Yes, sir, he thought, everyone jumps, everyone runs when I yell. It'll be a fine season.

He gave the town a last snap of his fingers.

Doors slammed open; people stepped out.

Summer 1928 began.

Ronna N. Welsh

"CAMP FOOD"

Summer camp is about nothing if it is not about escape—though "escape" may seem an odd word for it. Going to camp means embracing routines just as strict as those of school. In fact, the routines are stricter, for they govern every waking moment. The counselors live closer to you than a teacher, the food is more prescribed, the activities just as demanding. And yet, none of that seems a just description of summer camp.

Despite the prescriptions, camp is an escape from the expected, the ordinary, the regular. It is a movement away from those who know us so well that they can predict our responses—and so we give them those responses because they can be predicted; we can do nothing else. But summer camp is the opportunity to try the new: plunging into a waterfall, weaving lanyards, eating awful corn dogs, shooting a B.B. gun at a tattered paper target, identifying red oak leaves and white pine needles and—too late—poison sumach. It is a chance to explore, yes; to push ourselves, yes; to make new friends, yes. All these we expect. But perhaps most powerfully, it is also the chance to reinvent ourselves away from the questioning,

> *C*amp is an escape from the expected, the ordinary, the regular.

unbelieving, scornful eyes of those who would not allow such re-invention.

Ronna Welsh pictures summer camp as her opportunity to experience the world in ways that she could not in the confines of suburbia. Here, away from the literal and metaphoric bright lights, she discovers the stars, and food, and friendship, and vocation, and—herself. And now, as an adult looking back, she thinks of camp not with sentiment alone but with gratitude for the chance to escape and to come back changed.

"CAMP FOOD"

With the onset of summer, I feel oddly displaced. Disorienting heat aside, summer prescribes for me a potent dose of nostalgia which rattles my sense of the present. I ache for specific things: misty mountain air dusted with campfire smoke, toasted marshmallows. The memories of childhood and my first taste of freedom.

It was at overnight camp that I saw my first starlit sky. I was nine years old and clinically shy about advertising my myopia in public. I'd tote thick glasses to the occasional softball game, but never to the social canteen or anywhere else for public purview. Before I first wore glasses at night, my eyes had counted only three stars in the entire central Pennsylvania sky, a canvas permanently peppered with light. Once magnified, the web of constellations paralyzed me like a trapped insect. I remember standing and gazing at the field of storybook blue and gold and feeling true awe for the first time. Just as this moment acutely enlarged my universe, camp profoundly broadened my world.

At camp, I discovered bras and Maxi-pads, perfected *schmugee* making (wet toilet-paper pods that stuck to the ceiling), wore blue eye shadow and pink tube tops, and teased my friend's permed hair. Camp was about ear piercings, wedgies, pre-pubescent boys, and an aching devotion to Harry Chapin. It was about bad musicals that we all loved and great acoustic guitar. And camp was about Julie and Jamie, my seasonal best friends, and the solidarity of bunk number eight.

But mostly, camp was a study in kid spirit, sparked by the greatest freedom ever experienced by this young, shy girl. My world of chalkboards and suburbs, of mean boys and bratty girls, disappeared at the arbored entrance to this secluded space. At camp, I acquired a fluency in curse words and gave a go at humor. I led the Nutella Chocolate Sandwich Spread Movement, which left peanut butter stuck in the jar. And in an act of famed defiance, I consumed enough sugar cereal to compensate for what my parents refused me at home. Sure there were consequences: I eventually lost a filling to taffy sticks and a slim figure to Snickers bars. I invariably shamed my grandfather with my dirty mouth. But my disrepute was mine. I wore it proudly.

Camp was not about food, surely, but food inspired our greatest excesses. I consumed my weight in corn fritters each week, followed by binges on blueberry blintzes and sloppy joes. At camp, I roasted umpteen marshmallows and ate my first Neapolitan ice cream bar. But if camp food was indulgent (think sugar, think fried), it was also often disgusting. The top three worst things I've ever eaten in my life are Camp Reeta's brisket, green beans, and chicken pot pie.

Mealtime at Camp Reeta wasn't about the food, anyway. The dining hall became a forum for chanting and singing, for gossip, for food fights, and for girl chats. It was a place to break *challah* and drink "wine" juice on Shabbat. It was where we acquired domestic skills (how to scrape and stack plates) and where we practiced table decorum, including proper pleasantries ("Pass the ★!#★! Corn Puffs, PLEEEEZE!").

Generally, meals were a comfort, and only occasionally, like the time they served undercooked chicken in the summer of '78, a source of pain. "The bird," I wrote home, in what was to be the infamous birth of my food writing career, "was defective."

Maybe the "food poisoning" letter smacked of a familiar family satire or unveiled a precious attempt at precociousness. Maybe it reflected an endearing naïveté. In any case, my mom saved it. For me, today, it conjures up images of crisp rolls of white paper, unfurled atop mess hall tables. It evokes the smell of wet wood benches, soaked in Kool-Aid, and of chants from spirited girls, caught up in just being themselves.

I fold the letter with care. It belongs to my parents, and I implore them to preserve it well. "This is more of my childhood than you'll ever know," I want to explain, acutely aware, now, of the shortcomings of adult words in expressing kids' complex emotions. I want to tell them that camp was about becoming more of myself than my parents or schoolteachers or school friends ever realized, how it was my initiation into real girlhood, a community closed to shy preteens the rest of the year. I, at least, will cherish this letter as an artifact of immunity, a time when the choice to eat sugar cereal in defiance of a parental prohibition, much like the choice to leave my parents for two months each year, was a notably independent act.

Scott Cairns

"ACCEPTING BLOOD" AND "YELLOW"

The lazy, playful days of summer are often marked by the sharp intrusion of more painful realities, whether these be the memories of taunts from fellow campers or, as here in the first of Scott Cairns's poems, the sudden gush of blood from an injured arm. A day at the beach amidst the jostling rivalry of brothers turns suddenly into a panicked trip to the emergency room. Here at the hospital there are nurses and gauze and sutures and all the accoutrements of modern medicine. Yet, Cairns moves us more deeply into that day, that wound, those brothers: *accepting* blood mingles helplessness and responsibility, fragility and tenacity, knowing when to hold on and when to let go.

> *M*omentous decisions are not always bound up with momentous events; they may come upon us fleetingly in the casual afternoon of a hot summer day.

Such momentous decisions are not always bound up with momentous events; they may come upon us fleetingly in the casual afternoon of a hot summer day. The girl fingering the light yellow dress is caught, too, in a moment of decision. When we, with the poet, urge her to "try it on," we encourage her—and ourselves—toward hope and play, if only in the momentary grasping of beauty that will lighten our day.

Accepting Blood

As my brother lost his footing
along the slick weeds beside our
beach house, keeping his balance meant
shooting his arm through the glass
of a side window. His blood
was immediate and simple.
There wasn't time to pull back
his clothing, to inspect
the damage, or to give much thought
to anything, only time
to grip him where his coat
was reddest, and to grip him hard
at the hinge of his shoulder.
I held him like that until his blood
had colored most of what I wore,
until we reached the hospital,
where the nurse could finally
replace my hands with gauze,
and there was nothing left
to do, but let him go.

Yellow

The town is much larger than you recall,
but you can still recognize the poor.
They vote to lose every chance they get, their faces
carry the tattoo of past embarrassments,

they are altogether too careful. This girl,
here in the print dress, pretending to shop
for an extravagance, the too slow way
her hand lingers between the colors along

the rack, her tentative hold on the clasp—
sure signs she knows she has no business here.
Soon enough she'll go home again with nothing
especially new in her hand. But no one

needs to rush things. The afternoon itself
is unhurried, and the lighted air outside
the store has lilacs in it. Her hand finds
a yellow dress. I think she should try it on.

Jamaica Kincaid

"The Circling Hand"
from *Annie John*

For a schoolgirl on holiday, the rhythms of household life can be a soothing counterpoint to the stress and competition that lie in wait in the classroom. Bathing, eating, brushing teeth, buying the groceries, doing the laundry—these ordinary tasks link mother and daughter, bringing them together into a cozy conspiracy of domesticity. Jamaica Kincaid catalogues the gentle rituals, the leisurely pace that mark a Caribbean household.

> Summer's leisure offers a scale on which we balance the joys and failings of ordinary life, lived in ordinary families, in ordinary time.

But if summer strengthens family ties through shared leisure and shared work, its enhanced intimacy stretches these ties as well, thinning the fabric of faithfulness, opening up a seam of disappointment and incipient sorrow. A shared bath may become a defense against the pain of infidelity; a stroll through the marketplace, a glimpse into the knotted heart of love. Summer's leisure offers a scale on which we balance the joys and failings of ordinary life, lived in ordinary families, in ordinary time.

"The Circling Hand" from *Annie John*

During my holidays from school, I was allowed to stay in bed until long after my father had gone to work. He left our house every weekday at the stroke of seven by the Anglican church bell. I would lie in bed awake, and I could hear all the sounds my parents made as they prepared for the day ahead. As my mother made my father his breakfast, my father would shave, using his shaving brush that had an ivory handle and a razor that matched; then he would step outside to the little shed he had built for us as a bathroom, to quickly bathe in water that he had instructed my mother to leave outside overnight in the dew. That way, the water would be very cold, and he believed that cold water strengthened his back. If I had been a boy, I would have gotten the same treatment, but since I was a girl, and on top of that went to school only with other girls, my mother would always add some hot water to my bathwater to take off the chill. On Sunday afternoons, while I was in Sunday school, my father took a hot bath; the tub was half filled with plain water, and then my mother would add a large caldronful of water in which she had just boiled some bark and leaves from a bay-leaf tree. The bark and leaves were there for no reason other than that he liked the smell. He would then spend hours lying in this bath, studying his pool coupons or drawing examples of pieces of furniture he planned to make. When I came home from Sunday school, we would sit down to our Sunday dinner.

My mother and I often took a bath together. Sometimes it was just a plain bath, which didn't take very long. Other times, it was a special bath in which the barks and flowers of many different trees, together with all sorts of oils, were boiled in the same large caldron. We would then sit in this bath in a darkened room with a strange-smelling candle burning away. As we sat in this bath, my mother would bathe different parts of my body; then she would do the same to herself. We took these baths after my mother had consulted with her obeah woman, and with her mother and a trusted friend, and all three of them had confirmed that from the look of things around our house—the way a small scratch on my instep had turned into a small sore, then a large sore, and how long it had taken to heal; the way a dog she knew, and a friendly dog at that, suddenly turned and bit her; how a porcelain bowl she had carried from one eternity and hoped to carry into the next suddenly slipped out of her capable hands and broke into pieces the size of grains of sand; how words she spoke in jest to a friend had been completely misunderstood—one of the many women my father had loved, had never married, but with whom he had had children was trying to harm my mother and me by setting bad spirits on us.

When I got up, I placed my bedclothes and my nightie in the sun to air out, brushed my teeth, and washed and dressed myself. My mother would then give me my breakfast, but since, during my holidays, I was not going to school, I wasn't forced to eat an enormous breakfast of porridge, eggs, an orange or half a grapefruit, bread and butter, and cheese. I could get away with just some bread and butter and cheese and porridge and cocoa. I spent the day following my mother around and observing the way she did everything. When we went to the grocer's, she would point out to me the reason she bought each thing. I was shown a loaf of bread or a pound of butter from at least ten different angles. When we went to market, if that day she wanted to buy some crabs she would inquire from the person selling them if they came from near Parham, and if the person said yes my mother did not buy the crabs. In Parham was the leper colony. and my mother was convinced that the crabs ate nothing but the food from the lepers' own plates. If we were then to eat the crabs, it wouldn't be long before we were lepers ourselves and living unhappily in the leper colony.

How important I felt to be with my mother. For many people, their wares and provisions laid out in front of them, would brighten up when they saw her coming and would try hard to get her attention. They would dive underneath their stalls and bring out goods even better than what they had on display. They were disappointed when she held something up in the air, looked at it, turning it this way and that, and then, screwing up her face, said, "I don't think so," and turned and walked away—off to another stall to see if someone who only last week had sold her some delicious christophine had something that was just as good. They would call out after her turned back that next week they expected to have eddoes or dasheen or whatever, and my mother would say, "We'll see," in a very disbelieving tone of voice. If then we went to Mr. Kenneth, it would be only for a few minutes, for he knew exactly what my mother wanted and always had it ready for her. Mr. Kenneth had known me since I was a small child, and he would always remind me of little things I had done then as he fed me a piece of raw liver he had set aside for me. It was one of the few things I liked to eat, and, to boot, it pleased my mother to see me eat something that was so good for me, and she would tell me in great detail the effect the raw liver would have on my red blood corpuscles.

We walked home in the hot midmorning sun mostly without event. When I was much smaller, quite a few times while I was walking with my mother she would suddenly grab me and wrap me up in her skirt and drag me along with her as if in a great hurry. I would hear an angry voice saying angry things, and then, after we had passed the angry voice, my mother would release me. Neither my mother nor my father ever came straight out and told me anything, but I had put two and two together and I knew that it was one of the women that my father had loved and with whom he had had a child or children, and who never forgave him for marrying my mother and having me. It was one of those women who were always trying to harm my mother and me, and they must have loved my father very much, for not once did any of them ever try to hurt him, and whenever he passed them on the street it was as if he and these women had never met.

When we got home, my mother started to prepare our lunch (pumpkin soup with droppers, banana fritters with salt fish stewed in antroba and tomatoes, fungie with salt fish stewed in antroba and tomatoes, or pepper pot, all depending on what my mother had found at market that day). As my mother went about from pot to pot, stirring one, adding something to the other, I was ever in her wake. As she dipped into a pot of boiling something or other to taste for correct seasoning, she would give me a taste of it also, asking me what I thought. Not that she really wanted to know what I thought, for she had told me many times that my taste buds were not quite developed yet, but it was just to include me in everything. While she made our lunch, she would also keep an eye on her washing. If it was a Tuesday and the colored clothes had been starched, as she placed them on the line I would follow, carrying a basket of clothespins for her. While the starched colored clothes were being dried on the line, the white clothes were being whitened on the stone heap. It was a beautiful stone heap that my father had made for her: an enormous circle of stones, about six inches high, in the middle of our yard. On it the soapy white clothes were spread out; as the sun dried them, bleaching out all stains, they had to be made wet again by dousing them with buckets of water. On my holidays, I did this for my mother. As I watered the clothes, she would come up behind me, instructing me to get the clothes thoroughly wet, showing me a shirt that I should turn over so that the sleeves were exposed.

Over our lunch, my mother and father talked to each other about the houses my father had to build; how disgusted he had become with one of his apprentices, or with Mr. Oatie; what they thought of my schooling so far; what they thought of the noises Mr. Jarvis and his friends made for so many days when they locked themselves up inside Mr. Jarvis's house and drank rum and ate fish they had caught themselves and danced to the music of an accordion that they took turns playing. On and on they talked. As they talked, my head would move from side to side, looking at them. When my eyes rested on my father, I didn't think very much of the way he looked. But when my eyes rested on my mother, I found her beautiful. Her head looked as if it should be on a sixpence. What a beautiful long neck, and long plaited hair, which she pinned up around the crown of her head because when her hair hung down it made her too hot. Her nose was the shape of a flower on the brink of opening. Her mouth, moving up and down as she ate and talked at the same time, was such a beautiful mouth I could have looked at it forever if I had to and not mind. Her lips were wide and almost thin, and when she said certain words I could see small parts of big white teeth—so big, and pearly, like some nice buttons on one of my dresses. I didn't much care about what she said when she was in this mood with my father. She made him laugh so. She could hardly say a word before he would burst out laughing. We ate our food, I cleared the table, we said goodbye to my father as he went back to work, I helped my mother with the dishes, and then we settled into the afternoon.

G. K. Chesterton

"A Piece of Chalk" from *Tremendous Trifles*

What can be more delightful than the prospect of a whole day doing nothing? Why, an actual day doing nothing, of course! And how full those nothings can be—drinking the second cup of tea, stretching bare toes out on the barely warmed morning deck, stroking the cat as he wanders by, turning the first page of a long-awaited novel.

G. K. Chesterton takes us along on his day of doing nothing. He rustles up brown paper from his landlady, all the while musing on his own ineptitude in wrapping parcels and the capacious texture of that wrapping material. He puts some colored chalk in his pocket and idly contemplates the great English epic that might catalogue all the contents of that pocket. He sets out for a walk on the Sussex downs and sits down to draw.

And suddenly the nothingness of this leisurely day opens up to

> Suddenly the nothingness of this leisurely day opens up to the sky and down to the ocean, back to ancient writers and forward to eternity.

the sky and down to the ocean, back to ancient writers and forward to eternity—a piece of chalk beckoning us to recall and create, to wonder and laugh, at ourselves and our world.

"A Piece of Chalk"

I remember one splendid morning, all blue and silver, in the summer holidays when I reluctantly tore myself away from the task of doing nothing in particular, and put on a hat of some sort and picked up a walking-stick, and put six very bright-coloured chalks in my pocket. I then went into the kitchen (which, along with the rest of the house, belonged to a very square and sensible old woman in a Sussex village), and asked the owner and occupant of the kitchen if she had any brown paper. She had a great deal; in fact, she had too much; and she mistook the purpose and the rationale of the existence of brown paper. She seemed to have an idea that if a person wanted brown paper he must be wanting to tie up parcels; which was the last thing I wanted to do; indeed, it is a thing which I have found to be beyond my mental capacity. Hence she dwelt very much on the varying qualities of toughness and endurance in the material. I explained to her that I only wanted to draw pictures on it, and that I did not want them to endure in the least; and that from my point of view, therefore, it was a question, not of tough consistency, but of responsive surface, a thing comparatively irrelevant in a parcel. When she understood that I wanted to draw she offered to overwhelm me with note-paper, apparently supposing that I did my notes and correspondence on old brown paper wrappers from motives of economy.

I then tried to explain the rather delicate logical shade, that I not only liked brown paper, but liked the quality of brownness in paper, just as I liked the quality of brownness in October woods, or in beer, or in the peat-streams of the North. Brown paper represents the primal twilight of the first toil of creation, and with a bright-coloured chalk or two you can pick out points of fire in it, sparks of gold, and blood-red, and sea-green, like the first fierce stars that sprang out of divine darkness. All this I said (in an off-hand way) to the old woman; and I put the brown paper in my pocket along with the chalks, and possibly other things. I suppose every one must have reflected how primeval and how poetical are the things that one carries in one's pocket; the pocket-knife, for instance, the type of all human tools, the infant of the sword. Once I planned to write a book of poems entirely about the things in my pocket. But I found it would be too long; and the age of the great epics is past.

With my stick and my knife, my chalks and my brown paper, I went out on to the great downs. I crawled across those colossal contours that express the best quality of England, because they are at the same time soft and strong. The smoothness of them has the same meaning as the smoothness of great cart-horses, or the smoothness of the beech-tree; it declares in the teeth of our timid and cruel theories that the mighty are merciful. As my eye swept the landscape, the landscape was as kindly as any of its cottages, but for power it was like an earthquake. The villages in the immense valley were safe, one could see, for centuries; yet the lifting of the whole land was like the lifting of one enormous wave to wash them all away.

I crossed one swell of living turf after another, looking for a place to sit down and draw. Do not, for heaven's sake, imagine I was going to sketch from Nature. I was going to draw devils and seraphim, and blind old gods that men worshipped before the dawn of right, and saints in robes of angry crimson, and seas of strange green, and all the sacred or monstrous symbols that look so well in bright colours on brown paper. They are much better worth drawing than Nature; also they are much easier to draw. When a cow came slouching by in the field next to me, a mere artist might have drawn it; but I always get wrong in the hind legs of quadrupeds. So I drew the soul of the cow; which I saw there plainly walking before me in the sunlight; and the soul was all purple and silver, and had seven horns and the mystery that belongs to all the beasts. But though I could not with a crayon get the best out of the landscape, it does not follow that the landscape was not getting the best out of me. And this, I think, is the mistake that people make about the old poets who lived before Wordsworth, and were supposed not to care very much about Nature because they did not describe it much.

They preferred writing about great men to writing about great hills; but they sat on the great hills to write it. They gave out much less about Nature, but they drank in, perhaps, much more. They painted the white robes of their holy virgins with the blinding snow, at which they had stared all day. They blazoned the shields of their paladins with the purple and gold of many heraldic sunsets. The greenness of a thousand green leaves clustered into the live green figure of Robin Hood. The blueness of a score of forgotten skies became the blue robes of the Virgin. The inspiration went in like sunbeams and came out like Apollo.

But as I sat scrawling these silly figures on the brown paper, it began to dawn on me, to my great disgust, that I had left one chalk, and that a most exquisite and essential chalk, behind. I searched all my pockets, but I could not find any white chalk. Now, those who are acquainted with all the philosophy (nay, religion) which is typified in the art of drawing on brown paper, know that white is positive and essential. I cannot avoid remarking here upon a moral significance. One of the wise and awful truths which this brown-paper art reveals, is this, that white is a colour. It is not a mere absence of colour; it is a shining and affirmative thing, as fierce as red, as definite as black. When, so to speak, your pencil grows red-hot, it draws roses; when it grows white-hot, it draws stars. And one of the two or three defiant verities of the best religious morality, of real Christianity, for example, is exactly this same thing; the chief assertion of religious morality is that white is a colour. Virtue is not the absence of vices or the avoidance of moral dangers; virtue is a vivid and separate thing, like pain or a particular smell. Mercy does not mean not being cruel or sparing people revenge or punishment; it means a plain and positive thing like the sun, which one has either seen or not seen.

Chastity does not mean abstention from sexual wrong; it means something flaming, like Joan of Arc. In a word, God paints in many colours; but He never paints so gorgeously, I had almost said so gaudily, as when He paints in white. In a sense our age has realised this fact, and expressed it in our sullen costume. For if it were really true that white was a blank and colourless thing, negative and non-committal, then white would be used instead of black and grey for the funeral dress of this pessimistic period. We should see city gentlemen in frock coats of spotless silver satin, with top hats as white as wonderful arum lilies. Which is not the case.

Meanwhile, I could not find my chalk.

I sat on the hill in a sort of despair. There was no town nearer than Chichester at which it was even remotely probable that there would be such a thing as an artist's colourman. And yet, without white, my absurd little pictures would be as pointless as the world would be if there were no good people in it. I stared stupidly round, racking my brain for expedients. Then I suddenly stood up and roared with laughter, again and again, so that the cows stared at me and called a committee. Imagine a man in the Sahara regretting that he had no sand for his hour-glass. Imagine a gentleman in mid-ocean wishing that he had brought some salt water with him for his chemical experiments. I was sitting on an immense warehouse of white chalk. The landscape was made entirely out of white chalk. White chalk was piled more miles until it met the sky. I stooped and broke a piece off the rock I sat on: it did not mark so well as the shop chalks do; but it gave the effect. And I stood there in a trance of pleasure, realising that this Southern England is not only a grand peninsula, and a tradition and a civilisation; it is something even more admirable. It is a piece of chalk.

Richard Jefferies

"Meadow Thoughts" from *The Life in the Fields*

Summer is a time of stillness, if only we have the ears to hear it. And with stillness come broad spaces and long reaches of time—those expanses of infinity that both swallow up our own small selves and bear us out into the grand universe.

Richard Jefferies, a nineteenth-century novelist and essayist, takes us into the English meadows, and here, too, as in Chesterton's essay, we are dwarfed by nature. The natural world is not backdrop, canvas, or scroll—not even thick brown paper—onto which we scrawl our messy stories. It is its own immensity, filled with a "wondrousness" that words cannot begin to describe. Indeed, Jefferies finds it hard even to read in summer and impossible to concentrate on writing when he is sitting out of doors. "Such solace and solitude ... cannot be painted," nor written, nor even sung, perhaps.

> Summer is a time of stillness, if only we have the ears to hear it. And with stillness come broad spaces and long reaches of time—those expanses of infinity that both swallow up our own small selves and bear us out into the grand universe.

Yet, in the calm, deepening days of summer we may find our way back to the old house, the country road, the deserted garden, the great wall, to that centering of our selves within immensity, to an "abounding hope," which calls forth quiet Psalms of praise.

"Meadow Thoughts"

The old house stood by the silent country road, secluded by many a long, long mile, and yet again secluded within the great walls of the garden. Often and often I rambled up to the milestone which stood under an oak, to look at the chipped inscription low down—"To London, 79 miles." So far away, you see, that the very inscription was cut at the foot of the stone, since no one would be likely to want that information. It was half hidden by docks and nettles, despised and unnoticed. A broad land this seventy-nine miles—how many meadows and cornfields, hedges and woods, in that distance?—wide enough to seclude any house, to hide it like an acorn in the grass. Those who have lived all their lives in remote places do not feel the remoteness. No one else seemed to be conscious of the breadth that separated the place from the great centre, but it was, perhaps, that consciousness which deepened the solitude to me. It made the silence more still; the shadows of the oaks yet slower in their movement; everything more earnest. To convey a full impression of the intense concentration of Nature in the meadows is very difficult—everything is so utterly oblivious of man's thought and man's heart. The oaks stand—quiet, still—so still that the lichen loves them. At their feet the grass grows, and heeds nothing. Among it the squirrels leap, and their little hearts are as far away from you or me as the very wood of the oaks. The sunshine settles itself in the valley by the brook, and abides there whether we come or not. Glance through the gap in the hedge by the oak, and see how concentrated it is—all of it, every blade of grass, and leaf, and flower, and living creature, finch or squirrel. It is mesmerised upon itself. Then I used to feel that it really was seventy-nine miles to London, and not an hour or two only by rail, really all those miles. A great, broad province of green furrow and ploughed furrow between the old house and the city of the world. Such solace and solitude seventy-nine miles thick cannot be painted; the trees cannot be placed far enough away in perspective. It is necessary to stay in it like the oaks to know it.

Lime-tree branches overhung the corner of the garden-wall, whence a view was easy of the silent and dusty road, till over-arching oaks concealed it. The white dust heated by the sunshine, the green hedges, and the heavily massed trees, white clouds rolled together in the sky, a footpath opposite lost in the fields, as you might thrust a stick into the grass, tender lime leaves caressing the cheek, and silence. That is, the silence of the fields. If a breeze rustled the boughs, if a greenfinch called, if the cart-mare in the meadow shook herself, making the earth and air tremble by her with the convulsion of her mighty muscles, these were not sounds, they were the silence itself. So sensitive to it as I was, in its turn it held me firmly, like the fabled spells of old time. The mere touch of a leaf was a talisman to bring me under the enchantment, so that I seemed to feel and know all that was proceeding among the grass-blades and in the bushes. Among the limetrees along the wall the birds never built, though so close and sheltered. They built everywhere but there. To the broad coping-stones of the wall under the lime boughs speckled thrushes came almost hourly, sometimes to peer out and reconnoitre if it was safe to visit the garden, sometimes to see if a snail had climbed up the ivy. Then they dropped quietly down into the long strawberry patch immediately under. The cover of strawberries is the constant resource of all creeping things; the thrushes looked round every plant and under every leaf and runner. One toad always resided there, often two, and as you gathered a ripe strawberry you might catch sight of his black eye watching you take the fruit he had saved for you.

Down the road skims an eave-swallow, swift as an arrow, his white back making the sun-dried dust dull and dingy; he is seeking a pool for mortar, and will waver to and fro by the brook below till he finds a convenient place to alight. Thence back to the eave here, where for forty years he and his ancestors built in safety. Two white butterflies fluttering round each other rise over the limes, once more up over the house, and soar on till their white shows no longer against the illumined air. A grasshopper calls on the sward by the strawberries, and immediately fillips himself over seven leagues of grass blades. Yonder a line of men and women file across the field, seen for a moment as they pass a gateway, and the hay changes from hay-colour to green behind them as they turn the under but still sappy side upwards. They are working hard, but it looks easy, slow, and sunny. Finches fly out from the hedgerow to the over-turned hay. Another butterfly, a brown one, floats along the dusty road—the only traveller yet. The white clouds are slowly passing behind the oaks, large puffed clouds, like deliberate loads of hay, leaving little wisps and flecks behind them caught in the sky. How pleasant it would be to read in the shadow! There is a broad shadow on the sward by the strawberries cast by a tall and fine-grown American crab tree. The very place for a book; and although I know it is useless, yet I go and fetch one and dispose myself on the grass.

I can never read in summer out of doors. Though in shadow the bright light fills it, summer shadows are broadest daylight. The page is so white and hard, the letters so very black, the meaning and drift not quite intelligible, because neither eye nor mind will dwell upon it. Human thoughts and imaginings written down are pale and feeble in bright summer light. The eye wanders away, and rests more lovingly on greensward and green lime leaves. The mind wanders yet deeper and farther into the dreamy mystery of the azure sky. Once now and then, determined to write down that mystery and delicious sense while actually in it, I have brought out table and ink and paper, and sat there in the midst of the summer day. Three words, and where is the thought? Gone. The paper is so obviously paper, the ink so evidently ink, the pen so stiff; all so inadequate. You want colour, flexibility, light, sweet low sound—all these to paint it and play it in music, at the same time you want something that will answer to and record in one touch the strong throb of life and the thought or feeling, or whatever it is that goes out into the earth and sky and space, endless as a beam of light. The very shade of the pen on the paper tells you how utterly hopeless it is to express these things. There is the shade and the brilliant gleaming whiteness; now tell me in plain written words the simple contrast of the two. Not in twenty pages, for the bright light shows the paper in its common fibre-ground, coarse aspect, in its reality, not as a mind-tablet.

The delicacy and beauty of thought or feeling is so extreme that it cannot be inked in; it is like the green and blue of field and sky, of veronica flower and grass blade, which in their own existence throw light and beauty on each other, but in artificial colours repel. Take the table indoors again, and the book: the thoughts and imaginings of others are vain, and of your own too deep to be written. For the mind is filled with the exceeding beauty of these things, and their great wondrousness and marvel. Never yet have I been able to write what I felt about the sunlight only. Colour and form and light are as magic to me. It is a trance. It requires a language of ideas to convey it. It is ten years since I last reclined on that grass plot, and yet I have been writing of it as if it was yesterday, and every blade of grass is as visible and as real to me now as then. They were greener towards the house, and more brown tinted on the margin of the strawberry bed, because towards the house the shadow rested longest. By the strawberries the fierce sunlight burned them.

The sunlight put out the books I brought into it just as it put out the fire on the hearth indoors. The tawny flames floating upwards could not bite the crackling sticks when the full beams came pouring on them. Such extravagance of light overcame the little fire till it was screened from the power of the heavens. So here in the shadow of the American crab tree the light of the sky put out the written pages. For this beautiful and wonderful light excited a sense of some likewise beautiful and wonderful truth, some unknown but grand thought hovering as a swallow above. The swallows hovered and did not alight, but they were there. An inexpressible thought quivered in the azure overhead; it could not be fully grasped, but there was a sense and feeling of its presence. Before that mere sense of its presence the weak and feeble pages, the small fires of human knowledge, dwindled and lost meaning. There was something here that was not in the books. In all the philosophies and searches of mind there was nothing that could be brought to face it, to say, This is what it intends, this is the explanation of the dream. The very grass-blades confounded the wisest, the tender lime leaf put them to shame, the grasshopper derided them, the sparrow on the wall chirped his scorn. The books were put out, unless a screen were placed between them and the light of the sky—that is, an assumption, so as to make an artificial mental darkness. Grant some assumptions—that is, screen off the light—and in that darkness everything was easily arranged, this thing here and that yonder. But Nature grants no assumptions, and the books were put out. There is something beyond the philosophies in the light, in the grass-blades, the leaf, the grasshopper, the sparrow on the wall. Some day the great and beautiful thought which hovers on the confines of the mind will at last alight. In that is hope, the whole sky is full of abounding hope. Something beyond the books, that is consolation.

T'ao Ch'ien

"READING *THE BOOK OF HILLS AND SEAS*"

T'ao Ch'ien catalogues the joys of summer: green grasses and trees, birds and spring wine, garden produce and gentle rains, and—best of all—solitude and a good book. For T'ao Ch'ien tells a reverse tale to match the one told by Richard Jeffries's. If summer's unflinching sunlight can extinguish the words on the page, its quiet hours also invite us to lose ourselves in the stories those words can tell.

> *I*f summer's unflinching sunlight can extinguish the words on the page, its quiet hours also invite us to lose ourselves in the stories those words can tell.

The book T'ao Ch'ien is reading, *The Book of Hills and Seas,* recounts the story of King Chou, who lived in the tenth century B.C.E. One day the king is invited into the Western Paradise to dine with Si Wang Mu, the queen of the immortals. There among the mountains of Tibet, inside another walled garden, stands a peach tree, its branches extended to bear the weight of the whole universe, its fruit offering immortality to all who would eat. Yet, the peach tree itself needs the queen to care for it, to love it, to nurture and cultivate it.

As T'ao Ch'ien reads he wanders through paradise and glances into eternity. And as he reads he reminds us that summer is the time to turn off cell phones, unplug the television, nod vaguely to friends and family, and sink into the books that will take us into "the whole Universe." For where but in the old stories can our imaginations be restored, nurtured, cultivated?

And where is happiness, except in these?

READING *THE BOOK OF HILLS AND SEAS*

In the month of June the grass grows high
And round my cottage thick-leaved branches sway.
There is not a bird but delights in the place where it
rests:
And I too—love my thatched cottage.
I have done my ploughing:
I have sown my seed.
Again I have time to sit and read my books.
In the narrow lane there are no deep ruts:
Often my friends' carriages turn back.
In high spirits I pour out my spring wine
And pluck the lettuce growing in my garden.
A gentle rain comes stealing up from the east
And a sweet wind bears it company.
My thoughts float idly over the Story of King Chou
My eyes wander over the pictures of Hills and Seas.
At a single glance I survey the whole Universe.
He will never be happy, whom such pleasures fail to
please!

Anne Lamott

"ALTAR" FROM *TRAVELING MERCIES: SOME THOUGHTS ON FAITH*

It might seem that Anne Lamott and her son Sam building a birthday altar on the beach are far away from Greentown, Illinois, where Ray Bradbury puts Douglas Spaulding in *Dandelion Wine*. But perhaps not. As Anne Lamott struggles to hold on to her gift—as she struggles with the possibility of becoming one of those people that Douglas sees below him, moving about in the old, unvarying routines—she sees Sam and the magic that emerges from his "underground necessity." It is as though one of the people running below Douglas had looked up, seen him, and recognized the presence of—well, magic.

> *The* magic of summer may be something best seen by a child, but that does not mean that it must inevitably vanish.

Because this is exactly what happens to Anne Lamott. She sees Sam create something beautiful out of nothing—out of what lies around him and what others ignore. She sees the sandpipers, so well adapted, so intense, paying "necessary attention" to the world around them. And she sees herself and Sam building the sand altar that the changing tide will doom, and she recognizes that it is the making, not the made, that is permanent.

Perhaps the illusion of summer's permanence, Lamott suggests, is no illusion at all. The magic of summer may be something best seen by a child, but that does not mean that it must inevitably vanish. Maybe some parts of it can stay, as real as the oval of soft pink beach glass that Lamott holds as she writes words of love and gratefulness.

"Altar"

Sam and I were on the beach at San Quentin on the morning of his eighth birthday. He was having a party that afternoon at our best friends' house, and four of his friends from school were invited, but he'd agreed to come with me to the beach until then. It gave me a great excuse not to write—it was my kid's birthday, for God's sake. The truth, though, was that I'd hardly written in weeks, and then only pitiful little stream-of-consciousness writing exercises, like Job's wife trying to get the *Artist's Way* to work. I couldn't remember the point anymore; a lot of rewards had come my way, but I felt like a veteran greyhound at the racetrack who finally figures out that she's been chasing mechanical bunnies: all that energy, and it's not even a real rabbit. It was an awful predicament, to be so tired of doing what I do and, at the same time, worried that the jig was going to be up this time for sure, that I wasn't going to be *allowed* to do it anymore. That the authorities were going to call and say I'd blown my chance to be one of the writers—but they'd found me a new job, at the Laundromat. I was going to be the anxious woman who hands out change: "Here, here's some quarters. Don't use that machine, it overflows! Hey! That man's using your basket!"

But Sam at eight is fantastic, utterly magic. He's so much bigger than he was last year. His legs are nearly longer than mine, and he styles his hair now before he goes to school, moussifies it into a punk look sometimes, and other times slicks it back until, as he put it, "it looks fancy." His spiritual views are changing; sometimes he says he doesn't believe in only Jesus now. He says, "I believe in all the gods now," but that may be just to torture me. I'm not that concerned yet, but let me get back to you on this when he starts leaving *Eck Speaks!* pamphlets around for me to find.

Half the time he's so gentle and sweet that grown-ups smile and shake their heads at such a good child. With infinite patience, he has taught a number of children to ride two-wheelers over the years, and he gives them flattened bottle caps as medals of encouragement when they fail. But he can be terribly unfriendly with me, and he's got this new toughness, this teenage impersonation that he pulls out from time to time with varying effect. For instance, he told me not long ago, with rather nonchalant sadism, "No one thinks you're funny." Mostly this facade is pretty touching, though. I recently dropped him off for a couple of hours with our fourteen-year-old friend Rory, who is the coolest boy you've ever met, and Sam immediately went into this unconscious adolescent parody, a fifty-five pound Sean Penn, all slouchy tics and slanted eyes and bored derision. When I picked him up later at Rory's, he slouched out to the car with his bottom lip hanging down as if a lit cigarette were dangling from it, and as we drove off, Sam sneered, "He thinks he's so cool, but he doesn't even have the Disney Channel."

So there we were, my eight-year-old boy and I, building a something or other. It had begun as a castle but had morphed into a woolly-mammoth-shaped birthday altar with turrets. We spelled out his name on the sand in the center of the structure with letters made from tiny broken white shells. We stuck feathers, seaweed, beach glass, and shells in the turrets and humps.

Sam really has a gift for making things out of next to nothing. He has magic in those little monkey fingers. He sees things spacially. His last teacher, after expressing some concern about his handwriting, said, "He makes such amazing things out of ... of ... of," and I said, "Garbage?," and she said, "Yes!" He walks along looking in dirt and carpets and corners for discarded bits of metal or plastic, packaging, string, and then like somebody knitting very quickly, he fiddles these things into little contraptions. For instance, with a plastic container that had once held snack cheese and crackers, and a strand of maroon embroidery thread, a large bent paper clip, a popsicle stick, and a little ball of foil, he made an apparatus for hypnotizing animals, with a spring-lock closure so that any bad guys who stole it could never get it to work.

Sometimes I have a knee-jerk concern that he has so little interest in school. At the end of second grade, one of the mothers said, "Gee, he doesn't go much for homework, does he?," and I wanted to scream, "No, but he makes *inventions*, you dumb slut, out of *garbage*. While your kid is an obsequious little Type A suck."

I realize I may be the least bit sensitive.

Sam and I had built huge ramparts around our castle and had dug a moat to keep out the aliens and bad guys. He thinks and talks and dreams about bad guys all the time—also, monsters and dangerous animals. He looked so lost—and so found—in his work on the beach, his vision so clear and focused, while here I was in the middle of an emotional kaleidoscope. What a year: so much love, so many deaths and setbacks. It was all too much. I had begun to feel like when you're a kid, and you and your friends pretend to be outrunning hot lava and then all of a sudden it turns out that it has caught up to you and is swirling around your ankles. I looked over at Sam. He had just covered a turret with cannonballs of round beach pebbles. He still looks like a wood sprite, although definitely a more manly wood sprite.

We were working away side by side until Sam saw some sandpipers and got up to race down to the water, flapping his wings at them. They all flew away. Sam is built just like my father, whom we always called "Old Birdlegs." But he tans well. My father's legs were as pale as the moon.

The sandpipers landed fifty feet away, and Sam returned. He got back to work. But we both kept glancing up at them. They look so absurd; they're well adapted but you'd never know just by looking at them. You have to see them in action, right on the edge, trying to scrabble out a living. Now Sam left them alone and bounded around looking for useful items. I listened to the sandpipers' cries of alarm, took in their spindly legs, their masks of pure white, their features patterned like speckled brown eggs.

Walking and digging, walking and digging along the shore, poking their long pointed beaks into the sand, hoping there's food.

They're very naked. There's such intensity in them, too, the intensity of the moment—like the gypsies, they can't drift off or they might die, and because of this quality of necessary attention, they have a lovely precision, dancing a kind of comical ballet.

"You're not even going to believe what I just scored," Sam shouted on his return, cocky and pumped up like a very short boxer before a fight. He had things hidden behind his back and brought out his hands to reveal several really cruddy-looking clothespins. "Do you have a pen?" he asked breathlessly, and I did, in the back pocket of my jeans.

Sam took my pen and drew in faces, mustaches, hair. He took a bit of black pipe cleaner that was stuck in a turret and fashioned a machine gun out of it for one of the clothespin men. He surrounded his castle with the men he has nightmares about, men with guns, men who will hurt or save him; and he surrounded his castle with monsters made of Styrofoam and seaweed. His art springs out of bubbling underground necessity, as if he's somehow dipping himself into the river that gave him life; he's making dream material visible. I watched him carefully. He was making art because he has to, and because he's brave enough to try and make contact, right there on the edge of madness, where he dreams.

"We have to go," I told him. The party at our friends' house was going to start in an hour or so.

"No!" he wailed. "We can't. What about ... our creation? We can't just leave it here. We have to stay and protect it. We've worked so hard on it! The waves will come and wash it away."

"Honey," I said, "it was never meant to be permanent. You must have known the tide would come back in."

He thought about this for a minute. "I'm going to kick it all over, then," he said. "And I *hate* you," he added. "And I hate *everything.*"

I didn't say anything. He walked away from me and the altar, world weary, shuffling with dejection, head down. Sam, I wanted to explain, making the altar was a way to celebrate, to honor you today. The fact that it's going to wash away heightens how wonderful our *making* it was. The altar didn't hold as much animating spirit as our *making* it did, the gathering, the choices. It's like: We made it, we love it—oops, it's gone. But the best part is still here.

Of course I didn't say any of this, and he didn't in fact kick his birthday altar over. Some time later he came back to where I lay and asked if we could stay just a while more. I said yes, sure, and smoothed some sand off his face with my fingertips. He let me, and then walked off again. I lay back down and closed my eyes, and I guess I must have fallen asleep. Because later still he was tugging at my sleeve until I opened my eyes and sat up. He had his fists balled up, concealing something, and he wanted me to guess which hand the secret was in. I tapped the left fist, and he unfurled his fingers to reveal an oval of soft pink beach glass.

"Wow," I said, picking it out of his small palm. If you'd seen my face, you would have thought he'd just given me a Spanish doubloon. He stood there watching me with a long sideways look, his face turned slightly away, pleased with my reaction but determined not to show it. The glass was polished from the sea, and I put it in the pocket of my shorts. "Thank you," l said, and he shrugged. Then he actually chucked me under the chin, like one of my uncles used to do, and ran off again to the shore.

The waves haven't come for my smooth glass yet. In the meantime, it is right here in the front pocket of the jeans I am wearing now. I reach into my pocket for it a lot; it helps me write in some mysterious way I don't at all understand. But what I want to say is, happy birthday, Sam, Samuel John Stephen Lamott. And traveling mercies, too. I can't help but say again what I said on the beach that day, in a whisper this time and without even being exactly sure to whom I'm saying it: Thank you. Thank you. Thank you.

PSALM 100

Be joyful in God (all ye lands),
  serve the Lord with gladness,
  come before his presence with joy.
Be ye sure, that the Lord, he is God:
  it is he that hath made us,
  and not we ourselves.
We are but his people
  and the sheep of his pasture.

O go your way into his gates then
  with thanksgiving,
  and into his courts with praise.
Be thankful unto him
  and speak good of his name.

For the Lord is gracious,
  his mercy is everlasting,
  and his truth endureth
From generation to generation.

Mixed Greens and Walnuts

Ingredients:

8 ounces mixed salad greens
3/4 cup chopped walnuts
thinly sliced red onion
8 ounces Gorgonzola cheese, crumbled
2 tart green apples, cored and diced
8-ounce bottle of raspberry dressing

Assemble the lettuce on plates, then top with even amounts of each item. Drizzle with dressing or offer on the side.

PART TWO
Tillage and Cultivation

INTRODUCTION

In *Laddie: A True Blue Story*, a novel based on Gene Stratton-Porter's own childhood experiences in Wabash County, Indiana, the hero decides one morning to plow the west eighty acres with his mother's matched team of gray carriage horses. He loops red tulips over Jo's ears and yellow daffodils over Ned's, tunes up his imitation of a whippoorwill, and sets off to whistle, sing, and plow his way through the next two weeks:

> *See the merry farmer boy, tramp the meadows*
> > *through,*
> *Swing his hoe in careless joy, while dashing off the*
> > *dew.*
> *Bobolink in maple high, trills a note of glee,*
> *Farmer boy in gay reply now whistles cheerily.*

Even in the 1870s, even in rural Indiana, Laddie cuts a romantic and unrealistic figure, as well he knows. But he is out to prove a point to Pamela Pryor, the woman he loves and who unexpectedly has told him that the vocation of a farmer is no fit occupation for a man as talented as he—or for the man she intends to marry. He is putting on a spectacle to show her his other love—his love of the land, of farming, of cultivating, a love he wants her to share. He calls his spectacle "the pageant of summer."

And pageant is exactly the right word for what Laddie is doing and for what summer itself is. Because summer, which lies between the flurry of spring planting and the frenzy of the fall harvest, settles into the story that links the two, settles into the steady rhythm of in-between. The first act is over; the final one is yet to be. The story summer tells—or perhaps better, the story it shows—is the oldest one of all: a man and a woman tending a garden, eating its fruits, and walking with God in the cool of the day.

Cultivation returns us to the basics: We must have food, and food comes from the soil. Even if we don't grow our own, it is during the summertime that we eagerly plunder farmers' markets and stop at the roadside stand to buy white corn from children who picked it "just this morning." We look so longingly at our neighbor's tomatoes that she hands us a brown bag a bit damp on the bottom with just enough dirt inside to set off the rich reds of beefsteaks, Brandywines and Better Boys, Pink Girls, Jetstars and Juliets. And because the corn is so sweet and the tomatoes are so ripe and the blueberries stain our fingers and teeth, we take notice of what we are putting into our mouths. We pay attention. We bite into blessing.

And that, says the Jewish tradition, is what kashrut, keeping kosher, is all about. "Keeping kosher," says Lauren Winner, "transforms eating from a mere nutritional necessity into an act of faithfulness. If you keep kosher, the protagonist of your meal is not you; it is God."

When we are attentive to God, when we are faithful to God even in our eating, the extravagance of summer doesn't seem wasteful. The cornhusks and cucumber peels, the overripe plums and watermelon rinds fatten the compost heap or the woodchuck who lives under the shed. In warmer climates the seeds in the garbage dump begin to sprout—fruit from debris, life from death. And such hardihood reminds us that nature can get on quite well without us, thank you very much. Michael Pollan reminds us that weeds flourish inside—and outside—the garden. And Alice Meynell notes in her late Victorian prose that "The grass is always ready to grow in the streets—and no streets could ask for a more charming finish than your green grass. The gasometer even must fall to pieces unless it is renewed; but the grass renews itself. There is nothing so remediable as the work of modern man—'a thought which is also,' as Mr. Picksniff said, 'very soothing.' And by remediable I mean, of course, destructible. As the bathing child shuffles off his garments—they are few, and one brace suffices him—so the land might always in reasonable time, shuffle off its yellow brick and purple slate, and all the things that collect about railway stations. A single night almost clears the air of London."

And yet, though nature can shuffle off the detritus of civilization, cultivation remains one of our most basic vocations, perhaps our deepest calling, just as food remains our most basic need. But cultivation is not just the quickest means to the biggest end, a matter of calculating the technology that will deliver the greatest number of green bananas with the least amount of bruising to the greatest number of northern consumers. In fact, cultivation isn't really about means and ends at all, although there is a process and there is a goal. Cultivation is about growing; nurturing; being present to tender, fragile shoots of life—tending the garden, as Laddie tended his love for Pamela. "To tend" once meant "to listen," and that may be all we need to know about becoming master gardeners.

Cultivation is also the antidote for that great temptation of summer: laziness, which, like all great sins, lies in the shadow of its companion virtue, leisure. Whereas leisure allows time to pool, pauses in the headlong rush, stops to look—and listen—laziness counts out the minutes and flips them away. Leisure is generous; laziness, a spendthrift. We emerge from leisure refreshed, from laziness weary to the bone. Even a catalogue of laziness from the Chinese poet Po Chüi makes us tired:

> *I have got patronage, but am too lazy to use it;*
> *I have got land, but am too lazy to farm it.*

My house leaks; I am too lazy to mend it.
My clothes are torn; I am too lazy to darn them.
I have got wine, but am too lazy to drink;
So it's just the same as if my cellar were empty.
I have got a harp, but am too lazy to play;
So it's just the same as if it had no strings.

It is no accident that Po Chüi moves from land to house to clothes to drink to song. Barren idleness has a way of drifting through our lives, polluting as it goes. But the discipline of cultivation extends its tendrils as well. It is no accident that as Elinore Pruitt Stewart cultivates the land she cultivates a sturdy young daughter and a growing love for Mr. Stewart; it is no accident that as Gretel Ehrlich disciplines her body to the sheepherder's tasks she disciplines her heart, as well; it is no accident that Sherman Alexie learns to tell his own stories by cultivating his memories. Nor is it an accident that we speak of cultivating the virtues, for those qualities of mind and heart—and yes, of body—are not objects we possess, much less ends that we achieve. They are habits of being we slowly develop as we tend to the steady rhythm of our lives.

And if the greatest of virtues is love, perhaps its quiet cousin is kindness: the kindness that runs a mowing machine for a busy rancher; the kindness that tells a small story well; the kindness that, as we read here in the final selection, enables a busy doctor to hold the feet of homeless people and cut their toenails.

A Prayer

God of creating power, God of star and soil,
hear this prayer from creatures made from the
      dust of the earth,
but made also in your image:
human and humus, neither beast nor angel.

Hear us as we strive to till and keep,
as we work the land and labor for a blessing.
Bless the work of our hands and minds,
and bless the gifts entrusted to our care.

Shower us yet again with rain and warmth
so that spring may turn to summer,
      promise into fruition,
        hard work into harvest.

Remove the strife from our striving,
and bless all our striving that pleases you
and prospers your creation.

Bless us as we daily till and plant,
as we daily nurture and complete,
so that our striving becomes your Shalom.

God of creating power, complete in grace what
    we begin.
Attend to what we tend,
    in the earth,
    in words,
    in work,
    in deeds of love and kindness,
    and let it be very good in your sight.

Amen.

—JAMES VANDEN BOSCH

A Gathering of Farming Poems

It is easy to wax nostalgic about the joys of farming when you are not the one hoeing in hundred-degree weather or huddling under a haystack during a hailstorm or canning two hundred quarts of tomato sauce. But, nostalgia aside, there is something about summer that calls us back to the root meaning of cultivation: to till the land. The poets gathered here know that to till the land means to bestow labor and attention upon it, and the attention they bestow is both precise and generous.

> *There* is something about summer that calls us back to the root meaning of cultivation: to till the land.

These poems celebrate the joys of tilling the land, but they are not sentimental. Here is falling sweat and women rushing about; here are those who toil in the world. But if the poets recognize the hardships, they also know the joys of cultivation and the way it tugs on our hearts, as city and suburban dwellers. Why, asks Paul Laurence Dunbar, do we envy the farm boy as he whistles his way through his chores? It is not just because we sense a kind of primal freedom in his "artless song," although we do hear that. But it is also because in singing a song of lakes *and* land, work *and* rest, grief *and* merriment, he sings us back to the rhythms of life.

Summer

from *A Four-season Song on the Hardships and Joys of Farming Life*

CHEUNG HSIEH

Ripples of wheat toss in the wind,
It's again the early sprouting of grain seedlings,
    now halfway out.
Just watch those whirring spars above the dikes,
    Splattering silver streams, splashing milk!
Take off your straw hat, let the rain comb smooth
    the hair on your head;
While weeding, let your sweat fall on the root of the
    growing grain.
And busy at raising silkworms, women rush about,
    gathering mulberry leaves.
    Such are the hardships of farming life.

Flustering wind
Shakes the broad bamboo leaves;
Amid the rustling sound
Float down new bamboo-skins.
Just the season of green river-reeds on the surface of the water,
    And red pomegranate by the corner of the house.
    Boys giggle in the field picking melons,
    Wash their feet in the pond in the slanting sun.
In the evening breeze, everyone talks of nonsense.
    Such are the joys of farming life.

In Summer

PAUL LAURENCE DUNBAR

Oh, summer has clothed the earth
In a cloak from the loom of the sun!
And a mantle, too, of the skies' soft blue,
And a belt where the rivers run.

And now for the kiss of the wind,
And the touch of the air's soft hands,
With the rest from strife and the heat of life,
With the freedom of lakes and lands.

I envy the farmer's boy
Who sings as he follows the plow;
While the shining green of the young blades lean
To the breezes that cool his brow.

He sings to the dewy morn,
No thought of another's ear;
But the song he sings is a chant for kings
And the whole wide world to hear.

He sings of the joys of life,
Of the pleasures of work and rest,
From an o'erfull heart, without aim or art;
'Tis a song of the merriest.

O ye who toil in the town,
And ye who moil in the mart,
Hear the artless song, and your faith made strong
Shall renew your joy of heart.

Oh, poor were the worth of the world
  If never a song were heard,—
If the sting of grief had no relief,
  And never a heart were stirred.

So, long as the streams run down,
  And as long as the robins trill,
Let us taunt old Care with a merry air,
  And sing in the face of ill.

Elinore Pruitt Stewart

"A Busy, Happy Summer" from
Letters of a Woman Homesteader

The summer cultivation of a small garden may bring much pleasure—both to the gardener and to the visitor. Cultivation of a larger vegetable garden may bring just as much aesthetic pleasure, along with a sense that the gardener is contributing to the care and feeding of others. (It is no small thing that Henry David Thoreau's wedding present for Nathaniel and Sophia Hawthorne was a large vegetable garden he had planted just south of their front door.) But the cultivation of a ranch is both a mightier enterprise and a more uncertain one. And a century ago, its success or failure was determined by forces that few in North America, other than independent farmers, can appreciate.

> *The summer cultivation of a small garden may bring much pleasure—both to the gardener and to the visitor. Cultivation of a larger vegetable garden may bring just as much aesthetic pleasure, along with a sense that the gardener is contributing to the care and feeding of others.*

When Elinore Pruitt Stewart lost her husband in a train accident, she took the hand of her two-year-old daughter and went to Denver, determined to be her own support. There, she cleaned houses and washed laundry. Eventually she became the housekeeper for a Scotch cattleman, and, falling in love, married him. Together, they pioneered a quarter-section in Wyoming—a life that Stewart chronicled in letters back to a friend in Denver.

The life of summer cultivation that these letters depict is not an easy one. Mowing, milking, and putting up jams and jellies are tasks that are consuming and wearying, and certainly Stewart knows how overwhelming they can be. But there is also enormous pride in work well done, and a sense that having done those chores enables—not entitles, enables—one to experience the real joy of a remarkable day of leisure. The cultivations of summer, Stewart suggests, are a necessity—but these necessities lead to new sun-ups and glorious days.

"A BUSY, HAPPY SUMMER"

September 11, 1909.

Dear Mrs. Coney,—

This has been for me the busiest, happiest summer I can remember. I have worked very hard, but it has been work that I really enjoy. Help of any kind is very hard to get here, and Mr. Stewart had been too confident of getting men, so that haying caught him with too few men to put up the hay. He had no man to run the mower and he couldn't run both the mower and the stacker, so you can fancy what a place he was in.

I don't know that I ever told you, but my parents died within a year of each other and left six of us to shift for ourselves. Our people offered to take one here and there among them until we should all have a place, but we refused to be raised on the halves and so arranged to stay at Grandmother's and keep together. Well, we had no money to hire men to do our work, so had to learn to do it ourselves. Consequently I learned to do many things which girls more fortunately situated don't even know have to be done. Among the things I learned to do was the way to run a mowing-machine. It cost me many bitter tears because I got sunburned, and my hands were hard, rough, and stained with machine oil, and I used to wonder how any Prince Charming could overlook all that in any girl he came to. For all I had ever read of the Prince had to do with his "reverently kissing her lily-white hand," or doing some other fool trick with a hand as white as a snowflake. Well, when my Prince showed up he didn't lose much time in letting me know that "Barkis was willing," and I wrapped my hands in my old checked apron and took him up before he could catch his breath. Then there was no more mowing, and I almost forgot that I knew how until Mr. Stewart got into such a panic. If he put a man to mow, it kept them all idle at the stacker, and he just couldn't get enough men. I was afraid to tell him I could mow for fear he would forbid me to do so. But one morning, when he was chasing a last hope of help, I went down to the barn, took out the horses, and went to mowing. I had enough cut before he got back to show him I knew how, and as he came back manless he was delighted as well as surprised. I was glad because I really like to mow, and besides that, I am adding feathers to my cap in a surprising way. When you see me again you will think I am wearing a feather duster, but it is only that I have been said to have almost as much sense as a "mon," and that is an honor I never aspired to, even in my wildest dreams.

I have done most of my cooking at night, have milked seven cows every day, and have done all the hay-cutting, so you see I have been working. But I have found time to put up thirty pints of jelly and the same amount of jam for myself. I used wild fruits, gooseberries, currants, raspberries, and cherries. I have almost two gallons of the cherry butter, and I think it is delicious. I wish I could get some of it to you, I am sure you would like it.

We began haying July 5 and finished September 8. After working so hard and so steadily I decided on a day off, so yesterday I saddled the pony, took a few things I needed, and Jerrine and I fared forth. Baby can ride behind quite well. We got away by sunup and a glorious day we had. We followed a stream higher up into the mountains and the air was so keen and clear at first we had on our coats. There was a tang of sage and of pine in the air, and our horse was midside deep in rabbit-brush, a shrub just covered with flowers that look and smell like goldenrod. The blue distance promised many alluring adventures, so we went along singing and simply gulping in summer. Occasionally a bunch of sage chickens would fly up out of the sagebrush, or a jack rabbit would leap out. Once we saw a bunch of antelope gallop over a hill, but we were out just to be out, and game didn't tempt us. I started, though, to have just as good a time as possible, so I had a fish-hook in my knapsack.

Presently, about noon, we came to a little dell where the grass was as soft and as green as a lawn. The creek kept right up against the hills on one side and there were groves of quaking asp and cottonwoods that made shade, and service-bushes and birches that shut off the ugly hills on the other side. We dismounted and prepared to noon. We caught a few grasshoppers and I cut a birch pole for a rod. The trout are so beautiful now, their sides are so silvery, with dashes of old rose and orange, their speckles are so black, while their backs look as if they had been sprinkled with gold-dust. They bite so well that it doesn't require any especial skill or tackle to catch plenty for a meal in a few minutes.

In a little while I went back to where I had left my pony browsing, with eight beauties. We made a fire first, then I dressed my trout while it was burning down to a nice bed of coals. I had brought a frying-pan and a bottle of lard, salt, and buttered bread. We gathered a few service-berries, our trout were soon browned, and with water, clear, and as cold as ice, we had a feast. The quaking aspens are beginning to turn yellow, but no leaves have fallen. Their shadows dimpled and twinkled over the grass like happy children. The sound of the dashing, roaring water kept inviting me to cast for trout, but I didn't want to carry them so far, so we rested until the sun was getting low and then started for home, with the song of the locusts in our ears warning us that the melancholy days are almost here. We would come up over the top of a hill into the glory of a beautiful sunset with its gorgeous colors, then down into the little valley already purpling with mysterious twilight. So on, until, just at dark, we rode into our corral and a mighty tired, sleepy little girl was powerfully glad to get home.

After I had mailed my other letter I was afraid that you would think me plumb bold about the little Bo-Peep, and was a heap sorrier than you can think. If you only knew the hardships these poor men endure. They go two together and sometimes it is months before they see another soul, and rarely ever a woman. I wouldn't act so free in town, but these men see people so seldom that they are awkward and embarrassed. I like to put them at ease, and it is to be done only by being kind of hail-fellow-well-met with them. So far not one has ever misunderstood me and I have been treated with every courtesy and kindness, so I am powerfully glad you understand. They really enjoy doing these little things like fixing our dinner, and if my poor company can add to any one's pleasure I am too glad.

Gretel Ehrlich

"FROM A SHEEPHERDER'S NOTEBOOK: THREE DAYS" FROM *THE SOLACE OF OPEN SPACES*

The days of pioneering women are not yet over, certainly not in Wyoming, and certainly not on the ranches that sprawl across its mountains. Like Elinore Pruitt Stewart a century earlier, Gretel Ehrlich set out one day from her urban home, determined to make her own way in an unknown land. A filmmaker from California, she had never seen sheep up close, let alone tried to herd them. Yet, confronted with necessity—"There ain't nobody else around," her friend John told her abruptly—she packed a knapsack and headed out with a horse and a border collie.

Where but in the steady rhythm of work can we learn to understand our desires or find that thin thread that leads our heart toward home?

Ehrlich's three days on the high plains follow an archetypal pattern of temptation. She is alone and ill prepared for the cruel weather, bereft of human company, hat, and hand cream. The purpose of the exercise soon escapes her—should she move the sheep fast or slow, up or down?—and the immensity of the setting overwhelms her: it hardly matters which way you go, John tells her, because the ranch stretches for "thirty or forty miles in any direction." The sheep both need and mock her: a galloping lamb plunges over a cliff and hangs upside down, dead to all appearances, then nonchalantly returns to life and its placid dam. The dog is more intelligent than she.

And yet, where but in the steady rhythm of work, pressed into keeping commitments to John, to the untidy flock, to the dog, to the land itself can she—and we—learn to understand our desires or find that thin thread that leads our heart toward home?

"From a Sheepherder's Notebook: Three Days"

When the phone rang, it was John: "Maurice just upped and quit and there ain't nobody else around, so you better get packed. I'm taking you out to herd sheep." I walked to his trailerhouse. He smoked impatiently while I gathered my belongings. "Do you know *anything* about herding sheep after all this time?" he asked playfully. "No, not really." I was serious. "Well, it's too late now. You'll just have to figure it out. And there ain't no phones up there either!"

He left me off on a ridge at five in the morning with a mare and a border collie. "Last I saw the sheep, they was headed for them hills," he said, pointing up toward a dry ruffle of badlands. "I'll pull your wagon up ahead about two miles. You'll see it. Just go up that ridge, turn left at the pink rock, then keep agoing. And don't forget to bring the damned sheep."

Morning. Sagesmell, sunsquint, birdsong, cool wind. I have no idea where I am, how to get to the nearest paved road, or how to find the sheep. There are tracks going everywhere so I follow what appear to be the most definite ones. The horse picks a path through sagebrush. I watch the dog. We walk for several miles. Nothing. Then both sets of ears prick up. The dog looks at me imploringly. The sheep are in the draw ahead.

Move them slow or fast? Which crossing at the river? Which pink rock? It's like being a first-time mother, but mother now to two thousand sheep who give me the kind of disdainful look a teenager would his parent and, with my back turned, can get into as much trouble. I control the urge to keep them neatly arranged, bunched up by the dog, and instead, let them spread out and fill up. Grass being scarce on spring range, they scatter.

Up the valley, I encounter a slalom course of oil rigs and fenced spills I hadn't been warned about. The lambs, predictably mischievous, emerge dripping black. Freed from those obstacles, I ride ahead to find the wagon which, I admit, I'm afraid I'll never see, leaving the sheep on the good faith that they'll stay on their uphill drift toward me.

"Where are my boundaries?" I'd asked John.

"Boundaries?" He looked puzzled for a minute. "Hell, Gretel, it's all the outfit's land, thirty or forty miles in any direction. Take them anywhere they want to go."

On the next ridge I find my wagon. It's a traditional sheepherder's wagon, rounded top, tiny wood cookstove, bed across the back, built-in benches and drawers. The rubber wheels and long tongue make it portable. The camp tender pulls it (now with a pickup, earlier with teams) from camp to camp as the feed is consumed, every two weeks or so. Sheep begin appearing and graze toward me. I picket my horse. The dog runs for shade to lick his sore feet. The view from the dutch doors of the wagon is to the southeast, down the long slit of a valley. If I rode north, I'd be in Montana within the day, and next week I'll begin the fifty-mile trail east to the Big Horns.

Three days before summer solstice; except to cook and sleep I spend every waking hour outside. Tides of weather bring the days and take them away. Every night a bobcat visits, perched at a discreet distance on a rock, facing me. A full moon, helium-filled, cruises through clouds and is lost behind rimrock. No paper cutout, this moon, but ripe and splendid. Then Venus, then the North Star. Time for bed.

Are the sheep bedded down? Should I ride back to check them?

Morning. Blue air comes ringed with coyotes. The ewes wake clearing their communal throats like old men. Lambs shake their flop-eared heads at leaves of grass, negotiating the blade. People have asked in the past, "What do you do out there? Don't you get bored?" The problem seems to be something else. There's too much of everything here. I can't pace myself to it.

Down the valley the sheep move in a frontline phalanx, then turn suddenly in a card-stacked sequential falling, as though they had turned themselves inside out, and resume feeding again in whimsical processions. I think of town, of John's trailerhouse, the clean-bitten lawn, his fanatical obsession with neatness and work, his small talk with hired hands, my eyesore stacks of books and notes covering an empty bed, John smoking in the dark of early morning, drinking coffee, waiting for daylight to stream in.

After eating I return to the sheep, full of queasy fears that they will have vanished and I'll be pulled off the range to face those firing-squad looks of John's as he says, "I knew you'd screw up. Just like you screw up everything." But the sheep are there. I can't stop looking at them. They're there, paralyzing the hillside with thousands of mincing feet, their bodies pressed together as they move, saucerlike, scanning the earth for a landing.

Thunderstorm. Sheep feed far up a ridge I don't want them to go over, so the dog, horse, and I hotfoot it to the top and ambush them, yelling and hooting them back down. Cleverly the horse uses me as windbreak when the front moves in. Lightning fades and blooms. As we descend quickly, my rein-holding arm looks to me like a blank stick. I feel numb. Numb in all this vividness. I don't seem to occupy my life fully.

Down in the valley again I send the dog "way around" to turn the sheep, but he takes the law into his own hands and chases a lamb off a cliff. She's wedged upside down in a draw on the other side of the creek. It will take twenty minutes to reach her, and the rest of the sheep have already trailed ahead. This numbness is a wrist twisting inside my throat. A lone pine tree whistles, its needles are novocaine.

"In nature there are neither rewards nor punishments; there are only consequences." I can't remember who said that. I ride on.

One dead. Will she be reborn? And as what? The dog that nips lambs' heels into butchering chutes? I look back. The "dead" lamb convulses into action and scrambles up the ledge to find his mother.

Twin terrors: to be awake; to be asleep.

All day clouds hang over the Beartooth Mountains. Looking for a place out of the wind, I follow a dry streambed to a sheltered inlet. In front of me, there's something sticking straight up. It's the shell of a dead frog propped up against a rock with its legs crossed at the ankles. A cartoonist's idea of a frog relaxing, but this one's skin is paper-thin, mouth opened as if to scream. I lean close. "It's too late, you're already dead!"

Because I forgot to bring hand cream or a hat, sun targets in on me like frostbite. The dog, horse, and I move through sagebrush in unison, a fortress against wind. Sheep ticks ride my peeling skin. The dog pees, then baptizes himself at the water hole—full immersion—lapping at spitting rain. Afterward, he rolls in dust and reappears with sage twigs and rabbit brush strung up in his coat, as though in disguise—a Shakespearian dog. Above me, oil wells are ridge-top jewelry adorning the skyline with ludicrous sexual pumps. Hump, hump go the wells. Hump, hump go the drones who gather that black soup, insatiable.

We walk the fuselage of the valley. A rattlesnake passes going the other way; plenty of warning but so close to my feet I hop the rest of the day. I come upon the tin-bright litter of a former sheep camp: Spam cans flattened to the ground, their keys sticking up as if ready to open my grave.

Sun is in and out after the storm. In a long gully, the lambs gambol, charging in small brigades up one side, then the other. Ewes look on bored. When the lamb-fun peters out, the whole band comes apart in a generous spread the way sheep ranchers like them. Here and there lambs, almost as big as their mothers, kneel with a contagiously enthusiastic wiggle, bumping the bag with a goatlike butt to take a long draw of milk.

Night. Nighthawks whir. Meadowlarks throw their heads back in one ecstatic song after another. In the wagon I find a piece of broken mirror big enough to see my face: blood drizzles from cracked lips, gnats have eaten away at my ears.

To herd sheep is to discover a new human gear somewhere between second and reverse—a slow, steady trot of keenness with no speed. There is no flab in these days. But the constant movement of sheep from water hole to water hole, from camp to camp, becomes a form of longing. But for what?

The ten other herders who work for this ranch begin to trail their sheep toward summer range in the Big Horns. They're ahead of me, though I can't see them for the curve of the earth. One-armed Red, Grady, and Ed; Bob, who always bakes a pie when he sees me riding toward his camp; Fred, wearer of rags; "Amorous Albert"; Rudy, Bertha, and Ed; and, finally, Doug, who travels circuslike with a menagerie of goats, roosters, colts, and dogs and keeps warm in the winter by sleeping with one of the nannies. A peaceful army, of which I am the tail end, moving in ragtag unison across the prairie.

A day goes by. Every shiver of grass counts. The shallows and dapples in air that give grass life are like water. The bobcat returns nightly. During easy jags of sleep the dog's dream-paws chase coyotes. I ride to the sheep. Empty sky, an absolute blue. Empty heart. Sunburned face blotches brown. Another layer of skin to peel, to meet myself again in the mirror. A plane passes overhead—probably the government trapper. I'm waving hello, but he speeds away.

Now it's tomorrow. I can hear John's truck, the stock racks speak before I can actually see him, and it's a long time shortening the distance between us.

"Hello."

"Hello."

He turns away because something tender he doesn't want me to see registers in his face.

"I'm moving you up on the bench. Take the sheep right out the tail end of this valley, then take them to water. It's where the tree is. I'll set your wagon by that road."

"What road?" I ask timidly.

Then he does look at me. He's trying to suppress a smile but speaks impatiently.

"You can see to hell and back up there, Gretel."

I ride to the sheep, but the heat of the day has already come on sizzling. It's too late to get them moving; they shade up defiantly, their heads knitted together into a wool umbrella. From the ridge there's whooping and yelling and rocks being thrown. It's John trying to get the sheep moving again. In a dust blizzard we squeeze them up the road, over a sharp lip onto the bench.

Here, there's wide-open country. A view. Sheep string out excitedly. I can see a hundred miles in every direction. When I catch up with John I get off my horse. We stand facing each other, then embrace quickly. He holds me close, then pulls away briskly and scuffles the sandy dirt with his boot.

"I've got to get back to town. Need anything?"

"Naw ... I'm fine. Maybe a hat ..."

He turns and walks his long-legged walk across the benchland. In the distance, at the pickup, an empty beer can falls on the ground when he gets in. I can hear his radio as he bumps toward town. Dust rises like an evening gown behind his truck. It flies free for a moment, then returns, leisurely, to the habitual road—that bruised string which leads to and from my heart.

Sherman Alexie

"The Summer of Black Widows"

In "The Summer of Black Widows," the title poem of his collection, the Native American writer Sherman Alexie asks: Where does story come from? Alexie suggests that story is somehow inside the world—here, in the form of black widow spiders that emerge after a summer rainstorm.

The spiders carry stories, Alexie shows. And stories are everywhere. Here, the summer cultivation of story suggests the enormous fecundity of the world around us, where stories offer themselves to us hardly needing cultivation—except that we first need to pay attention to the offering.

> *H*ere, the summer cultivation of story suggests the enormous fecundity of the world around us, where stories offer themselves to us hardly needing cultivation—except that we first need to pay attention to the offering.

The Summer of Black Widows

The spiders appeared suddenly
after that summer rainstorm.

Some people still insist the spiders fell with the rain
while others believe the spiders grew from the damp
*   soil like weeds with eight thin roots.*

The elders knew the spiders
carried stories in their stomachs.

We tucked our pants into our boots when we walked
*   through fields of fallow stories.*
An Indian girl opened the closet door and a story fell
*   into her hair.*
We lived in the shadow of a story trapped in the ceil-
*   ing lamp.*
The husk of a story museumed on the windowsill.
Before sleep, we shook our blankets and stories fell to
*   the floor.*
A story floated in a glass of water left on the kitchen
*   table.*
We opened doors slowly and listened for stories.
The stories rose on hind legs and offered their red bel-
*   lies to the most beautiful Indians.*
Stories in our cereal boxes.
Stories in our firewood.
Stories in the pockets of our coats.
We captured stories and offered them to the ants, who
*   carried the stories back to their queen.*

Sherman Alexie

A dozen stories per acre.
We poisoned the stories and gathered their remains
with broom and pan.

The spiders disappeared suddenly
after that summer lightning storm.

Some people still insist the spiders were burned to ash
while others believe the spiders climbed the lightning
bolts and became a new constellation.

The elders knew the spiders
Had left behind bundles of stories.

Up in the corners of our old houses
we still find those small, white bundles
and nothing, neither fire
nor water, neither rock nor wind,
can bring them down.

Michael Pollan

"WEEDS ARE US" FROM *SECOND NATURE: A GARDENER'S EDUCATION*

Summertime cultivation is not a benign proposition. As any gardener knows, one does not simply drop in the seeds, cover the rows with soil, and allow Nature its own way—as though the goddess Natura cared about the aesthetics of the garden, or its productivity, or its sightliness. There are forces, Michael Pollan suggests, that verge on the malign, that are out to dominate and subdue, and that couldn't care less whether the annuals have their way. And these malignant forces are, ironically enough, those that endow weeds with such highly evolved techniques and capabilities that they are better at being plants than the plants lovingly tended by human effort.

> *E*ngagement with our world calls for responsibility in the world—a principle that leaps beyond gardens, and property boundaries, and towns, and states, and nations, and principalities.

No encounter with the earth, Pollan suggests, is neutral. The moment of encounter opens the way for a history of seeds to sprout and do whatever it is they wish to do. Our response may be to allow this, but in so doing, we are yielding and, in that yielding, abandoning our responsibility. Pollan does not suggest that everyone needs to be Elinore Pruitt Stewart and head out to a quarter-section in Wyoming; he does suggest that engagement with our world calls for responsibility in the world—a principle that leaps beyond gardens, and property boundaries, and towns, and states, and nations, and principalities.

"Weeds Are Us"

Ralph Waldo Emerson, who as a lifelong gardener really should have known better, once said that a weed is simply a plant whose virtues we haven't yet discovered. "Weed" is not a category of nature but a human construct, a defect of our perception. This kind of attitude, which comes out of an old American strain of romantic thinking about wild nature, can get you into trouble. At least it did me. For I had Emerson's pretty conceit in mind when I planted my first flower bed, and the result was not a pretty thing.

Having read perhaps too much Emerson, and too many of the sort of gardening book that advocates "wild gardens" and nails a pair of knowing quotation marks around the word *weed* (a sure sign of ecological sophistication), I sought to make a flower bed that was as "natural" as possible. Rejecting all geometry (too artificial!), I cut a more or less kidney-shaped bed in the lawn, pulled out the sod, and divided the bare ground into irregular patches that I roughly outlined with a bit of ground limestone. Then I took packets of annual seeds—bachelor's buttons, nasturtiums, nicotianas, cosmos, poppies (California and Shirley both), cleomes, zinnias, and sunflowers—and broadcast a handful of each into the irregular patches, letting the seeds fall wherever nature dictated. No rows: this bed's arrangement would be *natural*. I sprinkled the seeds with loose soil, watered, and waited for them to sprout.

Pigweed sprouted first, though at the time I was so ignorant that I figured this vigorous upstart must be zinnia, or sunflower. I had had no prior acquaintance with pigweed (it grew nowhere else on the property), and did not deduce that it was a weed until I noticed it was coming up in every single one of my irregular patches. Within a week the entire bed was clothed in tough, hairy pigweeds, and it was clear that I would have to start pulling them out if I ever expected to see my intended annuals. The absence of rows or paths made weeding difficult, but I managed to at least thin the lusty pigweeds, and the annuals, grateful for the intervention on their behalf, finally pushed themselves up out of the earth. Finding the coast relatively clear, they started to grow in earnest.

That first summer, my little annual meadow thrived, pretty much conforming to the picture I'd had in mind when I planted it. Sky-blue drifts of bachelor's buttons flowed seamlessly into hot spots thick with hunter-orange and fire-engine poppies, behind which rose great sunflower towers. The nasturtiums poured their sand-dollar leaves into neat, low mounds dabbed with crimson and lemon, and the cleomes worked out their intricate architectures high in the air. Weeding this dense tangle was soon all but impossible, but after the pigweed scare I'd adopted a more or less laissez-faire policy toward the uninvited. The weeds that moved in were ones I was willing to try to live with: jewelweed (a gangly orange-flowered relative of impatiens), foxtail grass, clover, shepherd's purse, inconspicuous Galinsoga, and Queen Anne's lace, the sort of weed Emerson must have had in mind, with its ivory lace flowers (as pretty as anything you might plant) and edible, carrotlike root. That first year a pretty vine also crept in, a refugee from the surrounding lawn. It twined its way up the sunflower stalks and in August unfurled white, trumpet-shaped flowers that resembled morning glory. What right had I to oust this delicate vine? To decide that the flowers I planted were more beautiful than ones the wind had sown? I liked how wild my garden was, how peaceably my cultivars seemed to get along with their wild relatives. And I liked how unneurotic I was being about "weeds." Call me Ecology Boy.

"Weeds," I decided that summer, did indeed have a bad rap. I thought back to my grandfather's garden, to his unenlightened, totalitarian approach toward weeds. Each day he patrolled his pristine rows, beheading the merest smudge of green with his vigilant hoe. Hippies, unions, and weeds: all three made him crazy then, an old man in the late sixties, and all three called forth his reactionary wrath. Perhaps because there was little he could do to stop the march of hippies and organized labor, he attacked weeds all the more zealously. He was one of those gardeners who would pull weeds anywhere—not just in his own or other people's gardens, but in parking lots and storefront window boxes too. His world then was under siege, and weeds to him represented the advance guard of the forces of chaos. Had he lived to see it, my little wild garden—this rowless plant be-in, this horticultural Haight-Ashbury—would probably have broken his heart.

My grandfather wasn't the first person to sense a social or political threat in the growth of weeds. Whenever Shakespeare tells us that "darnel, hemlock, and rank fumatory" or "hateful docks, rough thistles, kecksies, burrs" are growing unchecked, we can assume a monarchy is about to fall. Until the romantics, the hierarchy of plants was generally thought to mirror that of human society. Common people, one writer held in 1700, may be "looked upon as trashy weeds or nettles." J. C. Loudon, an early nineteenth-century gardening expert, invited his readers "to compare plants with men, [to] consider aboriginal species as mere savages, and botanical species ... as civilized beings."

The garden world even today organizes plants into one great hierarchy. At the top stand the hypercivilized hybrids—think of the rose, "queen of the garden"—and at the bottom are the weeds, the plant world's proletariat, furiously reproducing and threatening to usurp the position of their more refined horticultural betters. Where any given plant falls in this green chain of being has a lot to do with fashion, but there are a few abiding rules. In general, the more intensively a plant has been hybridized—the further it's been distanced from its wildflower origins—the higher its station in plant society. Thus a delphinium can lord it over a larkspur, a heavily doubled bourbon rose over a five-petaled rugosa. A corollary of this rule holds that the more "weedy" a plant is—the easier it is to grow—

the lower its place: garden phlox, heir to all the fungi, has greater status than indestructible coreopsis.

Color, too, determines rank, and white comes at the top. This is because pure white occurs only rarely in nature, and perhaps also because a taste for the subtleties of white flowers is something that must be acquired. (Gaudy colors have always been associated with the baser elements: gaillardia, a loud, two-toned cousin of the daisy, used to be called "nigger flower.") Just beneath white is blue, a color that has always enjoyed royal and aristocratic connections, and from there it is a descent downscale through the hot and flashy shades, by the all-too-common yellows, past the reds even bulls will take note of, on down to the very bottom: shunned, rebuffed, eschewed, embarrassing, promiscuous magenta. Magenta, the discount pigment with which nature has brushed a thousand weeds, has always been a mark of bad breeding in the garden world. The offspring of hybrid species that have been allowed to set seed will frequently revert to magenta, as base genes reassert themselves.

My own romance of the weed did not survive a second summer. The annuals, which I had allowed to set seed the previous year, did come back, but they proved a poor match for the weeds, who returned heavily reinforced. It was as though news of this sweet deal (this chump gardener!) had spread through the neighborhood over the winter, for the weed population burgeoned, both in number and in kind. Recognizing that what I now tended was a weed garden, and having been taught that a gardener should know the name of every plant in his care, I consulted a few field guides and drew up an inventory of my collection. In addition to the species I've already mentioned, I had milkweed, pokeweed, smart-weed, St.-John's-wort, quack grass, crabgrass, plantain, dandelion, bladder campion, fleabane, butter-and-eggs, timothy, mallow, bird's-foot trefoil, lamb's quarters, chickweed, purslane, curly dock, goldenrod, sheep sorrel, burdock, Canada thistle, and stinging nettle. I'm sure I've missed another dozen, and misidentified a few, but this will give you an idea of the various fruits of my romanticism. What had begun as a kind of idealized wildflower meadow now looked like a roadside tangle and, if I let it go another year, would probably pass for a vacant lot.

Since this had not been my aesthetic aim, I set about reclaiming my garden—to at least arrest the process at "country roadside" before it degenerated to "abandoned railroad siding." I would be enlightened about it, though, pardoning the weeds I liked and expelling all the rest. I was prepared to tolerate the fleabane, holding aloft their sunny clouds of tiny asterlike flowers, or milkweed, with its interesting seedpods, but bully weeds like burdock, Canada thistle, and stinging nettle had to go. Unfortunately, the weeds I liked least proved to be the best armed and most recalcitrant. Burdock, whose giant clubfoot leaves shade out every other plants for yards around, holds the earth in a death grip. Straining to pull out its mile-long taproot, you feel like a boy trying to arm-wrestle a man. Inevitably the root breaks before it yields, with the result that, in a few days' time, you have two tough burdocks where before there had been one. All I seemed able to do was help my burdock reproduce. I felt less like an exterminator of these weeds than their midwife.

That pretty vine with the morning glory blossoms turned out to be another hydra-headed monster. Bindweed, as it's called, grows like kudzu and soon threatened to blanket the entire garden. It can grow only a foot or so high without support, so it casts about like a blind man, lurching this way then that, until it finds a suitable plant to lean on and eventually smother. Here too my efforts at eradication proved counterproductive. Bindweed, whose roots may reach ten feet down, can reproduce either by seed or human-aided cloning. For its root is as brittle as a fresh snapbean; put a hoe to it and it breaks into a dozen pieces, *each of which will sprout an entire new plant*. It is as though the bindweed's evolution took the hoe into account. By attacking it at its root—the approved strategy for eradicating most weeds—I played right into the insidious bindweed's strategy for world domination.

Have I mentioned my annuals? A few managed to hang on gamely. California poppies and Johnny-jump-ups proved adept at finding niches among the thistles, and a handful of second-generation nicotianas appeared, though these had reverted to the hue of some weedy ancestor—instead of bright pink, they came back a muddy shade of pale green. For the most part, my annuals counted themselves lucky to serve as under-planting for the triumphant weeds. But whatever niches remained for them the grasses seemed bent on erasing. Stealthy quack grass moved in, spreading its intrepid rhizomes to every corner of the bed. Quack grass roots can travel laterally as much as fifty feet, moving an inch or two beneath the surface and pushing up a blade (or ten) wherever the opportunity arises. You pull a handful of this grass thinking you've doomed an isolated tuft, only to find you've grabbed hold of a rope that reaches clear into the next county—where it is no doubt tied by a very good knot to an oak.

Now what would Emerson have to say? I had given all my weeds the benefit of the doubt, acknowledged their virtues and allotted them a place. I had treated them, in other words, as garden plants. But they did not behave as garden plants. They differed from my cultivated varieties not merely by a factor of human esteem. No, they seemed truly a different order of being, more versatile, better equipped, swifter, craftier—simply more adroit at the work of being a plant. What garden plant can germinate in thirty-six minutes, as a tumbleweed can? What cultivar can produce four hundred thousand seeds on a single flower stalk, as the mullein does? Or hitch its seeds to any passing animal, like the burdock? Or travel a foot each day, as kudzu can? ("You keep still enough, watch close enough," southerners will tell you, "and damn if you can't see it move.") Or, like the bindweed, clone new editions of itself in direct proportion to the effort we expend trying to eradicate it? Japanese knot-weed can penetrate four inches of asphalt, no problem. Each summer the roots of a Canada thistle venture another ten feet in every direction. Lamb's-quarter seeds recovered from an archaeological site germinated after spending seventeen hundred years in storage, patiently awaiting their shot. The roots of the witchweed emit a poison that kills every other plant in its vicinity.

No, it can't just be my lack of imagination that gives the nettle its sting.

Eventually I came to see that my weed-choked natural garden was irresponsible. My garden plants had thrown in their lot with me, and I had failed to protect them from the weeds. So I ripped out my flower garden and began anew. This time, I cut a perfect rectangle in the grass, and planted my flower seeds in scrupulous rows, eighteen inches apart and as straight as a plumb line could make them. As the seedlings came up, I cultivated assiduously between the rows, using the Dutch hoe that my grandfather had given me. I didn't worry much about epistemology: whatever came up between the rows I judged a weed and cut it down. The rows began as a convenience— they make cultivation an easy matter—but I've actually come to like the way they look; I guess by now I am more turned off by romantic conceits about nature than by a bit of artifice in the garden. Geometry is man's language, Le Corbusier once said, and I am happy to have a garden that speaks in that tongue. I know better now than to think a less tended garden is any more natural; weeds are our words, too.

As I see it, the day I decided to disturb the soil, I undertook an obligation to weed. For this soil is not virgin and hasn't been for centuries. It teems with hundreds of thousands of weed seeds for whom the thrust of my spade represents the knock of opportunity. Not "nature," strictly speaking, these seeds are really the descendants of earlier gardeners. To let them grow, to do nothing, is tantamount to letting those gardeners plant my garden: to letting all those superstitious Rosicrucians and Puritans and Russian immigrants have their way here. To do nothing, in other words, would be no favor to me, or my plants, or to nature. So, I weed.

A GATHERING OF GARDENING POEMS

Nothing says "summer" quite so powerfully as garden smells—freshly turned earth, ripening berries, even the "blossoms of the dark pittosporum trees" that most of us have never sniffed. Summer smells are extravagant. Do we really need a hundred different rose scents? the pungent odor of chicken manure? astringent red tomatoes gently rotting in the sun? Yes, yes, and yes—because we live in a wild and wondrous world, and even a small garden reminds us of that fact.

> Summer smells are extravagant. Do we really need a hundred different rose scents? the pungent odor of chicken manure? astringent red tomatoes gently rotting in the sun? Yes, yes, and yes.

So gardens take us deep into the mysteries of pink peonies and black ants and out to the fringes of the circling trees. And they create those small Edens where we gather our breath along with the flowers and vegetables and then head back into the house, refreshed with love.

Peony

BARBARA CROOKER

Imagine the hard knot of its bud, all that pink
> *possibility.*
Day by day it visibly swells, doubles, until one morning
in June, it unfolds, ruffle after ruffle, an explosion of
> *silk.*
Imagine your breath, as it runs through your body,
how it ebbs and flows, a river of air. Imagine
The exotic bazaar of the kitchen, where fragrances
jostle—star anise, cloves, cardamom, fill
your nostrils with the colors of the orient. Imagine
a feather, how it kisses your eyelids, caresses your
shoulder blades, the place where wings
might have been. Imagine your heart, how it works
like a clock, midnight to noon, never punches in,
never takes a vacation, keeps tolling, keeps toiling,
like black ants on this peony, whose true job
is to gather all the sweetness they can muster,
to do their small part to carry the breath of the world.

The Garden

LEE ROBINSON

Now that the teenagers
have taken the house—
long legs, loud shoes, sarcastic
tongues, their paraphernalia
winding from chair

to floor to stair
like some perverse
unstoppable vine—I retire
to the garden.

Nothing here
talks back. I learn
a language the children
don't speak: lantana,
hosta, portulaca. *I have gloves*
but seldom use them.
I like the dirt
under my fingernails,
the roughness that comes
from pulling weeds,
churning the soil for new beds.

It's time
to pitch the rusty swing set,
to rid the shed of punctured
volleyballs, old bicycles,
a decade of water guns,
time to fill it with peat moss
and new tools:

spade, trowel, rake,
all shiny, all mine.

In a Southern Garden

DOROTHEA MACKELLAR

When the tall bamboos are clicking to the restless lit-
    tle breeze,
And bats begin their jerky skimming flight,
And the creamy scented blossoms of the dark pit-
    tosporum trees,
Grow sweeter with the coming of the night.

And the harbour in the distance lies beneath a purple
    pall,
And nearer, at the garden's lowest fringe,
Loud the water soughs and gurgles 'mid the rocks
    below the wall,
Dark-heaving, with a dim uncanny tinge

Of a green as pale as beryls, like the strange faint-
    coloured flame
That burns around the Women of the Sea:
And the strip of sky to westward which the camphor-
    laurels frame,
Has turned to ash-of-rose and ivory—

And a chorus rises valiantly from where the crickets
    hide,
Close-shaded by the balsams drooping down—
It is evening in a garden by the kindly water-side,
A garden near the lights of Sydney town!

Richard Selzer

"TOENAILS" FROM *LETTERS TO A YOUNG DOCTOR*

Perhaps it is the poet's eye that is best able to connect the concrete experience in our lives to the abstractions that guide our living. In this sense, the cultivations of summertime that Elinore Pruitt Stewart and Michael Pollan speak of are concretizations of larger cultivations—the cultivations of the spirit. Medieval writers talked of cultivating the Virtues—virtues such as justice, prudence, temperance, fortitude, faith, hope, and the greatest of them all: love. As we cultivate outwardly, such writers suggest, so too must we cultivate inwardly.

> Kindness is an act in which one person uses gifts and abilities and time to engage fully and personally with another.

This is why it is so apt that in "Toenails," the surgeon Richard Selzer writes of his summer vacation—a time when he is deliberately removed from the intensity of the critical practices that dominate the other eleven months of his year. He is simply reading, removed from responsibilities, when the opportunity arises for him to cultivate in a way that he had never expected: He may cut the toenails of someone in need.

Kindness is an act in which one person uses gifts and abilities and time to engage fully and personally with another. Feelings have little to do with it. Inclination has nothing to do with it. Kindness arises when the act is needed, and one human soul looks at another human soul and says, "You before me." In this essay, Selzer goes against all conventions and all inclinations—he's on vacation, for Pete's sake—to cultivate unselfconsciously a virtue in the middle of a library, in the middle of need, in the middle of summer.

"TOENAILS"

It is the custom of many doctors, I among them, to withdraw from the practice of medicine every Wednesday afternoon. This, only if there is no patient who demands the continuous presence of his physician. I urge you, when the time comes, to do it, too. Such an absence from duty ought not to win you the accusation of lèse responsibility. You will, of course, have secured the availability of a colleague to look after your patients for the few hours you will spend grooming and watering your spirit. Nor is such idleness a reproach to those who do not take time off from their labors, but who choose to scramble on without losing the pace. Loafing is not better than frenzied determination. It is but an alternate mode of living.

Long ago I made a vow that I would never again delve away the month of July in the depths of the human body. In July it would be my own cadaver that engaged me. There is a danger in becoming too absorbed in Anatomy. At the end of eleven months of dissection, you stand in fair risk of suffering a kind of rapture of the deep, wherein you drift, tumbling among the coils of intestine in a state of helpless enchantment. Only a month's vacation can save you. It is wrongheaded to think of total submersion in the study and practice of Medicine. That is going too far. And going too far is for saints. I know medical students well enough to exclude you from that slender community.

Nor must you be a priest who does nothing but preserve the

souls of his parishioners and lets his own soul lapse. Such is the burnt-out case who early on drinks his patients down in a single radiant gulp and all too soon loses the desire to practice Medicine at all. In a year or two he is to be found lying in bed being fed oatmeal with a spoon. Like the fruit of the Amazon he is too quickly ripe and too quickly rotten.

Some doctors spend Wednesday afternoon on the golf course. Others go fishing. Still another takes a lesson on the viola da gamba. I go to the library where I join that subculture of elderly men and women who gather in the Main Reading Room to read or sleep beneath the world's newspapers, and thumb through magazines and periodicals, educating themselves in any number of esoteric ways, or just keeping up. It is not the least function of a library to provide for these people a warm, dry building with good working toilets and, ideally, a vending machine from which to buy a cup of hot broth or coffee. All of which attributes a public library shares with a neighborhood saloon, the only difference being the beer of one and the books of the other.

How brave, how reliable they are! plowing through you-name-what inclemencies to get to the library shortly after it opens. So unbroken is their attendance that, were one of them to be missing, it would arouse the direst suspicions of the others. And of me. For I have, furtively at first, then with increasing recklessness, begun to love them. They were, after all, living out my own fantasies. One day, with luck, I, too, would become a full-fledged, that is to say *daily,* member. At any given time, the tribe consists of a core of six regulars and a somewhat less constant pool of eight others of whom two or three can be counted on to appear. On very cold days, all eight of these might show up, causing a bit of a jam at the newspaper rack, and an edginess among the regulars.

Either out of loyalty to certain beloved articles of clothing, or from scantiness of wardrobe, they wear the same things every day. For the first year or two this was how I identified them. Old Stovepipe, Mrs. Fringes, Neckerchief, Galoshes—that sort of thing. In no other society does apparel so exactly fit the wearer as to form a part of his persona. Dior, Balenciaga, take heed! By the time I arrive, they have long since devoured the morning's newspapers and settled into their customary places. One or two, Galoshes, very likely, and Stovepipe, are sleeping it off. These two seem to need all the rest they can get. Mrs. Fringes, on the other hand, her hunger for information unappeasable, having finished all of the newspapers, will be well into the *Journal of Abnormal Psychology*, the case histories of which keep her riveted until closing time. As time went by, despite that we had not yet exchanged a word of conversation, I came to think of them as dear colleagues, fellow readers who, with me, were engaged in the pursuit of language. Nor, I noticed, did they waste much time speaking to each other. Reading was serious business. Only downstairs near the basement vending machine would animated conversation break out. Upstairs, in the Reading Room, the vow of silence was sacred.

I do not know by what criteria such selections are made, but Neckerchief is my favorite. He is a man well into his eighties with the kind of pink face that even in July looks as though it has just been brought in out of the cold. A single drop of watery discharge, like a crystal bead, hangs at the tip of his nose. His gait is stiff-legged, with tiny, quick, shuffling steps accompanied by rather wild arm-swinging in what seems an effort to gain momentum or maintain balance. For a long time I could not decide whether this manner of walking was due to arthritis of the knees or to the fact that for most of the year he wore two or more pairs of pants. Either might have been the cause of his lack of joint flexion. One day, as I held the door to the Men's Room for him, he pointed to his knees and announced, by way of explanation of his slowness:

"The hinges is rusty."

The fact was delivered with a shake of the head, a wry smile and without the least self-pity.

"No hurry," I said, and once again paid homage to Sir William Osler, who instructed his students to "listen to the patient. He is trying to tell you what is the matter with him." From that day, Neckerchief and I were friends. I learned that he lives alone in a rooming house eight blocks away, that he lives on his Social Security check, that his wife died a long time ago, that he has no children, and that the *Boston Globe* is the best damn newspaper in the library. He learned approximately the same number of facts about me. Beyond that we talked about politics and boxing, which is his great love. He himself had been an amateur fighter sixty years ago— most of his engagements having been spontaneous brawls of a decidedly ethnic nature. "It was the Polacks against the Yids," he told me, "and both of 'em against the Micks." He held up his fists to show the ancient fractures.

The actual neckerchief is a classic red cowboy rag folded into a triangle and tied about his neck in such a way that the widest part lies at the front, covering the upper chest as a kind of bib. Now and then a nose drop elongates, shimmers, wobbles and falls to be absorbed into the neckerchief. Meanwhile a new drop has taken the place of the old. So quickly is this newcomer born that I, for one, have never beheld him unadorned.

One day I watched as Neckerchief, having raided the magazine rack, journeyed back to his seat. In one flapping hand the *Saturday Review* rattled. As he passed, I saw that his usually placid expression was replaced by the look of someone in pain. Each step was a fresh onslaught of it. His lower lip was caught between his teeth. His forehead had been cut and stitched into lines of endurance. He was hissing. I waited for him to take his seat, which he did with a gasp of relief, then went up to him.

"The hinges?" I whispered.

"Nope. The toes."

"What's wrong with your toes?"

"The toenails is too long. I can't get at 'em. I'm walkin' on 'em."

I left the library and went to my office.

"What are you doing here?" said my nurse. "It's Wednesday afternoon. People are just supposed to die on Wednesday afternoon."

"I need the toenail cutters. I'll bring them back tomorrow."

"The last time you took something out of here I didn't see it for six months."

Neckerchief was right where I had left him. A brief survey, however, told me that he had made one trek in my absence. It was *U.S. News & World Report* on his lap. The *Saturday Review* was back in the rack. I could only guess what the exchange had cost him. I doubted that either of the magazines was worth it.

"Come on down to the Men's Room," I said. "I want to cut your toenails." I showed him my toenail clippers, the heavy-duty kind that you grip with the palm, and with jaws that could bite through bone. One of the handles is a rasp. I gave him a ten-minute head start, then followed him downstairs to the Men's Room. There was no one else there.

"Sit here." I pointed to one of the booths. He sat on the toilet. I knelt and began to take off his shoes.

"Don't untie 'em," he said. "I just slide 'em on and off."

The two pairs of socks were another story, having to be peeled off. The underpair snagged on the toenails. Neckerchief winced.

"How do you get these things on?" I asked.

"A mess, ain't they? I hope I don't stink too bad for you."

The nail of each big toe was the horn of a goat. Thick as a thumb and curved, it projected down over the tip of the toe to the underside. With each step, the nail would scrape painfully against the ground and be pressed into his flesh. There was dried blood on each big toe.

"Jesus, man!" I said. "How can you walk?" I thought of the eight blocks he covered twice a day.

It took an hour to do each big toe. The nails were too thick even for my nail cutters. They had to be chewed away little by little, then flattened out with the rasp. Now and then a fragment of nail would fly up, striking me in the face. The other eight toes were easy. Now and then, the door opened. Someone came and went to the row of urinals. Twice, someone occupied the booth next to ours. I never once looked up to see. They'll just have to wonder, I thought. But Neckerchief could tell from my face.

"It doesn't look decent," he said.

"Never mind," I told him. "I bet this isn't the strangest thing that's happened down here." I wet some toilet paper with warm water and soap, washed each toe, dried him off, and put his shoes and socks back on. He stood up and took a few steps, like someone who is testing the fit of a new pair of shoes.

"How is it?"

"It don't hurt," he said, and gave me a smile that I shall keep in my safety-deposit box at the bank until the day I die.

"That's a Cadillac of a toe job," said Neckerchief. "How much do I owe ya?"

"On the house," I said. "And besides, what kind of a boy do you think I am?"

The next week I did Stovepipe. He was an easy case. Then, Mrs. Fringes, who was a special problem. I had to do her in the Ladies' Room, which tied up the place for half an hour. A lot of people opened the door, took one look, and left in a hurry. Either it was hot in there or I had a temperature.

I never go to the library on Wednesday afternoon without my nail clippers in my briefcase. You just never know.

PSALM 65

Hear us, O God our salvation,

 Thou that art the hope of all the ends of the earth and of the broad sea,

Who in your strength setteth fast the mountains

 and are girded about with power.

Who stilleth the raging of the sea,

 the roaring of his waters and the tumult of the peoples.

They that dwell in the uttermost parts are afraid at thy tokens,

Thou makest both the morning and the evening stars to praise thee.

Thou visitest the earth, thou waterest it, and makest it very plenteous.

 The river of God is full of waters.

Thou preparest man his corn,

 and thus thou providest for the earth.

Thou waterest her furrows, thou breakest the hard clots thereof.

Thou makest it soft with the drops of rain

 and blessest the increase of it.

Thou crownest the year with thy goodness and thy footsteps drip fatness.

 The dwellings of the wilderness are fat also, that they drip withal

 and the little hills are pleasant on every side.

The fields are full of sheep,

 the valleys stand so thick with corn that they laugh and sing.

Mary Ann's Spicy Herb Dip

Ingredients:

- 1 cup of mayonnaise
- 2 cups of sour cream
- 4 sprigs of fresh cilantro, chopped fine, or 2 tsp. dried cilantro
- 2 sprigs of fresh parsley, chopped fine, or 1 tsp. dried parsley
- at least a fist full of fresh garlic, chopped fine, or 2 Table-
    spoons dried garlic
- juice from 1/2 lime or 1 Tablespoon lime juice
- 1 tsp. cracked pepper
- Salt to taste
- 1/2 sweet red pepper, chopped fine
- 1/2 medium sweet onion, chopped fine
- 2 jalapeño or chipotle peppers, chopped, or 2 Tablespoons
    jalapeño sauce

Prepare at least 3 hours prior to serving. Mix all ingredients and refrigerate. Great dip for veggies or chips.

PART THREE
Family and Community

INTRODUCTION

One of the most important American documents associated with summer is the Declaration of Independence, a document that speaks much of community. "It becomes necessary for *one people*," it opens. "*We* hold these truths to be self-evident." "*We*, therefore, the Representatives of the United States of America, in *General Congress, Assembled* ..." "*We mutually* pledge to each other *our* lives ..." Over and over, the Declaration of Independence affirms the notion of the community of a people, banded together. In this sense, it looks back to one of the first great American documents, the Mayflower Compact, in which the pilgrims promised to "solemnly and mutualy in ye presence of God, and one of another, covenant and combine our selves together into a civill body politick." It also looks forward to the next great American document, our Constitution, which opens with the ringing declaration, "We, the people ..."

One of summer's profound spiritual gifts is the awareness that we are not alone: that others work with us, play with us, worship with us. There are others who live with us and love us. We see that even our smallest processes are aided by the larger community that builds roadways, establishes laws, carries our mail, defends, gathers and distributes food and clothing, founds libraries and schools. In winter, we may sit by the woodstove and read. But summer calls us away from solitude to an awareness of community, annually adding this new rhythm to our lives.

When John Milton wrote his "L'Allegro," a poem celebrating joy and mirth, he pictured those qualities as often occurring in community—and the images he chose come from summer. He imagines Mirth arriving "While the Plowman near at hand, / Whistles o'er the Furrow'd Land, / And the Milkmaid singeth blithe, / And the Mower whets his scythe, / And every Shepherd tells his tale / Under the Hawthorn in the dale." He imagines a clamorous festival, where the town bells are ringing, and the fiddles are playing "To many a youth, and many a maid, / Dancing in the Checker'd shade; / And young and old come forth to play / On a Sunshine Holiday." And he imagines an even larger throng: "Tow'red Cities please us then, / And the busy hum of men." Finally, he imagines a celebration of the most intense community, marriage: "There let Hymen oft appear / In Saffron robe, with Taper clear, / And pomp, and feast, and revelry, / With mask, and antique Pageantry." These, Milton concludes, are "Such sights as youthful Poets dream / On Summer eves by haunted stream."

The eighth-century Confucian poet Du Fu has a more meditative vision focused on the pleasures of his own family, which he, like Milton, pictures in the summer.

> *The clear river curves to embrace the village.*
> *Everything is relaxed here in long summer.*
> *Swallows come and go as they like in the hall,*
> *gulls are necking in the water.*
> *My old wife is drawing on a Go board on paper,*
> *my little son is hammering a needle into a fishing hook.*
> *As long as old friends give me daily supplies,*
> *what else could my humble body desire?*

Summer suggests that we embrace the communities of which we are a part—sometimes by choice, sometimes by happenstance, sometimes simply by virtue of being members of the human race. Such an embrace may be humbling; to embrace a community might be to recognize that we need that community—"old friends give me daily supplies"—and for North Americans weaned on Ralph Waldo Emerson's cry for self-reliance, this may be difficult to accept. Although our North American capitalistic culture teaches us to say "I need things," it does not encourage us to say "I need you."

But we live, summer insists, depending upon each other. We combine together "*mutually*," says the Mayflower Compact. "We *mutually* pledge to each other our lives," the Declaration of Independence asserts. To put it another way, summer points us to an embrace that is real and meaningful. Even as we are supported within communities, so too are we called to support others. That, too, is mutuality.

There is also a quality of community that points at affirmation of a shared past. Communities have histories just as individuals do. In 1839, John Hayward's *New England Gazetteer* collected articles solicited from towns across New England. One does not read far into this volume without getting a sense of a community's proud acclamation of its history and identity. Of New Portland, Maine, Hayward includes this description: "This is one of the finest farming towns in the county. It produced, in 1837, 10,451 bushels of wheat. Population, same year, 1,476. This town has a pleasant village, a number of saw mills and other manufactories." The correspondent from Lebanon, New Hampshire, wrote that his town's "first settlers were a hardy, brave people, tenacious of their principles: most of them were men of strong minds, good habits, correct principles, and good common education."

There is a pride of belonging in these writers, a sense that the community is larger than themselves—another perhaps humbling spiritual lesson of summer. When we stand by the parade routes, when we sit beneath the skies lit up by fireworks, when we visit at family reunions with the great-grandparent who remembers our grandparents as tiny children, when we hear stories of how our families first came to this country, when we hear tales of the war or the frontier or the immigration docks and how our ancestors strove mightily in those contexts, we recognize that we truly are a part of something much larger than we at times recognize. Summer calls us to a sense of the larger whole.

These selections explore the spiritual meanings of the communities that summertime brings to mind. Reading the Declaration of Independence brings with it the thrill of recognition—this is the document that began the great experiment in democracy—but as Frederick Douglass and Barbara Tuchman remind us, communities can go wrong; they can oppress and exclude. In so doing, they lose the spiritual goodness that comes from gathering together. Thomas Lynch reminds us that a community's history is a fluid thing, reinterpreted as it is given over into the keeping of each successive generation. Donald Hall and William Vande Kopple both write of the powerful ways neighbors and families shape our understandings of ourselves. And Carl Sandburg's poetry echoes with the celebration of the communal, "a rouse of voices reaching for the heart of the world."

"Hear O Israel, the Lord our God, the Lord is one," claims the Sh'ma, rooting this call to faith in the community that speaks of *our* God. "I believe in God the Father," begins the Apostles' Creed, "and in the Holy Catholic Church," calling for a faith that is both individual and rooted in the larger experience, tradition, and community of the Church. We live our lives as individuals, yes. But summer teaches us too that we live our lives as members of communities vast and small, and that an awareness of that belonging will affect how it is that we take meaning from the constellation of experiences that make up who we are and how we make our way in this world.

A Prayer

Covenant God, hear the creatures you have
    made,
creatures made to know you and enjoy you forever,
creatures who find their rest in you.

Creator of all beauty, you have made us in your
    image;
you have made us for pleasure;
you have made us for joy.

O God, you have made us in your image:
You have made us for community,
for communion, for love.

In our foolishness, we squander those gifts.
We desire what is less than beautiful,
what is less than good,
what is less than lovely.

We pay the price in lives that are marked by
    restless striving,
not joy,
in lives that are marked by loneliness and self-
    destruction,
not communion.

Out of community with you,
we cannot properly love our neighbors and
    ourselves.

Liberate us from those elements of our selves,
    loving God,
that keep us from loving you and our neighbors
    aright.

Grant us eyes to see and hearts to love
those you have given us to be our neighbors,
so that we see signs of your kingdom, your
    shalom,
in our lives together.

Amen.

—JAMES VANDEN BOSCH

Thomas Lynch

"THE OAK GROVE IMBROGLIO" FROM *BODIES IN MOTION AND AT REST*

Summer evokes images of picnics, of parades, of crowded stands watching baseball games, of concerts in the park, of townspeople gathering on blankets at night to watch a Fourth of July sky, of Rotary Club concerts and Sunday School outings, of neighborhood block parties and families gathering on a hot beach. All of these represent gatherings of communities, when people come together to celebrate, to worship, to play, to express patriotism, to affirm the common bands that connect them with one another.

The essayist and funeral director Thomas Lynch here evokes that sense of communal spirit as it is manifested in a town's attempt to represent its own past—a process that in some ways is at the center of both of Lynch's vocations. It is no easy matter. Communities may be like-minded, and they may, in fact, share many assumptions about how the world is and why it is that way. But communities are not monolithic, as we

> $\mathcal{L}$ike the summer, communities are not eternal; yet, like the summer, communities create histories long in the remembering.

discover when the town decides to celebrate its history by making use of the local graveyard. To whom does the cemetery belong? Lynch asks. Not an easy question.

Like the summer, communities are not eternal; yet, like the summer, communities create histories long in the remembering. The communal celebrations of summer, be they personal (a family reunion) or local (the baseball game between the Lutherans and the Baptists) or national (the Fourth of July), all work to reinforce connections between individuals, forming groups both large and small. If the individuals end up fussing at one another, well then, suggests Lynch, the village council will put it on its agenda and the matter will be resolved—and recounted in later years as a summertime story.

"THE OAK GROVE IMBROGLIO"

Lately, the local citizenry is vexed by questions of "usage" in the village graveyard. It seems nothing is self-evident anymore.

Thespians with time on their hands can be a peril. Years ago there'd have been factories and wars and children underfoot to fatigue them, but now they all have 401Ks and flex time, day care and Planned Parenthood and the Pax Americana. Add to this expanding idleness the appetites of history buffs and the booster-ism of chamber-of-commerce types and we get a sometimes toxic cocktail of "good ideas." There is a hybrid class of do-gooder on the loose for whom even the dead are not past improvement, god-helpus. Just such a consortium came up with the brainstorm, over the winter, for what they call a Cemetery Walk to disturb the peace of the third weekend in August on what *they* hope will be an annual basis.

They used to do this play in Central Park, under a big tent rented for the weekend. They called it *Milford Memories*. It was mostly about the good old days and the good old-timers who used to live here a good old century ago before sidewalks and indoor plumbing and Internet access made life complex. A band was hired, costumes made, lines learned at rehearsals. Posters were put up all around town. Tickets were sold in the local emporia. Mention was made from several pulpits.

The first year, of course, everyone came to see what their neighbors had wrought. The next year no one came back, not even for the free matinee on Sunday afternoon. Apparently the fascination with Victoriana has its limits and the local curiosities had been sated. The old days, it turns out, are a finite field of study. Even when it is costumed, dramatized and set to music, it is hard to compete with twentieth-century spectacles. The writers blamed the actors, the actors blamed the writers. Both groups looked with suspicion at the band.

It is a long-established truth of the theater that if the script cannot be improved upon and the actors are working at the top of their craft and still no one comes, then it must be the venue, the stage. If the *what* and *who* cannot be fixed, maybe the *where* is worth another look. This is when someone proposed a "Cemetery Walk." The troop turned its collective head as a water spaniel will when a strange noise is heard.

"We could do it in Oak Grove!" the visionary said. "Who needs props when you've got headstones and monuments, the names and dates and everything right there!"

Some naysayer said it would be hard to get folks to show up at a graveyard.

"Not if you take them by buckboard wagons!" said one of the crew. A certain contagion attends such brainstorms. "We could sell lemonade!" said another.

The hitherto crestfallen cast members began to nod and smile at one another. Same costumes, same script, same camaraderie, but a new and improved "stage." The director, who manages a local real estate franchise, said, "Location, location, location!"

An organizing committee was formed. One of the thespians was active with the Historical Society, which unanimously agreed to act as co-sponsor of the event. Another knew someone on the township board, which promptly granted its permission to use the cemetery without public hearing, for surely no one would take issue with such a worthy enterprise. A route was established to take advantage of the best old houses with their gingerbread and formal gardens. Banners and buntings appeared. The wholesale syndication of good intentions, good neighbors and good times resembled nothing so much as one of those Brueghel prints in which happy villagers turn their efforts to a common purpose, like *Hay Making* or *The Peasant Dance* or *Children's Games,* and live happily ever after.

When the day in August itself arrived, tickets were sold for seats in horse-drawn wagons hired from the local 4-H crowd that made their leisurely way through the old section of town, with docents from the Historical Society riding shotgun, pointing out en route some points of historical significance, architectural importance and local lore until they came to Oak Grove Cemetery, where actors in period costumes and paste-on beards jumped out from behind the headstones of our historical dead and told their stories. Civil war casualties, flu victims and Main Street merchants long since dead were "brought to life," so to speak, to a more or less captive audience of variously bewildered and wide-eyed wagoneers who, conditioned by the culture they lived in, felt, nonetheless, "entertained" or "edified" or, at the very least, part of a "meaningful shared experience."

The writers, directors and actors all agreed that the production was, well, "moving." That this may have had something to do with the horse-drawn wagons was a truth that remained, all the same, unspoken. The costly band had been replaced by taped music and a boom box. The tent rental and chair rental had been made redundant. To the extent that the ticket sales covered the cost of the livery charges, a little stipend to the cemetery maintenance fund and the wine-and-cheese cast party that inevitably followed, the project was fashioned a monumental if break-even success!

So it was with great distress that they received the news, in the form of a letter to the *Milford Times* the following week, that some of the people who had family buried in Oak Grove took issue with the use of their ancestors' final resting place as a "stage" of sorts. Had the organizers of this production no sense of decorum or respect for the dead?

But what better way to commemorate the dead, it was argued, than to educate the living about their lives? The place is full of history and "characters" and stories and art!

No, the other side argued, it is full of fathers and mothers and daughters and sons who have no obligation to educate or entertain or instruct the living. Museums and libraries, art galleries and public parks, serve these purposes. The bodies of the dead make Oak Grove a sacred space. The lessons of the grave are taught in stony quiet to those who go there for their hushed reasons, less for information than for contemplation, less for soliloquy than for interior monologue.

The thespians argued the merits of the play, its dignity and respect and artistic splendors, its value as a vehicle for history and local interests.

LOCATION, LOCATION, LOCATION, came the counter-charge. The right thing done in the wrong place is, in the end, a mistake. There are plenty of options available to the living. The high school, the Methodist church, the Masonic temple, all have stages. Central Park has an amphitheater and plentiful parking. The dead, long buried, are grounded, optionless, rooted to their graves in ways that could not be relieved or remedied. The issue of *choice* has reared its contentious head with shades of *Hamlet* and the late-century debates over zoning and privacy and barrier-free access.

Then there's the matter, ever a concern in the Middle West, of the slippery slope. If a Cemetery Walk for the Historical Society, why not a Cemetery Bird Watching for the Audubon Society? What possible harm is there in bird watching? If a Cemetery Walk for Milford Memories, why not a 5-K run through the cemetery to raise funds for disabled veterans? Is that not a noble purpose? What possible harm in a 5-K run? If a Cemetery Walk for the sake of history, why not a memorial band concert—what possible harm? And if a band concert, why not a folk concert, and if a folk concert, why not a rock concert, and if rock, why not reggae or rap or a bit of opera—who gets to choose, who gets to say which kind of concert is and isn't appropriate? Or why not a bake sale or wine tasting or memorial raft race—for Oak Grove is bordered by the mighty Huron too? Why not art shows or poetry readings or nature studies or ecology lectures? Why oughtn't the Rotary Club, which has several past members buried there, and an interest in the heritage of this place, have an annual picnic there to raise awareness about this town and the Rotary's involvement with it? Or why not the PTA, or the chamber of commerce, or the Thursday night bowling league? There's never a shortage of interest and a worthy cause. These are all good things, undertaken by good people for all the best reasons. And Oak Grove might well seem a good place for them. What possible harm?

The harm, of course, is that once the gate is opened it is hard to close, and lost forever is the sacred and dedicated space that is only a cemetery and needs be nothing more.

The Oak Grove imbroglio won't be settled soon. There's never a shortage of polemic or opinion here. Low inflation and a bull market have left us all with time on our hands to ponder the formerly imponderable questions. Should a graveyard be a graveyard only? Whose cemetery is it anyway? Are the dead left in the livings' care or in their indenture?

The village council has put the matter on the agenda for its October meeting. There will be a series of public hearings. Fundraisers are scheduled on both sides of the questions. Placards are being painted in folks' garages. The newspaper is planning a special series of reports.

Maybe if I took a funeral down through town—hearse and limousines, corpse and pallbearers, family and friends, cast and crew, all of us playing our long-practiced parts—but took a detour into Central Park and laid the dead guy out in the gazebo there and engaged one of the local clergy to hold forth on the mysteries of death and the promise of salvation, or buried the next few clients in the tennis courts, or burned a few locals in the barbecue and scattered their ashes in the horseshoe pits, or consigned the bodies to the deep of the wee pond there, or set them adrift on a blazing barge, Viking-style, in the middle of the mighty Huron River, which runs along the south edge of the village green; maybe folks would start to understand. If Oak Grove can be turned into a theater, can't Central Park be memorial gardens? Even the most noble of human endeav-ors can miss the mark by half a mile sometimes. Is there a chance the thespians will get the picture?

Still, maybe they'd turn up with their video-cams and patio chairs—ever ready for the movie version of a good idea—giving out with "Places everyone! Lights. Camera. Quiet on the set. Roll 'em!"

William J. Vande Kopple

"BRIGHT HOPE"

Communities are as large as nation-states, as small as individual families. And size has little to do with the passionate commitment to common bands. Whose heart does not sing when the Olympic flag is raised and one's country's national anthem is played in celebration and honor of athletic prowess? And whose heart does not hold still in its beating with the pleasure of a small child reading his first sentence, a spouse succeeding beyond hope in her profession, a grandparent telling a story of the old days? It is not good that the man should be alone, says the Lord God soon after Adam's creation. Our experience affirms the principle.

> *C*ommunities are as large as nation-states, as small as individual families. And size has little to do with the passionate commitment to common bands.

In "Bright Hope," essayist William J. Vande Kopple borrows a line from the old hymn "Great is Thy Faithfulness," to capture the joys and tensions that lie within the community of a family. The bands of love that connect one member to another have nothing to do with the passage of time, suggests Vande Kopple. They have everything to do with commitment, one to another. That commitment is expressed through mutual experience, mutual understanding, mutual kindness—all of which teach us what community and family really means.

"Bright Hope"

When my dad mentioned at breakfast on the next-to-last day of our family vacation that he was going to drive down to Grand Rapids to bring Grandpa Abe up for a half day of fishing, my little brothers and sister didn't even seem to hear him. As they raced through their cereal, leaving small pools of milk on the table with a Fruit Loop or two floating in them, all they talked about between their annoying crunches was getting out on the dock. There they would do what they had done for hours every day of the week so far—lie as quietly as possible on their stomachs and peer over the edge waiting for minnows and small sunfish that they tried to catch with violent swift swoops with partially torn butterfly nets.

But Dad got me wondering: Why would he drive from our cottage on Hess Lake to the city and back, later having to repeat the whole process? He would have to make four thirty-five minute drives in one day. Couldn't Grandpa do what he had always done before, drive his tank-like deuce and a quarter—with Grandma Reka when she was alive and by himself after she died—to spend part of a day with us while we were on our summer vacation? But I sensed that I had better keep still. Dad seemed fidgety, scraping at his lower lip first with one eyetooth, then the other, and I knew if I asked any question at all, he might respond with what I hated to hear: "Thirteen years old and already a worry wart—when are you going to learn how to trust?"

When they got back from Grand Rapids, I was in the boat making sure everything was set. I had three life jackets stowed in a little compartment in the bow. I had a cushion laid out on each seat. I had Dad's metal tackle/tool box under the middle seat and my plastic tackle box under the rear. I had a Johnson's silver minnow snapped on my rod, and I had checked my drag.

But Grandpa didn't carry his rods and tackle box directly out onto the dock and claim his favorite spot in the bow of the boat, as he always had in the past. Instead, he brought his gear to the edge of our beach, gave a plastic pail half-buried in the sand a nudge with his foot, and then turned to look for a lawn chair on the grass. Once in a chair, he seemed to be scanning the opposite shoreline, but I noticed that after a few minutes his head slumped forward as he fell into a little snooze.

After I had double-checked that everything was ready in the boat, I called to Dad and Grandpa, "Hey! Are we going to get out there or what? I've been waiting all morning. Not too many water skiers right now. And all the big bass are going to feel insulted if we don't pay more attention to them than this!"

So Dad walked over and nudged Grandpa, his head jerked up, and they gathered his gear and came out to the boat. I was surprised to see that Grandpa accepted some help from my dad in stepping down into the boat. "My left hip is pretty much a dud," he winced; "sometime soon, I guess, I'll have to see about getting a new one."

Once we were all settled in the boat and Dad had rowed us out of the shallows, Grandpa's unusual behavior continued. Always in the past he had been close to imperious during fishing excursions, telling us that he knew precisely where all the fish were and what they would bite on, directing my dad to position the boat according to his very specific directions, insisting that he get the first crack at casting to spots that he claimed held fish.

But this time when my dad asked him where he wanted to try first, all he said was "Oh, anywhere out here past the weeds. It's all about the same." So we drifted along the outside edge of the coontail, and I got busy casting to little pockets in the weeds. Dad made casts too, but very casually, as if he would be surprised to catch anything. But all Grandpa did was snap on a pre-rigged plastic night crawler and then lob it out behind the boat. More than once we told him that he needed to add some weight to his line and clean off his lure; we could see the crawler dragging about six inches below the surface only ten feet back of the boat, a couple of brownish weeds snagged on the rear hook. But he left the fouled crawler where it was, resting one spotted hand on the gunnel and staring down at the tiny whirlpools our keel stirred up as the wind pushed us along.

I fought and lost two nice bass in the first twenty minutes or so—it was the most action with big fish that I had had to that point that week—and then Dad asked Grandpa if he wanted to keep drifting. "You don't have to stay out here for my sake," Grandpa replied; "Bill got into some fish. And you said you might have had a hit or two. It doesn't seem to be my day. We might as well call it quits."

So we reeled up and headed in.

When we were tied up back at the dock, Dad gave Grandpa a hand getting out of the boat and then turned to grab equipment from me. As he did, he saw that I had noticed how wet Grandpa's seat cushion was; some of the liquid had run off the cushion onto the seat itself.

"I'll get a rag and wipe it all up," I said; "no has to know any difference."

"Good. Thanks. Grandpa's not been doing too good the last month or so. And you can't believe how embarrassed it all makes him. He refuses to talk about it—even to me when it's just the two of us."

"But he'll get better before too long, won't he?"

"This is a tough bit of business, Bill. We've been to more than one doctor. And the last one says he's pretty much run out of options for treatment."

"But summer has just started, and Grandpa and I usually fish together every week in the summer. Don't tell me I won't be able to get out on the water with him before school starts up again."

"You know what we say in this family about hope."

"Hope? You mean that line you say and sometimes even sing to yourself?"

"Yeah. Do you understand it?"

"Some of it, I guess."

About forty years later, long after I had graduated from rented row-boats to my own fishing boat, I occasionally found myself sharing it with one or more adolescent male relatives.

At the end of last August, our extended family spent a long weekend camping at Mullet Lake, and during lunch of the first day, my three sons—Jon, Joel, and Jason—and their two nephews—Tim and Matt—started some intense collective begging to get me to take all five of them out to try for pike on the flats of the Indian River, which they had heard noticeably successful fisherman talking about at the fish-cleaning house.

My sons knew how skittish I was about having the three of them, let alone the three of them plus their two male cousins, fishing together with me in one boat. So for the first couple of days I don't think they were too surprised when I put them off and pretended to have no interest in fishing a big new lake—left the boat on its trailer the first day, took all the women out for a ride checking out cottages the next. But those boys had worn me down more than once in the past, and they knew they could probably wear me down again.

"What's the point of having a boat called a 'fishing machine' if you don't even use it to fish?" Joel called from the edge of our campsite, where the five of them were taking turns juggling a soccer ball the afternoon of our last full day.

"Yeah," Jason added, "earlier this summer you told us this lake had pike and muskies down by the Indian River, and why would you say that and then not take us out to try for them? Doesn't the Bible have verses about parents not frustrating their kids?"

"I'm just afraid that having all five of you together in one boat is trouble, and that starts with a *T* and rhymes with *P*," I countered.

"Real funny!" Joel took another turn. "What's *The Sound of Music* got to do with taking us out in the boat? You think you can trick us by just sitting there quoting lines from songs, but you're wrong."

"*I'm* wrong?"

"Just think about it a little, Dad," Jon stepped in; "we talked to Tim and Matt about this trip a month or more ago, and they were so sure they would be able to try for pike that each of them went out and bought some expensive new lures. Would it really be fair to lead them to spend money for tackle they weren't going to be able to use?"

"Oh, I don't know. Is that true, Matt? Did you spend some of your own money on new lures?"

"I bought a couple. I've never caught a pike in my life. Not even sure I've seen one, except in pictures. And Jon, Joel, and Jason got me going with all their stories about your last trip to Les Cheneaux. So I took some of my lawn money and bought a big Rapala. And a red-and-white spoon—the package says it's guaranteed to catch fish."

"How about you, Tim?"

"I bought a couple of new spinner baits, but if you really don't want all of us in the boat with you, I'll try to find some other time to use them. I think my uncle on my mom's side has a canoe." He ended with a little shrug of resignation.

It was the shrug that did it. I could handle their sass and sarcasm. I could handle their arguments, in which they said the same thing over and over, increasing the volume with each repetition. I could even handle most of their whining. But I couldn't handle somber resignation. So I decided to take the chance and say yes to all six hundred and forty or so pounds of them.

And, in truth, they were close to angelic as we, probably over the limits of my boat's carrying capacity, headed away from the campground launch site south to the flats, the bow of the boat burrowing into the backside of one swell after the next. But once we got there and started rigging up to fish, they began to send up little flares that when the five of them were together, foolery or danger or both were never far off.

Joel and Jason liked to take big shiner minnows, position a jackknife on their spine behind their gills, slice their heads off at an angle, hook the decapitated bodies on jigs, and then cast and retrieve the jigs.

This, we all knew, was a very effective technique. The slanted cut on the shiner bodies would make them wobble enticingly in the water when retrieved slowly, and if there were any pike around, they usually could not resist such offerings.

The trouble started when Joel and Jason began to argue about who had made the most effective cut. As the argument developed, they started tossing bloody shiner bodies from one end of the boat to the other for inspection. While this was going on, the muscles in my neck and shoulders started to tighten up since every few seconds I had to look around and then do a little bob and weave to avoid being hit by the bloody body of a shiner. Alert as I was, I still ended up with a stain on the shoulder of my t-shirt.

When these two saw that the others had finished snapping on crank baits and were ready to fish, they finally decided to drop their squabble and get their baits in the water. But then my neck and shoulders tensed up even more. None of these kids was very big; Jason and Matt, the youngest, were only around five feet tall. But each of them was using a rod six feet long or longer, and in order for them to get their baits a ways out from the boat, they would swing the rod behind them to eight or nine o'clock and then whip it forward and release the line.

If they had had a tennis ball attached to the end of their line, I probably would have worried only a little about getting bopped in the back of the head. But since they all were whipping out over the water either a large jig hook or a lure with a pair of treble hooks, I feared having one or more hooks rip into my neck or the back of one of my ears. "Probably," I thought, "the older boys could take one of my ears right off."

"You've got to watch each and every back cast," I warned; "no exceptions! Else somebody will need to have hooks cut out of the back of his head—and you sure don't want that someone to be me." To their credit, they worked hard to cooperate; I could see them glancing over their shoulders to make sure they had a clear lane for their back casts.

Until one of them thought he had a strike. Then they all went into a casting frenzy—whup, whup, whup, whup, whup, their rods slicing the air as they raced to land a lure on the spot where they thought the fish had been. No attention to their back casts. No worry when a lure brushed through somebody's hair. Nothing but annoyance about wasted time when one of their lures hooked my baseball cap and took it sailing out over the water.

Sometimes, usually just after one of these casting frenzies had burned itself out, one of the boys, now feeling the effects of having drunk thirty or forty ounces of Mountain Dew in the last hour, would balance himself up on the gunnel, unzip, and noisily hit a spot in the water seven or eight feet away. Once one started, another usually followed, setting up a contest about who could hit the water farthest from the boat. The others would estimate distances and declare a winner, who would then sing out in a husky falsetto, carrying across the water, "Pop, pop, whiz, whiz. Oh, what a relief it is!"

After the song, they usually moved into a bragging and joking contest. A few of their jokes were clever. A few, I thought, were just plain stupid. Several approached the ribald, with allusions to parts of the human body that the youngest boys, somewhat awkward between childhood and early adolescence, clearly had not settled on names for.

I should have stopped them, I know. But they were almost manic in their attempts to one-up one another. Plus I was pretty sure that no one in any other boat or on the shore could hear them. And some late-developing part of my character, I have to admit, actually enjoyed some of their jokes; in fact, I often had to turn away and fake some coughing to cover my laughter.

As anglers say, we really got into some pike that night. Everybody fought and landed at least a couple—I had several razor-thin slits on my fingers from handling so many pike and getting too close to their teeth. Plus Jon caught his biggest fish of the summer—a thirty-seven-inch northern with such broad shoulders that he and Joel together had trouble holding it still while I took my pliers and got the hooks out.

As we plowed our way back to the launch site, I reminded the boys that since we had to pack up in the morning, I was going to trailer the boat that night and pull it to our campsite. Later, when I had finished backing the boat up next to our tent, I jumped out and told them: "I've got to hit the bathroom before I do anything else. You guys make sure you've got all your equipment out of the boat and do what you can to clean things up. Pick up all the bits of loose line. Don't leave any candy wrappers on the floor. And make double sure there are no hooks lying around!"

As I came back from the bathroom, Jason finished cramming a life jacket into one of the boat's side compartments, whispered something to his brothers and cousins, and walked up to me.

"We were wondering. We know it's the end of summer and you'll probably leave the boat in the garage as you start fishing the rivers for salmon whenever you have time on the weekends, but...."

"But what?"

"Well, we all had such a blast out there tonight—do you think you'll be willing to take the five of us out on the water again when it warms up next spring? It would stink if this was a one and only."

"You know what we say in this family about hope."

"Huh? Oh, right. I hear Grandpa with a line about hope every so often. Like last night, when I was helping him get the campfire going, I heard him singing. Let's see—what was that again? Yeah, I've got it: He was singing "strength for today, and bright hope for the morrow" under his breath. What's up with that?"

"Don't you understand it?"

"Maybe a little."

"You'll understand it better and better as you get older."

"You think so? What makes you say that?"

"Because look how old I am, and I learned something about it just tonight."

Carl Sandburg

A GATHERING OF POEMS

Summer is a time for solitary walks and long hours spent buried in a book, but summer also lures us back into the company of family, friends, and neighbors. We yawn together and talk together. We walk quietly with our lover or sit silently looking up at stars and out at the darkening lake. We head out to the Fourth of July celebration, clutching blankets and lawn chairs, handing out sparklers to delighted toddlers, agreeing with our newly made friends sitting on the roof of the car next to us that, yes, these are the best fireworks ever.

Perhaps summer is, as Carl Sandburg imagines it, the conductor of a great orchestra. It sets the whole world spinning and singing and shouting—and all to accompany and embrace the joyous leaps of a single exuberant dancer. Or perhaps summer itself is the orchestra, lovingly directed by One who knows the heart of the world—and the heart of each dancer.

> Perhaps summer is, as Carl Sandburg imagines it, the conductor of a great orchestra. It sets the whole world spinning and singing and shouting—and all to accompany and embrace the joyous leaps of a single exuberant dancer.

Village in Late Summer

Lips half-willing in a doorway.
Lips half-singing at a window.
Eyes half-dreaming in the walls.
Feet half-dancing in a kitchen.
Even the clocks half-yawn the hours
And the farmers make half-answers.

On the Breakwater

On the breakwater in the summer dark, a man and a
*   girl are sitting,*
She across his knee and they are looking face into face
Talking to each other without words, singing rhythms
*   in silence to each other.*

A funnel of white ranges the blue dusk from an out-
*   going boat,*
Playing its searchlight, puzzled, abrupt, over a streak
*   of green,*
And two on the breakwater keep their silence, she on
*   his knee.*

Summer Stars

Bend low again, night of summer stars.
So near you are, sky of summer stars,
So near, a long arm man can pick off stars,
Pick off what he wants in the sky bowl,
So near you are, summer stars,
So near, strumming, strumming,
So lazy and hum-strumming.

Mask

Fling your red scarf faster and faster, dancer.
It is summer and the sun loves a million green leaves,
masses of green.
Your red scarf flashes across them calling and a-calling.
The silk and flare of it is a great soprano leading a
chorus
Carried along in a rouse of voices reaching for the
heart of the world.
Your toes are singing to meet the song of your arms:

Let the red scarf go swifter.
Summer and the sun command you.

Silver Wind

Do you know how the dream looms? how if summer
  misses one of us the two of us miss summer—
Summer when the lungs of the earth take a long
    breath for the change to low contralto singing
    mornings when the green corn leaves first break
    through the black loam—
And another long breath for the silver soprano melody
    of the moon songs in the light nights when the
    earth is lighter than a feather, the iron moun-
    tains lighter than a goose down—
So I shall look for you in the light nights then, in the
    laughter of slats of silver under a hill hickory.
In the listening tops of the hickories, in the wind
    motions of the hickory shingle leaves, in the
    imitations of slow sea water on the shingle silver
    in the wind—
I shall look for you.

Goodnight

Many ways to spell good night.

Fireworks at a pier on the Fourth of July spell it with
red wheels and yellow spokes.
They fizz in the air, touch the water and quit.
Rockets make a trajectory of gold-and-blue and then
go out.

Railroad trains at night spell with a smokestack
mushrooming a white pillar.

Steamboats turn a curve in the Mississippi crying in
a baritone that crosses lowland cottonfields to a
razorback hill.

It is easy to spell good night.
Many ways to spell good night.

THE DECLARATION OF INDEPENDENCE

The Declaration of Independence—drafted by Thomas Jefferson, revised by Benjamin Franklin and John Adams, amended by the Second Continental Congress during a sweltering Philadelphia summer, and finally adopted by the Congress on July 4, 1776—is a ringing statement that establishes, among other principles, the nature of the connections that bind nations and peoples one to another. The Creator, the Declaration claims, endows all of us with unalienable rights. A government exists to support and protect those rights, to provide security and liberty and paths to happiness; thus, the only legitimate source of its authority is the consent of the governed. When the government no longer serves that purpose, then the community has been severed, and a people have the right to be independent and to form a new government that expresses mutual ties—a right that the signers of this Declaration took "with a firm reliance on the protection of divine Providence."

The opening lines of the Declaration still resound in the ears of Americans, as they do around the world among those who struggle for freedom: "We hold these truths to be self-evident."

For many years, this document was the stuff of grade school memorization—though that has passed with the loss of our taste for communal readings, as though they were mere rote recitations. But the opening lines of the Declaration still resound in the ears of Americans, as they do around the world among those who struggle for freedom: "We hold these truths to be self-evident." The powerful assertion by Jefferson and the other signers is what is celebrated each Fourth of July, the inception of the grand experiment in self-government that is America.

THE DECLARATION OF INDEPENDENCE

When in the Course of human events, it becomes necessary for one people to dissolve the political bands which have connected them with another, and to assume among the powers of the earth, the separate and equal station to which the Laws of Nature and of Nature's God entitle them, a decent respect to the opinions of mankind requires that they should declare the causes which impel them to the separation.

We hold these truths to be self-evident, that all men are created equal, that they are endowed by their Creator with certain unalienable Rights, that among these are Life, Liberty and the pursuit of Happiness.—That to secure these rights, Governments are instituted among Men, deriving their just powers from the consent of the governed,—That whenever any Form of Government becomes destructive of these ends, it is the Right of the People to alter or to abolish it, and to institute new Government, laying its foundation on such principles and organizing its powers in such form, as to them shall seem most likely to effect their Safety and Happiness. Prudence, indeed, will dictate that Governments long established should not be changed for light and transient causes; and accordingly all experience hath shewn, that mankind are more disposed to suffer, while evils are sufferable, than to right themselves by abolishing the forms to which they are accustomed. But when a long train of abuses and usurpations, pursuing invariably the same Object evinces a design to reduce them under absolute Despotism, it is their right, it is their duty, to throw off such Government, and to provide new Guards for their future security.— Such has been the patient sufferance of these Colonies; and such is now the necessity which constrains them to alter their former Systems of Government. The history of the present King of Great Britain is a history of repeated injuries and usurpations, all having in direct object the establishment of an absolute Tyranny over these States. To prove this, let Facts be submitted to a candid world.

He has refused his Assent to Laws, the most wholesome and necessary for the public good.

He has forbidden his Governors to pass Laws of immediate and pressing importance, unless suspended in their operation till his Assent should be obtained; and when so suspended, he has utterly neglected to attend to them.

He has refused to pass other Laws for the accommodation of large districts of people, unless those people would relinquish the right of Representation in the Legislature, a right inestimable to them and formidable to tyrants only.

He has called together legislative bodies at places unusual, uncomfortable, and distant from the depository of their public Records, for the sole purpose of fatiguing them into compliance with his measures.

He has dissolved Representative Houses repeatedly, for opposing with manly firmness his invasions on the rights of the people.

He has refused for a long time, after such dissolutions, to cause others to be elected; whereby the Legislative powers, incapable of Annihilation, have returned to the People at large for their exercise; the State remaining in the mean time exposed to all the dangers of invasion from without, and convulsions within.

He has endeavoured to prevent the population of these States; for that purpose obstructing the Laws of Naturalization of Foreigners;

refusing to pass others to encourage their migration hither, and raising the conditions of new Appropriations of Lands.

He has obstructed the Administration of Justice, by refusing his Assent to Laws of establishing Judiciary powers.

He has made Judges dependent on his Will alone, for the tenure of their offices, and the amount and payment of their salaries.

He has erected a multitude of New Offices, and sent hither swarms of Officers to harrass our people, and eat out their substance.

He has kept among us, in times of peace, Standing Armies without the Consent of our legislatures.

He has affected to render the Military independent of and superior to the Civil power.

He has combined with others to subject us to a jurisdiction foreign to our constitution, and unacknowledged by our laws; giving his Assent to their Acts of pretended Legislation:

For Quartering large bodies of armed troops among us:

For protecting them, by a mock Trial, from punishment for any Murders which they should commit on the Inhabitants of these States

For cutting off our Trade with all parts of the world:

For imposing Taxes on us without our Consent:

For depriving us in many cases, of the benefits of Trial by Jury:

For transporting us beyond Seas to be tried for pretended offences:

For abolishing the free System of English Laws in a neighbouring Province, establishing therein an Arbitrary government, and enlarging its Boundaries so as to render it at once an example and fit instrument for introducing the same absolute rule into these Colonies:

For taking away our Charters, abolishing our most valuable Laws, and altering fundamentally the Forms of our Governments:

For suspending our own Legislatures, and declaring

themselves invested with power to legislate for us in all cases whatsoever.

He has abdicated Government here, by declaring us out of his Protection and waging War against us.

He has plundered our seas, ravaged our Coasts, burnt our towns, and destroyed the lives of our people.

He is at this time transporting large Armies of foreign Mercenaries to complete the works of death, desolation and tyranny, already begun with circumstances of Cruelty & perfidy scarcely paralleled in the most barbarous ages, and totally unworthy the Head of a civilized nation.

He has constrained our fellow Citizens taken Captive on the high Seas to bear Arms against their Country, to become the executioners of their friends and Brethren, or to fall themselves by their Hands.

He has excited domestic insurrections amongst us, and has endeavoured to bring on the inhabitants of our frontiers, the merciless Indian Savages, whose known rule of warfare, is an undistinguished destruction of all ages, sexes and conditions.

In every stage of these Oppressions We have Petitioned for Redress in the most humble terms: Our repeated Petitions have been answered only by repeated injury. A Prince whose character is thus marked by every act which may define a Tyrant, is unfit to be the ruler of a free people.

Nor have We been wanting in attentions to our Brittish brethren. We have warned them from time to time of attempts by their legislature to extend an unwarrantable jurisdiction over us. We have reminded them of the circumstances of our emigration and settlement here. We have appealed to their native justice and magnanimity, and we have conjured them by the ties of our common kindred to disavow these usurpations, which, would inevitably interrupt our connections and correspondence. They too have been deaf to the voice of justice and of consanguinity. We must, therefore, acquiesce in the necessity, which denounces our Separation, and hold them, as we hold the rest of mankind, Enemies in War, in Peace Friends.

We, therefore, the Representatives of the united States of America, in General Congress, Assembled, appealing to the Supreme Judge of the world for the rectitude of our intentions, do, in the Name, and by Authority of the good People of these Colonies, solemnly publish and declare, That these United Colonies are, and of Right ought to be Free and Independent States; that they are Absolved from all Allegiance to the British Crown, and that all political connection between them and the State of Great Britain, is and ought to be totally dissolved; and that as Free and Independent States, they have full Power to levy War, conclude Peace, contract Alliances, establish Commerce, and to do all other Acts and Things which Independent States may of right do. And for the support of this Declaration, with a firm reliance on the protection of divine Providence, we mutually pledge to each other our Lives, our Fortunes and our sacred Honor.

Frederick Douglass

"WHAT TO THE SLAVE IS THE FOURTH OF JULY?"

Frederick Douglass was not the only orator who burned America's consciousness on the issue of slavery during the mid-nineteenth century, but his voice was certainly one of the most potent, having emerged from the chains of that crime. In 1838, Douglass escaped from Maryland and came to New Bedford, Massachusetts, and not long thereafter he traveled throughout the North as a lecturer for the Massachusetts Anti-Slavery Society. In 1845 he published the first volume of his autobiography, *Narrative of the Life of Frederick Douglass, An American Slave*—a book that became a huge best-seller and that may, with Harriet Beecher Stowe's *Uncle Tom's Cabin*, have been one of the strongest literary inducements toward the Civil War.

> *P*erhaps the listeners who came to hear Douglass deliver this Fourth of July speech were surprised at what they got—but they could never have denied its justice, or the prophetic quality of the voice that rang out on this summer day.

Douglass spent all of his life fighting for social justice, often through his hopefully entitled newspaper, *New National Era*, and often through his lectures and speeches. He urged that the vote be extended to newly emancipated slaves, that women be granted equal rights, and that working conditions for all be improved. The fire and passion of his rhetoric is suggested here in this lecture, given in 1852, when he took America to task for failing to live up to the promises and claims made in the Declaration of Independence. Perhaps the listeners who came to hear Douglass deliver this Fourth of July speech were surprised at what they got—but they could never have denied its justice, or the prophetic quality of the voice that rang out on this summer day.

"What to the Slave Is the Fourth of July?"

"For it is not light that is needed but fire...."

Fellow citizens: pardon me, and allow me to ask why am I called upon to speak here today? What have I or those I represent to do with your national independence? Are the great principles of political freedom and of natural justice, embodied in that Declaration of Independence, extended to us? And am I, therefore, called upon to bring our humble offering to the national altar, and to confess the benefits, and express devout gratitude for the blessings resulting from your independence to us?

Would to God, both for your sakes and ours, that an affirmative answer could be truthfully returned to these questions. Then would my task be light, and my burden easy and delightful. For who is there so cold that a nation's sympathy could not warm him? Who so obdurate and dead to the claims of gratitude, that would not thankfully acknowledge such priceless benefits? Who so stolid and selfish that would not give his voice to swell the halleluiahs of a nation's jubilee, when the chains of servitude had been torn from his limbs? I am not that man. In a case like that, the dumb might eloquently speak, and the "lame man leap like a hare."

But such is not the state of the case. I say it with a sad sense of

disparity between us. I am not included within the pale of this glorious anniversary! Your high independence only reveals the
immeasurable distance between us. The blessings in which you this
day rejoice are not enjoyed in common. The rich inheritance of
justice, liberty, prosperity, and independence bequeathed by your
fathers is shared by you, not by me. The sunlight that brought life
and healing to you has brought stripes and death to me. This Fourth
of July is *yours,* not *mine. You* may rejoice, *I* must mourn. To drag a
man in fetters into the grand illuminated temple of liberty, and call
upon him to join you in joyous anthems, were inhuman mockery
and sacrilegious irony. Do you mean, citizens, to mock me, by asking me to speak today? If so, there is a parallel to your conduct. And
let me warn you, that it is dangerous to copy the example of a
nation whose crimes, towering up to heaven, were thrown down by
the breath of the Almighty, burying that nation in irrecoverable
ruin. I can today take up the lament of a peeled and woe-smitten
people.

"By the rivers of Babylon, there we sat down. Yes! We wept
when we remembered Zion. We hanged our harps upon the wil-
lows in the midst thereof. For there they that carried us away captive, required of us a song; and they who wasted us, required of us
mirth, saying, Sing us one of the songs of Zion. How can we sing
the Lord's song in a strange land? If I forget thee, O Jerusalem, let
my right hand forget her cunning. If I do not remember thee, let
my tongue cleave to the roof of my mouth."

Fellow citizens, above your national, tumultuous joy, I hear the
mournful wail of millions, whose chains, heavy and grievous yesterday, are today rendered more intolerable by the jubilant shouts that
reach them. If I do forget, if I do not remember those bleeding children of sorrow this day, "may my right hand forget her cunning, and
may my tongue cleave to the roof of my mouth!" To forget them, to
pass lightly over their wrongs, and to chime in with the popular
themes, would be treason most scandalous and shocking, and would
make me a reproach before God and the world. My subject, then,
fellow citizens, is "American Slavery." I shall see this day and its

popular characteristics from the slave's point of view. Standing here, identified with the American bondman, making his wrongs mine, I do not hesitate to declare, with all my soul, that the character and conduct of this nation never looked blacker to me than on this Fourth of July. Whether we turn to the declarations of the past, or to the professions of the present, the conduct of the nation seems equally hideous and revolting. America is false to the past, false to the present, and solemnly binds herself to be false to the future. Standing with God and the crushed and bleeding slave on this occasion, I will in the name of humanity, which is outraged, in the name of liberty, which is fettered, in the name of the Constitution and the Bible, which are disregarded and trampled upon, dare to call in question and to denounce, with all the emphasis I can command everything that serves to perpetuate slavery—the great sin and shame of America! "I will not equivocate; I will not excuse"; I will use the severest language I can command, and yet not one word shall escape me that any man, whose judgment is not blinded by prejudice, or who is not at heart a slave-holder, shall not confess to be right and just.

At a time like this, scorching irony, not convincing argument, is needed. Oh! had I the ability, and could I reach the nation's ear, I would today pour out a fiery stream of biting ridicule, blasting reproach, withering sarcasm, and stern rebuke. For it is not light that is needed but fire; it is not the gentle shower, but thunder. We need the storm, the whirlwind, and the earthquake. The feeling of the nation must be quickened; the conscience of the nation must be roused; the propriety of the nation must be startled; the hypocrisy of the nation must be exposed; and its crimes against God and man must be denounced.

What to the American slave is your Fourth of July? I answer, a day that reveals to him more than all other days of the year, the gross injustice and cruelty to which he is the constant victim. To him your celebration is a sham; your boasted liberty an unholy license; your national greatness, swelling vanity; your sounds of rejoicing are empty and heartless; your denunciation of tyrants, brass-fronted impudence; your shouts of liberty and equality, hollow mockery; your prayers and hymns, your sermons and thanksgivings, with all your religious parade and solemnity, are to him mere bombast, fraud, deception, impiety, and hypocrisy—a thin veil to cover up crimes which would disgrace a nation of savages. There is not a nation of the earth guilty of practices more shocking and bloody than are the people of these United States at this very hour.

Go where you may, search where you will, roam through all the monarchies and despotisms of the Old World, travel through South America, search out every abuse and when you have found the last, lay your facts by the side of the every-day practices of this nation, and you will say with me that, for revolting barbarity and shameless hypocrisy, America reigns without a rival.

Barbara Tuchman

"ON OUR BIRTHDAY— AMERICA AS IDEA"

The historian Barbara Tuchman seems to hold the Declaration of Independence and Frederick Douglass's lecture "What to the Slave Is the Fourth of July?" in each hand. The community that is America, Tuchman claims, truly held for over a century a vision of freedom, independence, and self-government. However, no principle is immune from outside forces, and as America prospered, so too did the temptations of materialism and, with strength, the temptations of imperialism. Tuchman, who takes a long view of history, warns against the power of those forces, which have led America first toward arrogance, and then toward a loathing engendered by that arrogance—a loathing that is as powerful from within as from without.

> *N*o principle is immune from outside forces, and as America prospered, so too did the temptations of materialism and, with strength, the temptations of imperialism.

In such a situation, one might find cynicism and despair. But this is not where Tuchman leads. The bands of community are strong, she claims, and the optimistic conclusion to her piece is as stirring in its vision as anything that Jefferson or Douglass might have imagined.

"On Our Birthday—America as Idea"

The United States is a nation consciously conceived, not one that evolved slowly out of an ancient past. It was a planned idea of democracy, of liberty of conscience and pursuit of happiness. It was the promise of equality of opportunity and individual freedom within a just social order, as opposed to the restrictions and repressions of the Old World. In contrast to the militarism of Europe, it would renounce standing armies and "sheathe the desolating sword of war." It was an experiment in Utopia to test the thesis that, given freedom, independence, and local self-government, people, in Kossuth's words, "will in due time ripen into all the excellence and all the dignity of humanity." It was a new life for the oppressed, it was enlightenment, it was optimism.

Regardless of hypocrisy and corruption, of greed, chicanery, brutality, and all the other bad habits man carries with him whether in the New World or Old, the founding idea of the United States remained, on the whole, dominant through the first hundred years. With reservations, it was believed in by Americans, by visitors who came to aid our Revolution or later to observe our progress, by immigrants who came by the hundreds of thousands to escape an intolerable situation in their native lands.

The idea shaped our politics, our institutions, and to some extent our national character, but it was never the only influence at work. Material circumstances exerted an opposing force. The open frontier, the hardships of homesteading from scratch, the wealth of natural resources, the whole vast challenge of a continent waiting to be exploited, combined to produce a prevailing materialism and an American drive bent as much, if not more, on money, property, and power than was true of the Old World from which we had fled. The human resources we drew upon were significant: Every wave of immigration brought here those people who had the extra energy, gumption, or restlessness to uproot themselves and cross an unknown ocean to seek a better life. Two other factors entered the shaping process—the shadow of slavery and the destruction of the native Indian.

At its Centennial the United States was a material success. Through its second century the idea and the success have struggled in continuing conflict. The Statue of Liberty, erected in 1886, still symbolized the promise to those "yearning to breathe free." Hope, to them, as seen by a foreign visitor, was "domiciled in America as the Pope is in Rome." But slowly in the struggle the idea lost ground, and at a turning point around 1900, with American acceptance of a rather half-hearted imperialism, it lost dominance. Increasingly invaded since then by self-doubt and disillusion, it survives in the disenchantment of today, battered and crippled but not vanquished.

What has happened to the United States in the twentieth century is not a peculiarly American phenomenon but a part of the experience of the West. In the Middle Ages plague, wars, and social violence were seen as God's punishment upon man for his sins. If the concept of God can be taken as man's conscience, the same explanation may be applicable today. Our sins in the twentieth century—greed, violence, inhumanity—have been profound, with the result that the pride and self-confidence of the nineteenth century have turned to dismay and self-disgust.

In the United States we have a society pervaded from top to bottom by contempt for the law. Government—including the agencies of law enforcement—business, labor, students, the military, the poor no less than the rich, outdo each other in breaking the rules and violating the ethics that society has established for its protection. The average citizen, trying to hold a footing in standards of morality and conduct he once believed in, is daily knocked over by incoming waves of venality, vulgarity, irresponsibility, ignorance, ugliness, and trash in all senses of the word. Our government collaborates abroad with the worst enemies of humanity and liberty. It wastes our substance on useless proliferation of military hardware that can never buy security no matter how high the pile. It learns no lessons, employs no wisdom, and corrupts all who succumb to Potomac fever.

Yet the idea does not die. Americans are not passive under their faults. We expose them and combat them. Somewhere every day some group is fighting a public abuse—openly and, on the whole, notwithstanding the FBI, with confidence in the First Amendment. The U.S. has slid a long way from the original idea. Nevertheless, somewhere between Gulag Archipelago and the featherbed of cradle-to-the-grave welfare, it still offers a greater opportunity for social happiness—that is to say, for well-being combined with individual freedom and initiative—than is likely elsewhere. The ideal society for which mankind has been striving through the ages will remain forever beyond our grasp. But if the great question, whether it is still possible to reconcile democracy with social order and individual liberty, is to find a positive answer, it will be here.

PSALM 132

Behold, how good and joyful a thing it is, brethren,
     to dwell together in unity.
It is like the precious ointment upon the head,
     that ran down unto the beard,
     even unto Aaron's beard,
     and went down to the skirts of his clothing.
It is like the dew of Hermon, which fell upon the hill
     of Zion.
     For there the Lord promised his blessing
     And life for evermore.

Eggplant Spread

Ingredients:

1 eggplant
1 medium onion, peeled and diced
2 garlic cloves, minced
1 Tbsp. lemon juice
1 Tbsp. olive oil
1 tsp. dried oregano or 2 tsp. fresh, minced
salt and pepper to taste
2 Tbsp. fresh minced parsley

Bake eggplant whole (poke a few holes) at 350 degrees for 30–35 minutes. When it's cool enough, peel and dice the eggplant. Place it and remaining ingredients in a food processor and blend until it's a spread consistency. Chill until ready to serve. Serve with crackers, pita bread, or pita crisps.

PART FOUR
Nature and Grace

INTRODUCTION

Summer feels endless. It is not just that this season gives us the longest day of the year, but that we can physically feel the lengthening daylight—particularly in the northern latitudes or when we live at the western edge of an artificial time zone. There, as daylight stretches past 9:00 at night to 10:00 and even to 10:30 and the Fourth of July fireworks begin an hour before midnight, we feel indeed that we may never need to sleep again.

Nor is it only that we feel the long days in our very bones. Our minds, too, expand into a limitless capaciousness. Less pressed by the routines of autumn, the holidays of winter, or the reawakenings of spring, we experience a kind of timeless existence. "This is the very dead of summer," says Joseph Wood Krutch, and we fall into "Nature's own mood of somnolent content.... [We] can hardly believe that there was a spring or that there will ever be a winter." Of course, summers days are not really boundless, and the summer solstice itself marks the decline into darkness. Space and time inexorably contract, the edges of the horizon closing in upon us a little earlier each evening even through the suspended days of August.

But space and time also seem to expand, at least during the daylight hours. In summer we look around—and up and down—at the stars and katydids, at thunderclouds and common weeds. We notice things and the spaces things inhabit: the eggplant in its garden row, the birds fighting over the finch-seed sack, the swimmer in the middle of the lake. Even before Albert Einstein taught us to say "space-time," we recognized their intimate link.

"Had we but World enough, and Time," sings Andrew Marvell's young man to his love, "This coyness, Lady, were no crime. / We would sit down and think which way / To walk, and pass our long Love's Day." This young man does not think there is world enough and time for such leisurely lovemaking, but summertime invites us to believe otherwise. It is not so much that summer days are time-less as that they feel time-full, stuffed with round, opulent minutes. And in the time-full and space-full days of summer, nothing so invites us into the immensity—and intensity—of space-time as does the natural world.

And Charles Abbott directs our attention to the song-sparrow nestled into the dark recesses of a fence pile. When writers invite us to contemplate small things, they are small things that by their very compactness radiate an intensity of presence and demand an intensity of attention. But Celia Thaxter also makes us climb to the top of a high cliff to watch the sunrise over the sea, Ibn Abi I-Haytham asks us to look at the sun itself, and Walt Whitman points us to the stars. The immensity of nature—the limitless reaches of mountains and skies and seas—claims our attention, too, and sets us in our place. "What are humans," the Hebrew Psalmist asked, "that you, O God, are mindful of them?"

The great religious traditions recognize nature's magnetic power—its ability to draw us down into itself and then propel us outward to contemplate a Maker, a Creator, a Sustainer of life. During the festival of Janam Ashtami, celebrated in midsummer, devout Hindus remember the life of Sri Krishna by bathing in the holy spring at Guptganga or climbing nearby Mount Sareshwari. A Vedic hymn to Ushas, the dawn, announces that "she has opened for us the doors of the sky; setting in motion all moving things, she has revealed to us riches. Ushas has awakened all creatures." John Donne reminds us that we know authors by their books and then draws us down to one small page from the book of nature, "a farm, a garden, nay seven foot of earth, a grave, and that will be book enough. Go lower; every worm in the grave, lower, every weed upon the grave." He asks us to concentrate even more intensely and intimately upon our own bodies, our own pulse: "let thy pulse be intermitted, or stupefied, that thou feel not that, and do but think, and a worm, a weed, thy self, thy pulse, thy thought, are all testimonies, that All, this All, and all the parts thereof, are *Opus*, a work made, and *opus ejus*, his work, made by God.... God in that work."

Gerard Manley Hopkins, too, asks us to look closely, to see every bit of nature, kingfishers and dragonflies and "each mortal thing," as a round bell, perfectly tuned to sing out its own name, to "deal out" the secrets of existence—its own "indoors"—to the whole world, to speak and spell itself:

> *As kingfishers catch fire, dragonflies draw flame;*
> *As tumbled over rim in roundy wells*
> *Stones ring; like each tucked string tells, each hung*
> > *bell's*
> *Bow swung finds tongue to fling out broad its name;*
> *Each mortal thing does one thing and the same:*
> *Deals out that being indoors each one dwells;*
> *Selves—goes itself; myself it speaks and spells;*
> *Crying What I do is me: for that I came.*

And just hearing Nature's symphony of bells, listening to its great hymn of praise, its perfect pitch, might almost be enough. Almost. But Hopkins wants to say more; he wants to know more. Where do I stand within this great and resounding world? he asks. Who am I and what must I become?

> *I say more: the just man justices;*
> *Keeps grace: that keeps all his goings graces;*

> *Acts in God's eye what in God's eye he is—*
> *Christ, for Christ plays in ten thousand places,*
> *Lovely in limbs, and lovely in eyes not His*
> *To the Father through the features of men's faces.*

There is a glory to kingfishers and dragonflies, to the large and the small, to the silence and to the storm, to the busy buzzing of June and the somnolent days of August. But there is a glory, too, in being human: a glory sustained by grace, a glory that calls us to become what in God's eye we are. Summertime invites us into this glory, into the eternity that God has set in our hearts—although, as the Preacher reminds us, we cannot know the end from the beginning.

Perhaps not, but we can with enlarged vision and humble hearts make our way through the fullness of summertime, alert and awake, trembling in tune with nature's great symphony. We can be attentive to the life that pulses through nature, to the bells it rings so clearly, and to the One who gives and sustains that life.

A Prayer

God of grace,
grant us the further gift of noticing your grace
    every day.

In renewing sleep,
in food and drink,
in the dark sky and the fragile grass,
in the life of the senses,
in the passions of the mind,
in the love of a friend,
in the embrace of the family,
in the blessings of work and play,
in the breath of life,
may we feel the favor of your bounty.

God of grace,
grant us the further gift of responding to your
    grace every day

In gratitude for your gifts to us,
in valuing the gifts you have given to others,
in valuing the gifts that others are,
may we live lives that are graceful in return.

Bless us with graceful lives today and always—
lives that honor the source of grace,
lives that accept gifts humbly,
lives that pass the grace along,
lives alert for signs of grace and glory
throughout your great creation.

Make all our goings graces.

Amen.

—James Vanden Bosch

Luci Shaw

"RASPBERRIES" AND "SUMMER ROAD REMEMBERED"

When we become attentive to the little things around us, we may find surprising connections between the natural world and our own lives. Luci Shaw, for instance, finds a battleground in her seemingly innocuous raspberry patch. The birds advance first, scissoring their way into the thicket to snatch the jeweled fruit. Her neighbor, angry at the encroaching brambles, burns the patch to the ground. She herself emerges bloodied and fruit-stained from an afternoon's picking.

> *The heat of summer burns into the raspberry patch and burns up the long, thirsty, dog-tired highway.*

The heat of summer burns into the raspberry patch and burns up the long, thirsty, dog-tired highway. And yet here in the "dead of summer," as Joseph Wood Krutch calls it, arise the fresh tart juice of the raspberries and the promise of water—reminders of the food and drink, the "sum of summer," that will feed our bodies and nourish our souls.

Raspberries

Robins and chickadees, quick as
scissors, are there first,
sighting along the hairy stems,
slanting under leaves, darting
between thorns to the hearts,
pendant as jewels.

The birds think the berries
theirs, and us the shameless thieves.
Our human neighbor, too, is adversarial.
Always the primitive growth threatens
to prickle into his acre,
and last May he fired our canes
(while we were gone) not knowing
 you can't get rid of raspberries
that way—up from their small holocaust
they grew back twice as thick.

Today, undaunted by the scowl.
from next door, I hunker down, squinting,
against the sun, lifting aside
the leaves, plunging my whole arm
to a bush's heart, my skin crossed
with beaded wires of blood,
my palms bright with a sweet serum.
Thinking thorns, and blood, and fruit,
I take into my fingers, bit by bit,
the sum of summer.

Summer road remembered

head low, tongue
flagging the noon air, regular
pads reprinting
the old pattern
heading north
a trotting dog rises to mind
to signal the hot stretch
between Beloit and Madison

on the shoulder of the road
there is gravel
and a flourish of cow parsley
but mostly I see the steady
dog trot
and the corners of the mouth
pulled back for water

Walt Whitman

SELECTIONS FROM *SPECIMEN DAYS*

Walt Whitman's descriptions of the countryside near Camden, New Jersey, may seem at first a simple catalogue of simple pleasures: an old rail fence (reminiscent of Charles Abbott's favorite haunt), kingfishers and dragonflies, common weeds and stately trees, stars in the summer sky. But what appears so ordinary, perhaps so mundane, is stretched across a terrifying abyss. For Whitman records these observations after a decade of national and personal pain. He began working in the army hospitals following the wounding of his brother, George, at the first Battle of Fredericksburg on December 13, 1862, and continued until the cessation of hostilities in 1865. He writes:

> *To sit quietly, then, is not then an escape from "real life" but the way back into it. Nature offers as cure the message that Life is larger, more expansive, longer lasting than our individual lives.*

Of that many-threaded drama, with its sudden and strange surprises, its confounding of prophecies, its moments of despair, the dread of foreign interference, the interminable campaign, the bloody battles, the mighty and cumbrous and green armies, the drafts and bounties—the immense money expenditure, like a heavy-pouring constant rain.... Think how much, and of importance, will be ... buried in the grave, in eternal darkness.

Nor did the darkness end with the peace: on the national level, the country coped with the assassination of Lincoln, the rebuilding of the South, the enormous wartime debt; on the personal level, Whitman eventually succumbed to mental and physical exhaustion.

To sit quietly, then, is not then an escape from "real life" but the way back into it. Nature offers as cure the message that Life is larger, more expansive, longer lasting than our individual lives. That Life, created and sustained, is always a gift, always a blessing.

SELECTIONS FROM SPECIMEN DAYS

Entering a Long Farm-Lane

[*1876, '77*] As every man has his hobby-liking, mine is for a real farm-lane fenced by old chestnut-rails gray-green with dabs of moss and lichen, copious weeds and briers growing in spots athwart the heaps of stray-pick'd stones at the fence bases—irregular paths worn between, and horse and cow tracks—all characteristic accompaniments marking and scenting the neighborhood in their seasons—apple-tree blossoms in forward April—pigs, poultry, a field of August buckwheat, and in another the long flapping tassels of maize—and so to the pond, the expansion of the creek, the secluded-beautiful, with young and old trees, and such recesses and vistas.

Summer Sights and Indolencies

June 10th.—As I write, 5 1/2 P.M., here by the creek, nothing can exceed the quiet splendor and freshness around me. We had a heavy shower, with brief thunder and lightning, in the middle of the day; and since, overhead, one of those not uncommon yet indescribable skies (in quality, not details or forms) of limpid blue, with rolling silver-fringed clouds, and a pure-dazzling sun. For underlay, trees in fullness of tender foliage—liquid, ready, long-drawn notes of birds—based by the fretful mewing of a querulous cat-bird, and the pleasant chipper-ing-shriek of two kingfishers. I have been watching the latter the last half hour, on their regular evening frolic over and in the stream; evi-dently a spree of the liveliest kind. They pursue each other, whirling and wheeling around, with many a jocund downward dip, splashing the spray in jets of diamonds—and then off they swoop, with slanting wings and graceful flight, sometimes so near me I can plainly see their dark-gray feather-bodies and milk-white necks.

Mulleins and Mulleins

Large, placid mulleins, as summer advances, velvety in texture, of a light greenish-drab color, growing everywhere in the fields—at first earth's big rosettes in their broad-leav'd low cluster-plants, eight, ten, twenty leaves to a plant—plentiful on the fallow twenty-acre lot, at the end of the lane, and especially by the ridge-sides of the fences—then close to the ground, but soon springing up—leaves as broad as my hand, and the lower ones twice as long—so fresh and dewy in the morning—stalks now four or five, even seven or eight feet high. The farmers, I find, think the mullein a mean unworthy weed, but I have grown to a fondness for it. Every object has its lesson, enclosing the suggestion of everything else—and lately I sometimes think all is con-centrated for me in these hardy, yellow-flower'd weeds. As I come down the lane early in the morning, I pause before their soft wool-like fleece and stem and broad leaves, glittering with countless dia-monds. Annually for three summers now, they and I have silently return'd together; at such long intervals I stand or sit among them, musing—and woven with the rest, of so many hours and moods of partial rehabilitation—of my sane or sick spirit, here as near at peace as it can be.

Three of Us

July 14.—My two kingfishers still haunt the pond. In the bright sun and breeze and perfect temperature of to-day, noon, I am sitting here by one of the gurgling brooks, dipping a French water-pen in the limpid crystal, and using it to write these lines, again watching the feather'd twain, as they fly and sport athwart the water, so close, almost touching into its surface. Indeed there seem to be three of us. For nearly an hour I indolently look and join them while they dart and turn and take their airy gambols, sometimes far up the creek disappearing for a few moments, and then surely returning again, and performing most of their flight within sight of me, as if they knew I appreciated and absorb'd their vitality, spirituality, faithfulness, and the rapid, vanishing, delicate lines of moving yet quiet electricity they draw for me across the spread of the grass, the trees, and the blue sky. While the brook babbles, babbles, and the shadows of the boughs dapple in the sunshine around me, and the cool west by-nor'-west wind faintly soughs in the thick bushes and tree tops.

Among the objects of beauty and interest now beginning to appear quite plentifully in this secluded spot, I notice the hummingbird, the dragon-fly with its wings of slate-color'd gauze, and many varieties of beautiful and plain butterflies, idly flapping among the plants and wild posies. The mullein has shot up out of its nest of broad leaves, to a tall stalk towering sometimes five or six feet high, now studded with knobs of golden blossoms. The milk-weed, (I see a great gorgeous creature of gamboge and black lighting on one as I write,) is in flower, with its delicate red fringe; and there are profuse clusters of a feathery blossom waving in the wind on taper stems. I see lots of these and much else in every direction, as I saunter or sit. For the last half hour a bird has persistently kept up a simple, sweet, melodious song, from the bushes. (I have a positive conviction that some of these birds sing, and others fly and flirt about here, for my especial benefit.)

Hours for the Soul

July 22d, 1878.—Living down in the country again. A wonderful conjunction of all that goes to make those sometime miracle-hours after sunset—so near and yet so far. Perfect, or nearly perfect days, I notice, are not so very uncommon; but the combinations that make perfect nights are few, even in a life time. We have one of those perfections to-night. Sunset left things pretty clear; the larger stars were visible soon as the shades allow'd. A while after 8, three or four great black clouds suddenly rose, seemingly from different points, and sweeping with broad swirls of wind but no thunder, underspread the orbs from view everywhere, and indicated a violent heat-storm. But without storm, clouds, blackness and all, sped and vanish'd as suddenly as they had risen; and from a little after 9 till 11 the atmosphere and the whole show above were in that state of exceptional clearness and glory just alluded to. In the northwest turned the Great Dipper with its pointers round the Cynosure. A little south of east the constellation of the Scorpion was fully up, with red Antares glowing in its neck; while dominating, majestic Jupiter swam, an hour and a half risen, in the east—(no moon till after 11.) A large part of the sky seem'd just laid in great splashes of phosphorus. You could look deeper in, farther through, than usual; the orbs thick as heads of wheat in a field. Not that there was any special brilliancy either—nothing near as sharp as I have seen of keen winter nights, but a curious general luminousness throughout to sight, sense, and soul. The latter had much to do with it. (I am convinced there are hours of Nature, especially of the atmosphere, mornings and evenings, address'd to the soul. Night transcends, for that purpose, what the proudest day can do.) Now, indeed, if never before, the heavens declared the glory of God. It was to the full the sky of the Bible, of Arabia, of the prophets, and of the oldest poems. There, in abstraction and stillness, (I had gone off by myself to absorb the scene, to have the spell unbroken,) the copiousness, the removedness, vitality, loose-clear-crowdedness, of that stellar concave spreading overhead, softly absorb'd into me, rising so free, interminably high, stretching east, west, north, south—and I, though but a point in the centre below, embodying all.

As if for the first time, indeed, creation noiselessly sank into and through me its placid and untellable lesson, beyond—O, so infinitely beyond!—anything from art, books, sermons, or from science,

old or new. The spirit's hour—religion's hour—the visible suggestion of God in space and time—now once definitely indicated, if
never again. The untold pointed at—the heavens all paved with it.
The Milky Way, as if some superhuman symphony, some ode of
universal vagueness, disdaining syllable and sound—a flashing glance
of Deity, address'd to the soul. All silently—the indescribable night
and stars—far off and silently.

Charles C. Abbott

"A FENCE-RAIL FANCY" FROM *IN NATURE'S REALM*

August, that "lazy month, when comfortable idleness is more desired than riches," offers Charles Abbott a chance to sit by a pile of old fence rails and think about the life summed up in those slats of wood. A century ago, he muses, they were living trees; a few seasons ago, a highway for wildlife, and now they harbor busy mice and songbirds. As the weather cools they will fuel his fireplace, but, like summer itself, they lie for a moment suspended in time, evoking only memories.

> *P*erhaps it is just these insubstantial flights of fancy that will sustain us in the present and—if we cherish them—guide us into the future.

This cedar was once one of many that clotted the plain; this chestnut, the cousin of an ancient tree that still stands proudly along the path. This whiff of wood conjures up cedar chests and polished wainscoting in old houses, colonial carpenters and Quakers and childhood.

These are only memories—the vagaries of an idle August. But perhaps it is just these insubstantial flights of fancy that will sustain us in the present and—if we cherish them—guide us into the future.

"A Fence-rail Fancy"

Homely as was the old rail fence of other days, every panel thereof had a history no skill of man has ever yet been able to worthily record, and, coming to less complex objects, a single rail, whether the entire trunk of a tapering cedar or split from a chestnut log, has its own history that teems, perhaps, with those colonial times of which so often we say a great deal and know exceedingly little. Be all this as it may, I would now rather go back to the pile of old rails in the field corner than rest for the time in any kickshaw-crowded parlor. It was honest news that the rail pile had to tell, and this we do not always hear between four walls.

In the vacation days of August, the lazy month, when comfortable idleness is more desired than riches, it is good luck beyond reasonable hope to find a novel point of view. I think I found it in a pile of fence rails. Not one of these rails but was part of a living tree a good deal more than a century ago; that fact counts for something. Not one but bears evidences of strange experiences since, and this concerns us now, when on natural history bent. The fence-rail is the highway of more forms of animal life than any living tree, and often can boast of more travelers than the ground beneath or air above it. A rail fence, with its grassy or weedy angles, is a wild country, and saying this, we say everything.

It was not so long ago that this pile of rails reached across the wide field in orderly disarray, and all save the topmost one of each panel was hidden during August by weeds that overtopped half the little cedars and squatty sassafras saplings that were struggling to become trees; stout weeds that boasted of storm-defying strength and waved majestically in the passing breeze until effectually snubbed by frost. Then and always was this fence wild-life's highway. I have seen the squirrels, weasels, mice and larger mammals, more rarely, pass along it, and many a "Bob-white" that hid, at last, by squatting close to the bottom rail. Here, in mid-winter, were brave-hearted sparrows, and in February, when the sunshine hinted of spring, were warbling bluebirds, and I thought that half the glory of the fields would be gone if the fence were ever taken away; but the weather-beaten, lichen-coated rails, piled in the corner, have drawn unto them all the good things of the dear, old days.

In mid-December last I often lingered long on the sunny side of the rail pile. The sun's rays entered there and it seemed like summer. Not for a moment did I find myself alone. Even insect life was active. Now, in August, it is the shady side that I find more comfortable, and the wild-life of the field is like-minded. The birds come and go continually, and what busy creatures are the wrens that thread its tangled maze, running to and fro like frightened mice. Song-sparrows also have a fancy for the deep, dark recesses near its base, and after each exploratory tour these birds mount the topmost rail and sing exultantly. In vain do I peer into the long, narrow spaces between the rails. I can see nothing distinctly, yet I know that here are a hundred homes of creatures as diverse as birds, mice and spiders.

Strange it seems, when all that makes the world so entertaining is about me in abundance, that I should turn with such eagerness to these fence rails and consider them exclusively. To pass from natural history to humanity is perhaps excusable,—tastes differ; but to ignore a singing bird and give heed to a fence-rail savors of absurdity. Many men of many minds, and in August one is seldom studiously disposed. Vagaries assume importance when idle fancy is the limit of exertion. Here is a cedar rail, and the tall, tapering cedar-tree that still is a feature of the landscape was once to be numbered among the more prominent characteristics of old New Jersey. The level fields were then cedar-dotted plains. Peter Kalm mentions them as growing (1748) in dry, poor soil, and very slowly increasing in girth; usually scattered about singly, but sometimes "standing together in clusters." Perhaps the latter marked an abandoned Indian corn-field. I think this probable.

Kalm mentions a cedar, eighteen inches in diameter, that was two hundred and fifty years old. If he was not in error, the tree now in sight is quite two centuries old, yet does not stand out prominently. Still, close examination of the tree shows evidence of age. Little cedars like little men ever grow old and ugly. Mere size counts for nothing.

This particular cedar rail was cut more than a century ago, and the tree of which it was a part then was old; yet the country was settled. This now fast-decaying rail points, as it seems to me, to the still living trees of its kind, and I am closer linked to times long ago. The odor of cedars carries me back to chests and wainscoting of that wood, the workmanship of colonial carpenters. Old houses now are few, and rarer still to find them unmarred by modern furnishings, but a good, old-fashioned atmosphere clings to even this old cedar rail, and a whiff thereof conjures up a house I well remember.

But what of a chestnut rail? I am sitting now on one that has been deftly split from some stately tree in the dry, upland woods. I know this because the grain is straight and there is not a trace of a branch ever having grown from it. Close-grained and so firm, too, the rail came from the main trunk and not from some far out-reaching limb, the squirrels' highway when October ripened the nuts.

Peter Kalm, already quoted, makes scanty reference to the chestnut-tree, yet I cannot believe it was not in his day, as now, conspicuous beyond nearly every other growth. Huge white oaks in Quaker meeting-yards and chestnuts of as great size amid fields or along country roads are known to everybody, and though there were more forests than open land in Indian days, I am surprised that Kalm should have seen no chestnut-trees that strongly impressed him. Not far away still stands a splendid tree of this kind. It is seven feet in diameter, and in flourishing condition. How old? I often ask, and get various estimates. A common reply is that of a hundred years. People are given to mentioning this lapse of time as the climax of antiquity. It is of little significance in the age of trees. I own a rose-bush nearly that old, and lilac bushes that are older. The chestnut I spoke of is probably in its third century, and well advanced in it, too.

The old rail fence had to give way to modern improvements, so often a sad marring of a lovely landscape, but as a pile of rails in a field corner it has had its eventful little day. The farmer has been kept at arm's length, so to speak, and patient nature here resumed her sway. Scarcely a known weed but has found a root-hold here, and many have bloomed in a sweet, wild way more charming than the pretentious flowers of a trim garden.

Bright roses attracted the butterflies, and the gaudy trumpet-creeper brought the humming-birds from far and near. Later, when the cool autumn days have come and these old fence rails are fire-wood, as I sit before the andirons what glorious pictures of the overfull seasons, winter, spring and summer will float before me. Better that in this vague way we live over again some hours that are gone than not to live them over again at all.

A GATHERING OF SUMMER POEMS
FROM AROUND THE WORLD

To choose a gathering of summer poems seems almost presumptuous. To choose a gathering of summer poems about the natural world seems almost ludicrous. The natural world in summer is one of the most evocative experiences of the human condition, and it has led to more poetic responses than could ever be collected. How to make a choice from among the multitude?

Abandoning all hope of being exhaustive or even representative, we offer a collection of poems from the

> $\mathcal{S}$tars fall into the water, and each summer, each day, each minute might be the last.

Western, Islamic, and Oriental perspectives, each celebrating the given world as it is manifested in summer. Summer, in these poems, is remarkably intense; it is green and living and powerful. It is a splash of beauty, a day marked by "amplitude." It is so very alive that poets must resort to personification, so that the sun becomes a "gold eyebrow," and the trees dream.

But so too these poets recognize that this mortal world must pass, that while summer suggests fullness, it also suggests the transitory state of our being. Summer may seem eternal to Douglas Spaulding, but the evidence we see from the natural world is to the contrary. Stars fall into the water, and each summer, each day, each minute might be the last.

Butterflies

SIEGFRIED SASSOON

Frail travellers, deftly flickering over the flowers;
O living flowers against the heedless blue
Of summer days, what sends them dancing through
This fiery-blossom'd revel of the hours?

Theirs are the musing silences between
The enraptured crying of shrill birds that make
Heaven in the wood while summer dawns awake;
And theirs the faintest winds that hush the green.

And they are as my soul that wings its way
Out of the starlit dimness into morn:
And they are as my tremulous being—born
To know but this, the phantom glare of day.

Idyll

SIEGFRIED SASSOON

In the grey summer garden I shall find you
With day-break and the morning hills behind you.
There will be rain-wet roses; stir of wings;
And down the wood a thrush that wakes and sings.
Not from the past you'll come, but from that deep

Where beauty murmurs to the soul asleep:
And I shall know the sense of life re-born
From dreams into the mystery of morn
Where gloom and brightness meet. And standing
    there
Till that calm song is done, at last we'll share
The league-spread, quiring symphonies that are
Joy in the world, and peace, and dawn's one star.

Living

DENISE LEVERTOV

The fire in leaf and grass
so green it seems
each summer the last summer.

The wind blowing, the leaves
shivering in the sun,
each day the last day.

A red salamander
so cold and so
easy to catch, dreamily

moves his delicate feet
and long tail. I hold
my hand open for him to go.

Each minute the last minute.

Ephemera

BARBARA CROOKER

For who has despised the day of small things?

—Zechariah 4:10

It's just a day when dusty sycamore leaves
flash silver as they scull in the wind,
when high clouds journey across the sky,
huge white blossoms going to seed.
It's summer, and the world exhales its green breath.
For once, the humidity machine's been shut off,
and the air feels like a lover's caress.
My grouchy white cat stalks through the high grass,
twines once around my legs, then sits nearby,
as close as he's ever going to get. A spider
casts her filaments on a frond of Russian sage,
finches go to work on the sunflower heads,
nodding and bobbing. In the meadow, the traffic of
ants and bees....

The sun, no longer last week's red hot griddle,
casts us in a bronzy light, turns the air to syrup.
I neither want to be here, nor there. The afternoon
grows radiant around the edges. Dinner on the porch,
a thick steak, matchstick asparagus, many-grained bread.
A wedge of chocolate cake, cut in two, a handful
of raspberries. Arid, in the twilight, swallows scissor
the air over the orchard, cutting scraps in the cloth of light,
as we sip the last few mouthfuls of wine,
The small pleasures of the night, the amplitude of the day.

Late Summer

TADA CHIMAKO

In the gentle evening of the summer,
which is tired with the festival,
the water is clear
and the fish are at the bottom.

Holding leftover wreaths
in their languid arms,
trees are
already dreaming.

The last bird has flown by,
holding a black sound
in its beak.

Farewell, summer,
quicken your pace as you go ...
Stars fall quietly into the water ...

Sun

IBN ABI I-HAYTHAM

Look at the beautiful sun.
Rising it shows one gold eyebrow,
plays the miser with the other,
but we know it won't be
stingy. Soon it will splash its veil
of beauty everywhere.

A mirror of wonder
out of the East
hides again in dusk.

The horizon
is desolate at its escape
and puts on mourning robes,

Falling stars
are tears
of iron.

Celia Thaxter

FROM *AMONG THE ISLES OF SHOALS*

Celia Thaxter's *Among the Isles of Shoals* has been a New England classic since its publication in 1873. Certainly one reason for its continuing popularity is that the coastline Thaxter so lovingly details has been, for the most part, preserved, so that even today, on a bright blue summer morn, one could head out to the nine islands along the southern edge of Maine and see their rocky coasts as Thaxter saw them while growing up on White Island, where her father was the lighthouse keeper.

When Thaxter wrote, she was recalling her childhood—though every summer of her adult life she brought her family back to nearby Appledore Island to live at a hotel her father had built. But even from the distance created by time, Thaxter writes of the "infinite variety of beauty," a beauty that filled her with "an absorbing, unreasoning joy." She sets her piece in midsummer and pictures herself leaving the house in the morning, returning at dusk, and finding the most extraordinary things in the smallest of spaces.

> *T*he infinite variety of beauty that Thaxter describes is all associated with the sea, at that harsh place where the salt waves batter the gray rocks and beauty is born.

The infinite variety of beauty that Thaxter describes is all associated with the sea, at that harsh place where the salt waves batter the gray rocks and beauty is born. Some is unusual beauty: the cobweb, the spider, the bat that bites through her palm, the starfish that throws pieces of itself away. And there are also the small red petals of the pimpernel, the gold and purple of the elder, the pale yellow bud of the primrose—each of which chooses its moment to show itself. The message beneath Thaxter's description is the message that the fecundity of summer suggests: Pay Attention!

FROM *AMONG THE ISLES OF SHOALS*

Very soon I learned how richly [Nature] repays in deep refreshment the reverent love of her worshipper. With the first warm days we built our little mountains of wet gravel on the beach, and danced after the sandpipers at the edge of the foam, shouted to the gossiping kittiwakes that fluttered above, or watched the pranks of the burgomaster gull, or cried to the crying loons. The gannet's long, white wings stretched overhead, perhaps, or the dusky shag made a sudden shadow in mid-air, or we startled on some lonely ledge the great blue heron that flew off, trailing legs and wings, stork-like, against the clouds. Or, in the sunshine on the bare rocks, we cut from the broad, brown leaves of the slippery, varnished kelps, grotesque shapes of man and bird and beast that withered in the wind and blew away; or we fashioned rude boats from bits of driftwood, manned them with a weird crew of kelpies, and set them adrift on the great deep, to float we cared not whither.

We played with the empty limpet-shells; they were mottled gray and brown, like the song-sparrow's breast. We launched fleets of purple mussel-shells on the still pools in the rocks, left by the tide,—pools that were like bits of fallen rainbow with the wealth of the sea, with tints of delicate sea-weeds, crimson and green and ruddy brown and violet; where wandered the pearly eolis with rosy spines and fairy horns; and the large, round sea-urchins, like a boss upon a shield, were fastened here and there on the rock at the bottom, putting out from their green, prickly spikes transparent tentacles to seek their invisible food. Rosy and lilac starfish clung to the sides; in some dark nook, perhaps, a holothure unfolded its perfect ferns, a lovely, warm buff color, delicate as frost-work; little forests of coralline moss grew: up in stillness, gold-colored shells crept about, and now and then flashed the silver-darting fins of slender minnows. The dimmest recesses were haunts of sea-anemones that opened wide their starry flowers to the flowing tide, or drew themselves together, and hung in large, half-transparent drops, like clusters of some strange, amber-colored fruit, along the crevices as the water ebbed away. Sometimes we were cruel enough to capture a female lobster hiding in a deep cleft, with her millions of mottled eggs; or we laughed to see the hermit-crabs challenge each other, and come out and fight a deadly battle till the stronger overcame, and, turning the weaker topsy-turvy, possessed himself of his ampler cockle-shell, and scuttled off with it triumphant. Or, pulling all together, we dragged up the long kelps, or devil's-aprons; their roots were almost always fastened about large, living mussels; these we unclasped, carrying the mussels home to be cooked; fried in crumbs or batter, they were as good as oysters. We picked out from the kelp-roots a kind of starfish which we called sea-spider; the moment we touched it an extraordinary process began. One by one it disjointed all its sections,—whether from fear or anger we knew not; but it threw itself away, bit by bit, until nothing was left of it save the little, round body whence the legs had sprung!

With crab and limpet, with grasshopper and cricket, we were friends and neighbors, and we were never tired of watching the land-spiders that possessed the place. Their webs covered every window-pane to the lighthouse top, and they rebuilt them as fast as they were swept down. One variety lived among the round gray stones on the beach, just above high-water mark, and spun no webs at all. Large and black, they speckled the light stones, swarming in the hot sun; at the first footfall they vanished beneath the pebbles.

All the cracks in the rocks were draped with swinging veils like the window-panes. How often have we marvelled at them, after a fog or a heavy fall of dew, in the early morning, when every slender thread was strung with glittering drops,—the whole symmetrical web a wonder of shining jewels trembling in the breeze! Tennyson's lines,

> *"The cobweb woven across the cannon's throat*
> *Shall shake its threaded tears in the wind no more,"*

always bring back to my mind the memory of those delicate, spangled draperies, more beautiful than any mortal loom could weave, that curtained the rocks at White Island and "shook their threaded tears" in every wind.

Sometimes we saw the bats wheel through the summer dusk, and in profoundly silent evenings heard, from the lighthouse top, their shrill, small cries, their voices sharper and finer than needle-points. One day I found one clinging to the under side of a shutter,—a soft, dun-colored, downy lump. I took it in my hand, and in an instant it changed to a hideous little demon, and its fierce white teeth met in the palm of my hand. So much fury in so small a beast I never encountered, and I was glad enough to give him his liberty without more ado.

A kind of sandhopper about an inch long, that infested the beach, was a great source of amusement. Lifting the stranded sea-weed that marked the high-water line, we always startled a gray and brown cloud of them from beneath it, leaping away, like tiny kangaroos, out of sight. In storms these were driven into the house, forcing their way through every crack and cranny till they strewed the floors,—the sea so encircled us! Dying immediately upon leaving the water from which they fled, they turned from a clear brown, or what Mr. Kingsley would call a "pellucid gray," to bright brick-color, like a boiled lobster, and many a time I have swept them up in ruddy heaps; they looked like bits of coral.

I remember in the spring kneeling on the ground to seek the first blades of grass that pricked through the soil, and bringing them into the house to study and wonder over. Better than a shop full of toys they were to me! Whence came their color? How did they draw their sweet, refreshing tint from the brown earth, or the limpid air, or the white light? Chemistry was not at hand to answer me, and all her wisdom would not have dispelled the wonder. Later the little scarlet pimpernel charmed me. It seemed more than a flower; it was like a human thing. I knew it by its homely name of poor-man's weatherglass. It was so much wiser than I, for, when the sky was yet without a cloud, softly it clasped its small red petals together, folding its golden heart in safety from the shower that was sure to come! How could it know so much? Here is a question science cannot answer. The pimpernel grows everywhere about the islands, in every cleft and cranny where a suspicion of sustenance for its slender root can lodge; and it is one of the most exquisite of flowers, so rich in color, so quaint and dainty in its method of growth. I never knew its silent warning fail. I wondered much how every flower knew what to do and to be; why the morning-glory didn't forget sometimes, and bear a cluster of elder-bloom, or the elder hang out pennons of gold and purple like the iris, or the golden-rod suddenly blaze out a scarlet plume, the color of the pimpernel, was a mystery to my childish thought. And why did the sweet wild primrose wait till after sunset to unclose its pale yellow buds; why did it unlock its treasure of rich perfume to the night alone? Few flowers bloomed for me upon the lonesome rock; but I made the most of all I had, and neither knew of nor desired more. Ah, how beautiful they were! Tiny stars of crimson sorrel threaded on their long brown stems; the blackberry blossoms in bridal white; the surprise of the blue-eyed grass; the crowfoot flowers, like drops of yellow gold spilt about among the short grass and over the moss; the rich, blue-purple beach-pea, the sweet, spiked germander, and the homely, delightful yarrow that grows thickly on all the islands. Sometimes its broad clusters of dull white bloom are stained a lovely reddish-purple, as if with the light of sunset. I never saw it colored so elsewhere. Quantities of slender, wide-spreading mustard-bushes grew about the house; their delicate flowers were like fragrant golden clouds. Dandelions, buttercups, and clover were not denied to us; though we had no daisies nor violets nor wild roses, no asters, but gorgeous spikes of golden-rod, and wonderful wild morning-glories, whose long, pale, ivory buds I used to find in the twilight, glimmering among the dark leaves, waiting for the touch of dawn to unfold and become each an exquisite incarnate blush,—the perfect color of a South Sea shell. They ran wild, knotting and twisting about the rocks, and smothering the loose boulders in the gorges with lush green leaves and pink blossoms.

Many a summer morning have I crept out of the still house before any one was awake, and, wrapping myself closely from the chill wind of dawn, climbed to the top of the high cliff called the Head to watch the sunrise. Pale grew the lighthouse flame before the broadening day as, nestled in a crevice at the cliff's edge, I watched the shadows draw away and morning break. Facing the east and south, with all the Atlantic before me, what happiness was mine as the deepening rose-color flushed the delicate cloudflocks that dappled the sky, where the gulls soared, rosy too, while the calm sea blushed beneath. Or perhaps it was a cloudless sunrise with a sky of orange-red, and the sea-line silver-blue against it, peaceful as heaven. Infinite variety of beauty always awaited me, and filled me with an absorbing, unreasoning joy such as makes the song-sparrow sing,—a sense of perfect bliss. Coming back in the sunshine, the morning-glories would lift up their faces, all awake, to my adoring gaze. Like countless rosy trumpets sometimes I thought they were, tossed everywhere about the rocks, turned up to the sky, or drooping toward the ground, or looking east, west, north, south, in silent loveliness. It seemed as if they had gathered the peace of the golden morning in their still depths even as my heart had gathered it.

In some of those matchless summer mornings when I went out to milk the little dun cow, it was hardly possible to go farther than the doorstep, for pure wonder, as I looked abroad at the sea lying still, like a vast, round mirror, the tide drawn away from the rich brown rocks, a sail or two asleep in the calm, not a sound abroad except a few bird voices; dew lying like jewel-dust sifted over everything,—diamond and ruby, sapphire, topaz, and amethyst, flashing out of the emerald deeps of the tufted grass or from the bending tops. Looking over to the mainland, I could dimly discern in the level sunshine the depths of glowing green woods faintly revealed in the distance, fold beyond fold of hill and valley thickly clothed with the summer's splendor. But my handful of grass was more precious to me than miles of green fields, and I was led to consider every blade where there were so few.

SELECTIONS FROM PSALM 104

Praise the Lord, O my soul. O Lord my God, thou art become exceeding glorious. Thou art clothed with majesty and honor. Thou causest the wells to spring up among the valleys and the waters run among the hills, that all the beasts of the field may have drink, and that the wild asses may quench their thirst.

Above upon the hills have the fowls of the air their habitation, and sing among the branches. Thou waterest the hills from above, the earth is filled with the fruits of thy works. Thou bringest forth grass for the cattle and green herb for the service of men. Thou bringest food out of the earth; wine to make glad our hearts, oil to make our countenance cheerful, and bread to strengthen our heart.

The trees of the Lord are full of sap, even the trees of Lebanon, which he hath planted. There make the birds their nests, and the fir trees are a dwelling for the stork. The hills are a refuge for the wild goats and so are the stony rocks for the conies.

Thou hast appointed the moon for certain seasons, the sun knoweth his going down. Thou makest darkness, that it may be night, wherein all the beasts of the forest do move. Yea, and the young lions which roar after their prey and seek their meat from God. But when the sun ariseth, they get them away together and lie them down in their dens. Then goeth man forth to his work, and to till his land until the evening.

O Lord, how manifold are thy works, right wisely hast thou made them all; yea the earth is full of thy riches. They wait all upon thee, that thou mayest give them meat in due season. When thou givest it them, they gather it; when you openest thine hand, they are filled with good.

African Squash and Yams

Ingredients:

1 onion, chopped
2 tablespoons oil
1 pound Hubbard squash, pared and cut into 1-inch pieces
2 yams, or sweet potatoes, pared & cut into 1-inch pieces
1 cup coconut milk
1/2 teaspoon salt
1/2 teaspoon ground cinnamon
1/4 teaspoon ground cloves

Cook and stir onion in oil in 10-inch skillet over medium heat until tender. Stir in remaining ingredients. Heat to boiling. Reduce heat. Cover and simmer 10 minutes. Simmer, uncovered, stirring occasionally, until vegetables are tender, about 5 minutes longer.

PART FIVE
Retreat and Return

INTRODUCTION

Summer retreat—the phrase seems almost redundant. For summer is preeminently the season when we pack our suitcases, load up the car, and retreat to lakes and beaches and grandma's house and the stash of books we bought in January. We leave the office early, take long weekends, and stop reading the daily newspaper. We shed the accumulation of the school months as easily as our winter coats and spring sweaters.

There is always some element of escape to our summer retreats. Ada Louise Huxtable, speaking for all busy urbanites, welcomes summer days at a cottage where "every minute of the day isn't a hassle," and "every encounter isn't a joust with survival." And we need to escape from the relentless schedules that, all too often, we have created for ourselves. The immensity of summer—its seemingly endless days, the wide swatches of time that empty out across the hours—frees us from the routines of daily existence, from the tick, tick, tick of the clock we think we control.

But retreats cannot simply be escapes. They cannot merely be "away from." They must also be a "going to," and that is why we so often think of a retreat in terms of a particular place. It may be a place that we associate with sanctuary, like the Franciscan monastery to which Patricia Hampl retires, or it may be a rather unexpected place, like Barbara Hurd's Cranesville Swamp. But just as often a retreat is a familiar place, a place—the place—to which our hearts and bodies are pulled again and again: our grandparents' house, a family cottage, a beloved farmhouse, or even just the vegetable patch behind the house, turned over year after year and planted with the same carrots, the same radishes, the same cucumbers, the same beans, with an eggplant and some of those new melon seeds thrown in for a bit of dash. Sarah Orne Jewett goes back to Dunnet Landing, Robert Clark to Lake Superior in northern Wisconsin, Madeleine L'Engle to Crosswinds, Scott Momaday to Rainy Mountain.

Retreats take us back to places where we can be renewed, but that renewal often comes at a cost. A retreat is a descent, a little death. It is a letting go not just of our accumulated possessions but also of our accumulated preconceptions—our assumption that we can take life for granted, that it will always run in the smooth course we have set for it; our confidence that we can protect ourselves and those we love from any harm. Summer's spaciousness invites us to lay down our spurious omnipotence, to look out and ahead unafraid, but with refreshed and humbled eyes. Barbara Hurd reminds us of Thomas Merton's wise words: "My Lord God, I have no idea where I am going. I do not see the road ahead of me. I cannot know for certain where it will end."

But retreats also take us off that road, at least for a little while. So a retreat is holy, it is "set apart," sanctified. Sometimes it is set apart because we have work to do, a wrestle with the holy that we have long postponed. Jacob, whose biblical story so often parallels our own, barrels through life, grasping for every advantage and side-stepping God at every turn. Until that night when, all alone and trapped into retreat at the River Jabbok, he wrestles with an angel until daybreak. Bless me, he says, and he is blessed, though the mark of that blessing is a scar, a limp. Jacob will return to his journey, but he will never walk the same again.

Sometimes we retreat because we simply need to rest, to breathe, to create a pause in the action, to wake one morning refreshed again.

"The far East glows," wrote Toru Dutt, the nineteenth-century Hindu poet, "The morning wind blows fresh and free. / Should not the hour that wakes the rose / Awaken also thee?"

And sometimes we come away to a retreat because the year has taken its toll on us and we need to learn again just how to rejoice. Mary Sidney Herbert puts it this way:

> *Make over me thy mercy's streams to flow,*
> *So shall my whiteness scorn the whitest snow.*
> *To ear and heart send sounds and thoughts of*
> > *gladness,*
> *That bruised bones may dance away their sadness.*

Retreats, as Herbert's poem reminds us, do not require a special place as much as they demand—indeed, create—a special space. They are not so much about vacation as vocation, about heeding the call to worship, the call to come apart to sing and pray, to become song and prayer. Scott Momaday's grandmother, Aho, never traveled far from her childhood home, but she created a holy space each night in her bedroom, a retreat that set her apart even from her family. As her grandson recalls, "She made long, rambling prayers out of suffering and hope, having seen many things. I was never sure that I had the right to hear, so exclusive were they of all mere custom and company."

It is out of Aho's past that her hope is forged, for retreats also do the work of memory and of hope. And when our own memories fail, we turn to the memory of God, that "unlimited, infinite memory," Madeleine L'Engle tells us, in which "no atom of creation is ever forgotten ... always is; cared for; developing; loved." In summertime, as indeed in all the seasons of life, it is God who blesses our going out and our coming in. In the small "now" of our present lives, we reach back to reclaim promises of steadfast love and reach forward in hope to the love that will yet sustain us.

These are truths of which we need to be reminded frequently. In Islam, believers perform the ritual prayer, Salat, five times a day in public recognition that God is steadfast and sovereign. Yet, even this is not enough. Each Friday Muslims are called away to participate in a special noon prayer at a mosque. In the Jewish and Christian traditions the weekly retreat, the sanctified time, is the Sabbath—that "certain holy vacation" as a sixteenth-century catechism puts it. "Call the Sabbath your delight," says the prophet Isaiah, and Nan Fink, a young convert to Judaism, explains it this way: "Shabbat is like nothing else. Time as we know it does not exist for these twenty-four hours, and the worries of the week soon fall away. A feeling of joy appears. The smallest object, a leaf or a spoon, shimmers in a soft light, and the heart opens. Shabbat is a meditation of unbelievable beauty."

The Sabbath sets up a weekly rhythm of retreat and return. We rest, we meditate, we wrestle with God, we rejoice, we realign our priorities, we remember. But then we return to our work, our families, our challenges, even our failures. We take up tasks with renewed vigor but also with anticipation that yet again, just next week, there will be another Sabbath, another retreat, another day of rest.

So, too, summer is the Sabbath of the seasons, and as it fades "as imperceptibly as grief" we reach forward to the autumn, knowing that next year summer will come again.

A Prayer

Eternal and infinite God,
bless your finite creatures here,
who live and breathe on earth a while,
until we live and breathe no more.

All-glorious God,
protect your people here and prosper us.
You know our coming in and our going out,
the many ways we number our days.
Grant us wise hearts, to know your will,
and strong wills, to serve you wisely and well.

When the daily routine is too much with us,
bring us seasons of refreshment
so that we can serve you more fully and love
        you more clearly.

When our lives are chaotic and without shape,
bring us seasons of insight,
seasons of clarity,

so that we may serve you more fully and love
you more clearly.

Lord of time and space, our days are in your
hands.
Grant us wisdom to live our days aright.
Grant us grace to see ourselves in your light.
Give us days to sing your praise,
In work, in play, in every season of our lives.

Amen.

—JAMES VANDEN BOSCH

Barbara Hurd

"REFUGIUM" FROM *STIRRING THE MUD: ON SWAMPS, BOGS, AND HUMAN IMAGINATION*

When we first hear the word "retreat," we may imagine a quiet room, prayers, thoughts ascending to God, bells, whispering angel wings. Barbara Hurd imagines a swamp, specifically the Cranesville Swamp in western Maryland. As she tramps about Cranesville Swamp with her friend Michael, who is quietly dismantling his former life to live deliberately as a hermit, she discovers some unsettling truths about refuges.

> *R*etreats are not about shutting out the world but letting more of it back in.

To be sure, they provide safety, silence, a place to stop and withdraw from daily pressures—but they are also dangerous. They call us to forsake the scaffolding that usually keeps our lives erect and to sink our roots back into the real stuff of the world. They upset our perspective. Retreats are not about shutting out the world but letting more of it back in. When a genuine retreat intrudes, Hurd discovers, "Everything I feel about comfort starts to rattle." And, of course, retreats in and of themselves are not necessarily virtuous, nor do they automatically make us better persons. Scoundrels, thieves, and traitors, as well as would-be saints, seek refuge in a swamp; what we find on a retreat is closely related to what we bring in.

Most of us will not become hermits—we'll take our isolation in smaller doses, retreating to a lake cottage, a beloved stretch of beach, a favorite mountain trail, the well-worn library chair. But even here as we draw away for a little while, we will look for the strength that makes us a bit more courageous, a bit more kind, a bit more attentive to the world to which we will soon return.

"REFUGIUM"

At first that June day I thought I was seeing a small cat doing a weak imitation of an inchworm. It undulated in a strange combination of hunch-and-slink along the edge of Cranesville Swamp. Covered with dark fur, its chin dabbed with white, it reminded me of what theologians say about the life of the personality being horizontal, craving community; and that of the soul, vertical, needing solitude. This mink, going from one alder to another, manages both landscapes, traces with its lustrous back a pattern of swell and subside, evokes an image of Muslims prostrating themselves and standing, Catholics kneeling and rising, pale green inchworms arching and stretching along my forearm. We are gardeners, all of us, our hands broadcasting seeds in the spring, our arms in autumn clutching the harvested wheat. We mingle and retreat, seek company and refuge. We are the tide, the continuous going out and coming in that is the rhythm of our lives.

I have been thinking a lot about refuge, how the swamp has a long history as hideaway for scoundrels, debtors, enchanted women who guide lost hunters back to firm ground, runaway slaves, and hermits. When I saw the mink, a solitary creature who tolerates other minks only enough to breed and give birth, I had been slogging in Cranesville Swamp, Nature Conservancy land, on the western border of Maryland. I was with a hermit friend who has sold his house, his car, his bike, who is dismantling his identity as an artist living by the edge of the swamp. When he sold his studio, a nearby gallery took his work, including a drawing in which the hair of the goddess's attendants is replaced by a waterfall. You study it and try to puzzle out where their heads end and the waterfall begins. Michael is after an intimacy in his life that has nothing to do with sex. It's a bit disconcerting to sit with a man, his hazel eyes clear, his beard and hair neatly trimmed, who has no concerns about mortgage payments and insurance premiums or how he'd introduce himself at a campground social. Everything I feel about comfort starts to rattle. He tells me, quietly, "I want to live like an animal, close to the earth, self-sufficient, doing as little harm as possible." And ten minutes later: "And I want to live like Christ, close to God, detached, open to the unknown."

We talk for hours on the boardwalk at Cranesville. Michael isn't going into hiding; he's retreating from a path that wasn't headed toward what, for him, is being fully human. He's not sure what that means except a quiet letting go, a deliberate choice to go toward some kind of refuge that nourishes his spirit. All the great spiritual leaders have done it, from Buddha to Christ to Gandhi. They've withdrawn for a few days or weeks to sit in caves and under trees, to wander in deserts, alone, packing as little as possible into their knapsacks. They're after, I think, some moments of trackless quiet, a chance to blur the footprints, the sense of having been someplace, of having someplace to get to. A chance to see what happens when the past and the future stop tugging on the leash and the present opens like a well.

Those who are fond of retreats—writers, ecstatics, parents with young children—often comment on the silence such time away allows. Silence becomes something present, almost palpable. The task shifts from keeping the world at a safe decibel distance to letting more of the world in. Thomas Aquinas said that beauty arrests motion. He meant, I think, that in the presence of something gorgeous or sublime, we stop our nervous natterings, our foot twitchings and restless tongues. Whatever that fretful hunger is, it seems momentarily filled in the presence of beauty. To Aquinas's wisdom

I'd add that silence arrests flight, that in its refuge, the need to flee the chaos of noise diminishes. We let the world creep closer, we drop to our knees, as if to let the heart, like a small animal, get its legs on the ground.

The mink has disappeared into the underbrush. If I had been blindfolded and plunked down in this pocket of cool air and quaking ground, spiked by tamaracks and spruce, home to hermits and minks, and tried to figure out just where I was, I would guess a bog in Canada somewhere, far north of the noise of Quebec and Montreal. And Canada was probably the original home of Cranesville Swamp, which now straddles the Maryland–West Virginia border. We don't think of landscapes on the run, though we know birds fly south in the fall, mountain goats trek up and down the Rocky Mountain passes from season to season, and eel journey from the Sargasso Sea in the middle of the Atlantic Ocean to North America or Europe in search of fresh waters. But stand back far enough in geologic time and you can watch biomes migrating north and south across the globe as giant glaciers drag and push their icy fingers up and down the Northern Hemisphere. Almost twenty thousand years ago, the last intrusion shoved a wide band of boreal forest south to the mid-Atlantic region. When it withdrew, some ten thousand years later, most of those dark forests withdrew also, reestablishing themselves in Canada while southern deciduous forests reclaimed their usual position in Maryland. But in a few isolated pockets protected in high altitude bowls surrounded by higher ridges, boreal forests hunkered down, sank their damp feet into poorly draining clay and rock, and stayed.

And now they couldn't migrate north if they wanted to, for around them is a hostile world—too warm, too dry, the water flushing too fast through the underground aquifers. Dug up and replanted just a mile to the south, the tamaracks would wither, cranberry and sphagnum would curl and crisp, cotton grass would scorch and wilt in what would feel to them like brutally tropical air. This is an area known as a refugium—a particular ecosystem that cannot survive in surrounding areas.

Historically, refuges are retreats, shelters from danger or distress, and a refugee is one who flees to such shelter for safety. Something in the "outside" world threatens, presses too close, cannot accept the refugee's color or ethnicity or religion or eccentricity, the need for so much water and cool air. Something in the refuge spells protection. If you can hack, float, stagger, climb your way into the jungle, swamp, desert, or mountain, the color of your skin and how you worship won't matter. But something else will. Mohammed in his cave knew this, and Jesus in the desert, the Buddha under the Wisdom Tree. Michael in the swamp does too.

Refuge means a certain amount of quiet, a retreat from what frazzles and buzzes, from what sometimes feels in the mind like the continuous replay of the final minutes of a tied Super Bowl game, bleachers sagging with spectators whooping and jeering about wins and losses, voices hoarse, the players' one-point attention on flattening whatever comes between them and the triumph of a square yard of pigskin flying over the goal line. On an ordinary day, the human ear is bombarded with sound—anything and everything: the whine of a mosquito, the neighbor's lawn mower, the ratchety clock movement, sirens, seagulls, an old dog's snoring, car engines, and the popping roll of tires on hot pavement. Our minds, of course, automatically filter much of this hubbub. But at what cost? What happens to that filtered material? Cleaning the filter in my clothes dryer yields fuzzy bedding of dog hair, threads, shredded kleenex, and, once, a striking black-and-white feather, small and striped, cleaned and surely destined for more than the trash. I run my fingers across the lint trap, gathering the clean down. Scraped and softened linen like this was once used as dressings for wounds—a buffer between raw wound and the barrage of bacteria. Too much buildup of lint, though, and the wound can't breathe, the dryer will catch fire, your house will burn down. Does the human mind work the same way? Are there long screens we need occasionally to pull from our heads, run our fingers up, gathering into a pleated, linty accordion the excesses of noise we haven't processed? Do we need occasionally the silence of refuge for the way it lets our minds breathe a bit more easily?

Part of the appeal of a refuge may be its isolation. Here nobody can see you still weeping over a lover who hunched off with another some thirty years ago. Nobody notices how you suck in your stomach when someone of the opposite sex struts by. Or how you don't. A refuge is like a locked bathroom door where you can practice the fine art of extending your tongue until you can finally touch the tip of your nose, which you feel free to pick as thoroughly as you want. Nobody's watching; you can do whatever you want.

Consider, for instance, the hermit found in 1975 by a sheriff and his deputies in Florida's Green Swamp. This solitary Asian man had been so overwhelmed by metropolitan chaos, he'd fled to the cypress and black water a few miles from the roller coasters and virtual reality of Disney World and lived off alligators and armadillos. Hiding with white ibis and leopard frogs among wild orange trees, he was dubbed by the few who saw him "Skunk Ape." I like to think he earned this nickname. That in the relative safety of the Green Swamp, he indulged in some childhood fantasies of branch swinging, chest beating, that it was his dark silky hair against a pale back they saw as he scurried away. Nicknames don't always trivialize and they aren't always meant to humiliate. Consciously or not, perhaps the puzzled observers named his most salient characteristics, the ones that needed the tangled and private understory and the mournful cry of night herons in order to surface.

Of course it wasn't always the chanting of prayer or rumors of escape echoing through the refuge. In Cold Spring Swamp in New Jersey during the Revolutionary War, it was the raucous whoops of a bunch of men calling themselves the Refugees, who thought of themselves as British loyalists but who were, in reality, a band of thugs, terrorizing housewives and stagecoach travelers and then hightailing it back to the swamp to gloat over their booty. Scoundrels all of them, they counted on the inaccessibility of their hideout on a small island in the middle of the swamp. Revolutionary War soldier Francis Marion, swatting mosquitoes, made a different and openly partisan use of a swamp: he used Four Holes Swamp of South Carolina to elude the British. Known as the Swamp Fox, Marion and his band of men could disappear into the cypress and stay hidden for weeks. The Narragansett Indians holed up in the Great Swamp of Rhode Island beyond the reach of white men bent on retaliating for Indian raids. Until December of 1675, when the swamp froze over in an early New England cold snap and what had been almost impenetrable to the white men was transformed, overnight, into a smooth array of patios and sidewalks. They simply walked in and what followed was the greatest massacre in Rhode Island history. What had protected the Narragansetts for so long turned suddenly cold and hard and the enemy got in.

For all the reasons that make most people avoid the swamps—poisonous cottonmouths, saw grass so razor sharp it can slit a horse's legs, alligators that can devour a human whole, that sense of the plant-sky bearing down, the need to stay crouched and wary—they make great places of refuge. And if you add to the poison, the sedge swords, the carnivores, the prospect of being lost for decades, it's easy to see why no matter how determined your pursuer is, he often paces at the edge of the swamp, plucking off leeches, and wondering whether plunging into such unmapped and trackless territory is worth it. Of course, the same goes for you. In a canoe, the water closes silently behind you. On land, your footprint in the mud fills and vanishes.

Runaway slaves knew this, hidden in Great Dismal Swamp making shingles for years, and so did the Seminoles, who fled into the Everglades after the white man booted them from their homes in the Okefenokee Swamp of South Georgia. Unwilling to negotiate, surrender, or flee, the Seminoles took advantage of the white man's horror of the infested waters of the Glades. They established villages on hummocky islands in the midst of quagmires, built small canoes that could glide over shallow water, and used the dense vegetation for cover. In pursuit, the U.S. navy in the 1830s sent a Lieutenant Powell, whose men tried pushing and poling their boats, their boots and sticks slurping and sucking in the mud, the vast prairie sea of saw grass closing in on them. When a Lieutenant McLaughlin in Florida tried to succeed where Powell had failed, he led his men into Big Cypress Swamp on the western side of the state, where dense overhead vegetation blocks sunlight and the still water is thick with spinachy trailings. When the men in their big boots stirred the dark water, they kicked up noxious vapors that made them retch. But more disconcerting than that, circuitous streams destroyed their sense of direction. They wandered, retracing and detouring, unable to use the stars as navigational help because the canopy was so thick. Where water was low, they portaged again and again, stumbling over cypress knees and dead stumps, always on the lookout for snakes. Mist rose, steamy and blinding, from the muck, and when it cleared, the men had only the labyrinthine mirrors of black water, the almost impenetrable green walls of Spanish moss and cypress, no way to distinguish "here" from "there." From the top of a pine one of the men might climb, he'd gaze down on a maze of channels, a nightmare of fractals and mirrors, a kaleidoscope of water and thicket that disorients not because it shifts at the far end of your telescope but because it doesn't, and still you don't know where you are. "My Lord God," Thomas Merton wrote, "I have no idea where I am going. I do not see the road ahead of me. I cannot know for certain where it will end."

Sometimes, Rilke says, a man has to get up from his table and walk. Walk where? Does it matter? Moses and Jesus wandered into the desert. Mohammed hiked up the mountain. Michael is considering wandering from one coast to the other. *Solvitur ambulando*—the difficulty will be solved by walking. Rousseau knew it, Thoreau, Wordsworth, Nietzsche, and Austen. They walked out into the hills, country paths, and shorelines, philosophical tramps, all of them, seeking some sort of refuge, finding it, some of them, in the walk itself, and some in the desert landscapes stripped of the extraneous where they wrestled with the holy, and others in the muck and ooze of swamplands from Florida to Rhode Island where they holed up in the thick entanglements, the mucky waters, the trackless shallow waters that twist and bend for miles between overhanging cypress.

What countermovement? What return?

I wonder whether Michael worries about his retreat being a one-way street. What if, twenty years from now, he wanders out of the swamps and mountains and finds so much of the world has changed that he cannot even buy a book without access to the Internet, which requires a computer, which he sold when he sold his house, his car, his bike, and his kayak. What if he emerges with a passion for hand-knotted Persian carpets and caviar and no way to make a living? What if he emerges and nothing, absolutely nothing, has changed?

Out of the desert, Jesus emerged, the Devil's temptations strewn and parched over the sands behind him. Out of the wilderness, Moses' people wandered into the Promised Land. Under the Wisdom Tree, the Buddha finally stood and stretched his legs. Out of its cocoon in the pitcher plant, the *Exyria rolandiana* moth unfurls its wings. It had found refuge there weeks ago and reinforced the safety of its retreat by spinning a tight girdle around the neck of the plant's hood. The girdling caused the hood to choke and eventually to flop over the throat, sealing off the pitcher from outside intruders, much like closing the hatch on a boat against threatening seas. Inside, the caterpillar spun its cocoon in a dry haven. Today it emerges, its wings the color of claret, epaulets of saffron.

Does creation begin or end in the refuge of the fringed world? Did God start in a swamp somewhere, making mossy tendrils first, moving on to the mink's eyelashes, clumsy at first with this medium of land and water and then growing more proficient? Did he learn eventually to step out into the world, turning the brush and sweeping it just so, so that by the end of the semester, the broad Pacific was smooth, the prairies even and lush, the South drooping and luxuriant? Or did he begin with the broad strokes? Did he practice first with an airbrush on the vastness of ocean, high sweeps of the Himalayas, the way beginning art students do, stepping back from the easel, trying to get the broad outlines of their subjects, the feel of paint swiped across a mural? And did he then, as he grew more skilled, hunch over the canvas, end up with a miniature brush for the detailed work of wetlands, the fine scrim of sedges around a burnished lily-padded pool he must make appear and disappear with the seasons?

Do we begin or end in refuge? Which is the going out? Which is the coming in?

Standing at vanishing end of this boardwalk. I think of the water shrew, whose fringed hind toes can actually trap air bubbles that allow him to scamper across the surface of the water—a sort of built-in pontoon system that eliminates any need for him to stand here debating whether this is the beginning or the end of this boardwalk. The mink is hiding. Around the edges of the bog, the solitary white flower of *Coptis groenlandica* rises from its thready golden stem, which runs underground in a vast, lacy interlocking, its juice a balm for canker sores and irritated eyes. And Michael, here again, is knee-deep in the earth, showing me sundew plants, those glistening carnivorous circles the size of thumbtacks that look like the childhood drawings of hundreds of suns, cut out and glittered and strewn across the swamp.

Sarah Orne Jewett

"THE BACKWARD VIEW" FROM *THE COUNTRY OF THE POINTED FIRS*

Though she grew up in the picturesque village of South Berwick, Maine, not far from the coast, near houses whose eyes had seen inhabitants come and go long before the Revolution, Sarah Orne Jewett was not a writer interested in nostalgia, or sentiment, or the pretty picture. She was interested in the close observation and articulation of those things that lay very closely around her. This meant that she looked around South

> *Even as a child, Jewett had the ability to do what every writer must do: observe acutely.*

Berwick as a place full of life: a kind of life that she knew intimately because of her childhood there and because of her frequent excursions with her father, a doctor, to farms and fishing shacks in the area. Even as a child, Jewett had the ability to do what every writer must do: observe acutely.

In this short selection from her masterpiece, these powers show as she says farewell for a time to both a season and a summer. She leaves the summer house in Dunnet Landing half-reluctantly, recognizing that this was in some ways more truly a home than her other world "in which I feared to find myself a foreigner." But as our experience tells us, summers and summer retreats come to an end, and we must return out of that world to face autumn and winter.

"The Backward View"

At last it was the time of late summer, when the house was cool and damp in the morning, and all the light seemed to come through green leaves; but at the first step out of doors the sunshine always laid a warm hand on my shoulder, and the clear, high sky seemed to lift quickly as I looked at it. There was no autumnal mist on the coast, nor any August fog; instead of these, the sea, the sky, all the long shore line and the inland hills, with every bush of bay and every fir-top, gained a deeper color and a sharper clearness. There was something shining in the air, and a kind of lustre on the water and the pasture grass,—a northern look that, except at this moment of the year, one must go far to seek. The sunshine of a northern summer was coming to its lovely end.

The days were few then at Dunnet Landing, and I let each of them slip away unwillingly as a miser spends his coins. I wished to have one of my first weeks back again, with those long hours when nothing happened except the growth of herbs and the course of the sun. Once I had not even known where to go for a walk; now there were many delightful things to be done and done again, as if I were in London. I felt hurried and full of pleasant engagements, and the days flew by like a handful of flowers flung to the sea wind.

At last I had to say good-by to all my Dunnet Landing friends, and my homelike place in the little house, and return to the world in which I feared to find myself a foreigner. There may be restrictions to such a summer's happiness, but the ease that belongs to simplicity is charming enough to make up for whatever a simple life may lack, and the gifts of peace are not for those who live in the thick of battle.

SELECTIONS FROM *MY GRANDFATHER'S HOUSE: A GENEALOGY OF DOUBT AND FAITH*

Like Sarah Orne Jewett, Robert Clark associates summer with a house—a place where he went as a child during those warm months. In *My Grandfather's House*, Clark chronicles a journey of faith through five centuries of his family, beginning with the birth of the Anglican Church and culminating in his own personal return to faith centered on the house "in a forest of jack pine and spruce."

> *The retreat out of the world is not simply* away. *It is* to *something, or else it is simply an escape.*

The retreat out of the world is not simply *away*. It is *to* something, or else it is simply an escape. For Clark as a child, the summer retreat is to wonder, as he comes to a world that he identifies first as one of "inexhaustible goodness." But later, the house becomes a place of revelation. Here Clark comes to understand that the natural world may be spectacularly beautiful, but that such beauty can become expected and mundane. Here he sees that the woods and forest can be welcoming but also hostile. Here he comes into self-consciousness, the awareness of himself as himself. Here he becomes aware of the hunger of desire. Here he loses faith, and finds it again.

SELECTIONS FROM *MY GRANDFATHER'S HOUSE*

When I was a boy, my grandfather Griggs had a house in a forest of jack pine and spruce on Lake Superior in northern Wisconsin, and although I spent at most two months a year there, it seems to me the setting of my whole childhood. On three sides of the house the earth was stony and russet and flocked with pine needles; on the fourth there was a lawn leading down to the lake. The earliest photograph I possess of myself is set there: I am perhaps four months old, belly down on the grass, and my sister is entertaining me with a toy turtle. My parents are dressed as if for tennis; they are young and attractive and gazing at their children. How could we not have been—all of us—anything other than happy?

The house itself was sheathed in white clapboards with double-hung mullioned windows and dark green shutters. There was a front door surmounted by a pediment, a flagpole and a bull's-eye window. That no one ever used this front door speaks to my family's Puritan, New England origins; that the front door was at the side of the house speaks to some particularity I cannot quite put my finger on, a penchant for the oblique and the indirect, no matter how obviously straightforwardness might commend itself.

The house's true entrance was through the kitchen porch, itself reached by a one-by-twelve flung across the pine duff like a drawbridge. In wet weather it kept our feet out of the puddles and gumbo; in dry, it served as a level track for the wheels of the barbecue and the croquet set as well as a place to clean fish, whose viscera the raccoons carried off into the woods.

It was by no stretch of the imagination a wilderness. Before us and before the house, the place had been logged at least once and perhaps more, and was studded with the random clearings and tangled forest understory that suggested that the land had not known much peace of late. Still, we were blessed in such wildlife as presented itself: Birds sang their hours on the edge of the woods; garter snakes patrolled the foundation of the house; and deer stood outside the dining room windows regarding my grandmother as she skimmed her toast with marmalade and warmed her feet before the tangerine coils of the electric fire.

It was not, in retrospect, very much, but to me then it was an enchanted world and there was nothing before it in my life that I could or would have wanted to remember. In the scent and the heat rising in the sunlight from the pine needles, in the ratcheting of the crickets and the rustling of the wind, in its minute and myriad particularities, it seemed to almost pulse with beauty and excitement, with an inexhaustible goodness. My wonder in the face of it was bottomless.

Nor was this sense confined to the natural world. In fact, my grandparents' landscape was primarily interior. The walls of the house—a compressed-sawdust compound called beaverboard—were painted in light pastel colors and the rooms were furnished with simple, slightly worn furniture. Since they'd first arrived in 1930, the house had not so much undergone decoration as it had accreted its details organically, their immutable and sedate permanence disturbed only by eruptions of my grandfather's indomitable bad taste. Despite being raised in a locally distinguished family and receiving a prep school and Ivy League education, my grandfather reveled in artificial flowers, Reader's Digest Condensed Books, novelty neckwear, and "Sing Along with Mitch" records. When company was expected my grandmother and aunts swept the public rooms like a bomb squad, excising polyethylene hyacinths, ashtrays emblazoned with amiable drunks, priapic duck hunters, pissing urchins and miniature toilets with fur-covered seats and pearl-encrusted trim.

My grandfather's bad taste was, I think, more than a lapse or a quirk. Despite defeat after defeat at the hands of his wife and daughters, he pursued his taste as though impelled by a driving vision, a creative, even spiritual quest. He was scarcely an artist: He sold insurance, which perhaps encourages the cultivation of dread and rumination on last things. And so perhaps he sought to make an often senseless world cohere, to vanquish chaos and tragedy through whimsy.

During my childhood he began to impose a few such talismans and objets outside the house, as though trying to establish a point of contact or a portal into the natural world—into the wilderness—in terms that would be understandable to both it and him. He had a small yellow-and-black sign painted with the legend "Hoochy Goochy Gulchy" and nailed it on a tree next to the deep creek that ran along the border of the woods. And between the kitchen porch and the little cabin where the male grandchildren slept when they were old enough, he set up a little painted-plywood mother skunk and four kittens mounted on croquet wickets. After the summer was over and all of us had gone back home to the city for the winter, I would imagine the house empty, echoing and cold, and the skunk and her kittens buried under the snow. Then, when we arrived at the start of summer, they were the first thing I sought out; if any had been knocked down in the nine months since I'd seen them last, I set them upright. I was a child, the skunk kittens were as children, and so too, I think, was my grandfather in his fashion. But each year there seemed to be one less kitten, seemingly vanished together with the previous winter's snow, and by the time I was old enough to sleep alone in the cabin and too old to care about them any longer, there were none at all.

When I was four or five years old, when my father lay dying on the shore of the Atlantic, my grandfather Griggs had what was known as a picture window installed in the southwest corner of the house. I don't remember the carpenters coming, but they must have been some days at work—tearing out the old double-hung windows and their frames and fitting a six-foot-long header in their place—and when they were done, our relation to the world outside the house was irrevocably changed. What was once outside was now in some sense inside; by day, the green light poured into the living room, and at night the incandescence from our lamps streamed amber like oil across the lawn and into the trees.

In the first few years after the window went in, whenever guests came to visit my grandfather would guide them to it, beaming like a new father at the hospital nursery. It was as though he had acquired a Vermeer. In fact, he had merely ordered up the frame and the glass, but there was no separating them from what they contained. Two miles of water lay between us and the lake's opposite shore, a palisade of ruddy stone cliffs easing into hills of aspen and birch. These things had always been there, and I suppose we had always seen them. They had been many things, not one thing, but now they were bound together. Now we had what people called a view. It sat in our living room like the handsome portrait of a favorite son, of friend or kin of whom we were terribly proud.

It seemed as often as not my grandfather could be found at the window, looking through it or standing just in front of it on the patio he had had built. He was a man of habits, dressed in brown oxfords, pleated trousers of gray wool or gabardine, and a yellow V-neck sweater. If it was midday, he held a gin and tonic in a tall frosted glass; if it was evening, he had scotch and water or an old-fashioned with a maraschino cherry in it that looked like the sun going down in a forest fire.

The view turned him into a connoisseur of sunsets and he fed bolts of Kodachrome through his camera to record them. He must have made hundreds of exposures, all much the same: a border of spruce, a horizon of water, and the dusk's strata layered over them, saffron, crimson, and streaky as bacon. Later, as an adolescent, I wondered what he saw in what seemed to me so little, the sun's imperceptible decline, the acres of ruched and dimpled water, as tirelessly regarded as by a sailor's wife. My grandfather had been to sea once, when he was nineteen, on his way to France to drive an ambulance on the Western Front. His ship traveled in a convoy; when it reached France, he wrote his mother a letter and told her how the Gironde opened itself into the Atlantic above Bordeaux to receive them. He spent a year around Verdun, ferrying the wounded and the dying, swabbing out the blood from his ambulance, debating the merits of Protestantism versus Catholicism with the local priest. He met a beautiful girl with wavy bobbed hair and serene eyes in Epernay. He returned to the Midwest for good in 1918, and he kept her picture in the back of a desk drawer for the rest of his life. I think this, like many things in his life, was a keeping of faith, just like maintaining his voluminous correspondence and researching the Griggs family genealogy, honoring the past, doing memory's labor. I never heard him utter a devout or pious sentiment, but he clearly believed the world was more good than evil, and he was mightily content in it. That he had once met a pretty girl in France and that he now had a picture window were signs of grace enough for him.

We were children then—my sister, my cousins, and I—and while our elders confined themselves mostly to the house, the patio, and the lawn, we pressed the edges of our place in the world a few feet at a time: to the ditch on the other side of the road; to the stony, driftwood-tangled cove beyond the breakwater; into the woods to the far verge of the property. The earth was terra incognita but benign; barring ill weather, a little more of it could become home each day. We cached pennies and dolls and whistles in the bases of trees, and the forest gave us gifts in return: shelter in the rain, stones and berries, and—once and best of all—the white, perfectly preserved skull of a squirrel. It was enchanted, in the root sense of the word, "cantare": The world sang to us, it rocked us in its great soft arms.

One day when I was about nine years old, on a morning like any other, I heard screaming in the forest. The sunlight fell in shafts between the jack pines, and the air was still and resinous and warm. My cousin Cathy ran out of the woods, shrieking, raking wasps from her hair. She fell among the pine needles and lay on her stomach, writhing. Welts bloomed like tiny strawberries on her arms and legs. The screen door to the kitchen porch yawned and slammed again and again. She was encircled by adults and her cries became sobs and keening. She had stumbled into a wasps' nest in the woods; the stings were few and scarcely toxic, and she would be fine. She would not cry again with such ferocity for another eight or nine years, when a boy she loved forsook her.

I think it was not her body but her heart that pained her; her heart was broken that day. She had believed, until then, that the natural world was good—that it was a friend, itself a child as innocent and well-intentioned as she, and perhaps even a guardian, a protector. Now she had discovered it was cruel, arbitrary, and venomous. It repaid faith with caprice, with wounds. And the betrayal reverberated through everything she believed and thought she knew. For if the world was not good, why had not someone told her? Why, more important, had no one protected her? We were children; our lives were grounded in our faith in the wisdom and beneficence of adults, and beyond them, in the goodness of God. We had been misled, and perhaps lied to. In memory, the anger and the sting of betrayal were tangible as stone, as sour in our mouths as iron, as sharp as copper. They inscribed themselves on our lives as private martyrologies and *kindermärchen*. As in a Grimm's fairy tale, we suspected we had been abandoned, left in the forest. No one would save us, and we were children lost among other children, in the woods among the stones, the berries, the wasps, and the tiny white skull, creatures forsaken by our creator.

Thereafter, we approached the forest with wariness, or, as we grew older, with cocky heedlessness that hid an anxious, fearful belligerence. Needless to say, we sought revenge. Insects of all descriptions could be found trapped in the kitchen porch, flailing against the screens, their motions increasing in pitch and frenzy as the afternoon heat rose. We beat them with rolled newspapers and fly swatters, hosed them with water and insecticides drawn from brown bottles, asphyxiated them in clouds of gas. They buzzed in fury and agony and wheeled their bodies in pointless circles, like draw horses tethered to a mill.

I think we understood that we were cruel, but our cruelty was irresistible, like candy, like the desires in our bodies that we could not name and that we were scarcely learning to tease and sate. I myself spent more and more time by the picture window, not looking out of it, but sprawled beneath it on the sofa, reading books about expeditions, sea voyages, and sailors' knots. Sometimes a wasp or a blackfly would find its way into the house. I suppose they were drawn to the light of the window, or to the illusion that it was a passage to the outside. Or perhaps it was not an illusion, for no one could deny that the outside was clearly before them in the window, no matter how obdurate and impenetrable the window itself proved to be. They buzzed against it like drillers on a rock face of diamond, perhaps in frustration, perhaps in incomprehension, perhaps in sheer terror. I heard them, and I would get up and find a canister of insecticide and pump it onto their bodies until there was not a trace of their voices, until the poison mounted up like sea foam on the windowsill.

I can still see myself, a child clad in shorts and a T-shirt and high-topped sneakers, performing this liturgy of annihilation, and I know I could see myself doing it then. It was that very self-awareness, that watching myself do it, that gave the act its savor, the newfound thrill of performing on the stage of one's self-consciousness. And it was that that took my actions out of the childhood realm of mischief, disobedience, or thoughtlessness, past that of sin—of simply failing to be good—and into the realm of evil, of not merely causing misfortune but creating it, fashioning a self that was evil's author, setting that creature in motion as God did Adam, and watching it go about its work.

That was a discovery I made long ago, when I was scarcely a decade old, in the world before this one. But it seems to me that every human life reenacts the story of Eden, usually in childhood—an age in which there is no evil or falsehood or death, where seeming and being are one beautiful and numinous thing, where we are both wholly free and completely in accord with the creation we inhabit. One's own self and its expression seem identical with the world's will, with God's word, his self-utterance. Then, as Emerson put it, "It is very unhappy, but too late to be helped, the discovery we have made that we exist. That discovery is called the Fall of Man." And in the Fall, what we steal is not simply the fruit of the tree of knowledge, but specifically that of self-knowledge and the kind of self-expression that follows from it. In my lifetime self-expression has been regarded as one of the highest goods, and so it often can be. But in the Fall, we cease to differentiate between our use of this faculty and God's. The product of God's self-awareness is self-expression as pure being, as that which is wholly good. It's because of this that the expression "God is love" is more than a syrupy truism. For in a rigorously philosophical definition, love is that which lacks nothing—which wants nothing for itself but simply wills the existence of its object—and is therefore perfect being, which is to say God. God's self-expression is the Love from which we and his creation are engendered.

Our self-discovery leads elsewhere, not to joyful self-contemplation but, at least in part, to the end of our innocence. The loss of innocence seems to me less the gaining of forbidden knowledge than the discovery of desire—the sense that far from being blessed by both unimaginable grace and freedom, we are inadequate and also enslaved by what we lack; and the amelioration of that lack becomes our life's work. This is the knowledge that initiates our discontent, our disenchantment, our sense that we have been stripped of grace, that we are no longer loved. And that is, perhaps, why desire so often feels like love, or like the longing for it.

I know it was at my grandfather's house, after the wasps, that I discovered desire. For a long time before that, and some time after, life and the world felt emptied out, hollow, comfortable for the most part, full, in fact, of temporary satisfactions, but devoid of wonder. It seems to me now to have been a continuation and escalation of that sense of betrayal, of unwanted and unbidden knowledge, that first came upon me that summer when I was nine. Thereafter, my life did not lack joy or excitement, but they came not through the mere acceptance of the gift that that earlier enchanted world had seemed to me, but through the fulfillment of desire; of discovering an urge and acting on it, of making what I wanted to happen happen.

I think desire was in my body before it was in my mind. I first recollect it from around age ten: lying half-awake in bed in the cabin, conscious of a tension in my body, a sort of vibrant, manic itch, a delicious ache that on the one hand demanded to be eased—but how?—and on the other to be perpetually sustained. For the first time in my life, I didn't want to get straight up and play or go into the house or out into the woods. I wanted to stay here with this feeling for as long as it would go on.

In retrospect, I know that I was merely pressing my proto-adolescent morning erection against the mattress, but it took me some time to connect what I was feeling with my genitals or even with my body in a specific way, still less with the bodies of others. And I think at least a year went by before I understood that the sensation could be induced, coaxed, manipulated, and brought to a kind of epiphany, albeit not one that truly sated the underlying desire. That was what I came to understand about it, and in a general way about all desire: that it is not an itch that can ever really be scratched, because its savor, its substance—everything that we crave—depends on absence, unfulfillment, lack. What we truly covet is the hunger on the verge of being sated, the flash of the synapse between wanting and having. To possess it is to spoil it, and so we must start all over again.

Thus was desire a little akin to the wonder I had previously felt. Perhaps it is what grownups have, or at least cultivate, instead of enchantment. It has the joyful vibrancy of wonder, but not its placid givenness. Indeed, desire is not given but must be pursued, urged, and driven, its objects forever time-bound and scarce, and perhaps our pursuit of it implies something is in turn pursuing us, for which we believe desire is the remedy. We are unlikely to ask whether it is a fair substitute for what we have lost, but that itself is in the nature of the desire: to seem to be what we want. And to sense the lack, the unbeing, at the heart of desire is perhaps the adult equivalent of what I discovered in the woods when I was nine, my first loss of faith.

It was in the wake of these things that I underwent my first conversion, to Episcopalianism and being "good," at the age of twelve. Now, it seems nothing so much as an attempt to recover the inborn faith I had lost in the woods by my grandfather's house; an attempt, it also seems to me now, that was predicated not on love but on desire and so was as misguided as it was well-intended. When I saw myself, I saw what I was not and wanted to be. My conversion was less about a turning to God—the root meaning of the word "conversion"—than about the construction of a new self in which I was both creator and creature. This is not the intended task of religion, and it is not surprising that I drifted away from it and toward psychology and the neo-Transcendentalist program of the sixties and early seventies, which promised to bring about exactly the change I desired.

If my life of the next twenty years had a theme, it was self-discovery. Of course, I had discovered myself long before, but I had not much liked what I'd seen. My notion of my self was an autonomous person, not an object—a being whose essence was a given, created thing—but a subject. My person might be, as psychology taught, determined by the interactions of culture, politics, and power, but it was also somehow infinitely malleable if I wanted to undertake changing it. I did not see the contradiction in that, or wonder exactly what agent—which *me*—stood still performing all these operations while my personhood underwent its constant renovation and improvement.

I still visited my grandfather's house during these years, less perhaps for its current attractions than as a museum of the boy I used to be. But in my dreams it was still a refuge, still the world before this one, unfallen. Sometimes I held its image in my mind in the form of snow cave, the den of a hibernating creature, a heart—somehow warm and without fear or care—beating in the middle of the still and frozen world.

In fact, I never saw snow at my grandfather's house until I was older, eighteen years old. During the winter, squirrels had invaded the attic, and my grandfather and his handyman got the idea to drive them out by burning sulfur candles. One night in March, one of the candles fell, or was knocked over, and the house caught fire. When it was wholly in flames, someone across the lake, two miles away, saw the conflagration and called the fire department. But it was too late. The next day the earth where the house had stood hissed and buzzed with the snow, melted from the center of the fire outward, ringing it at a distance. I came a few days later. I would have liked to find the mother skunk and her kittens at some distance from the house, fallen, perhaps half buried in the duff, but safe, but they had disappeared years before. There was nothing left but two chimneys, some broken pieces of pottery where the kitchen had stood, and a few black shards of glass in the southwest corner. Someone told me the picture window would have exploded like a bomb.

I always wondered if the fire broke my grandfather's heart, if it effected some transformation or epiphany in his life. But I never knew his secrets, least of all that of his vast and placid contentment. I do know, as it later emerged, that despite his career in the insurance business, he had never bothered to put an insurance policy on the house in the woods.

He built a new house in its place, but it was not the same. I had my own house by then, and a career and a wife and a child. These things occupied me, and gradually took the place of the conscious self-fashioning I had been so busy with during my adolescence and twenties. Or rather, they became my person, they were who I was, until the shape and buttressing they had given my life began to fall away in my thirties. In the space of two years, I lost my job, my marriage, and my financial assets. The month I turned thirty-nine a close friend was diagnosed with a brain tumor, which would have to be removed by a long and complicated but not terribly perilous operation. Her surgery was in Pittsburgh, and at the moment it was taking place, I was driving down a highway in Wyoming, on my way to a magazine writing assignment.

I did not want to do the assignment and I did not want to be in Wyoming. The road ran through treeless high country, still winterbound, and the snow snaked on and off the shoulders in ribbons across the highway. From the west, black-bellied clouds were pressing down against the horizon, moving toward me, bearing, perhaps, an imminent blizzard. I thought of that, of all the things that had recently befallen my life, and of my friend on the operating table in Pittsburgh, and I said, aloud, not having given Him a thought in years, "Please, God—no more.'"

There was more. The weather held, but my friend never awoke from her surgery. The tumor was larger and the operation more difficult than predicted. She lingered for a week, and then she died.

I cannot say that, like Henry Adams with the death of his sister in 1870, I lost my faith at that moment. I had already lost my faith in any conscious form years before, and was, for lack of any other belief, a sort of fatalist. Fatalism—accepting that, lacking anything else, randomness and chance constitute a system—may be the dominant religion among educated, worldly-wise members of my generation. Provided your luck holds and you are not so old as to need to give much thought to death (which in this view merely returns the body to the soil, a kind of composting that is both appealing in its circularity and ecologically public-spirited), as creeds go you could do worse. If it's not strictly held—and it is not the sort of belief anyone bothers to hold systematically—moments of particular success can be construed, in the more traditional American manner, as having been deserved or earned. All in all, it is a swell religion for the fortunate and the smug.

When things turn really bad, however, no one wants to be a fatalist. The mind does not easily tolerate effects without causes, events without explanations. That is why jilted fatalists become cynics; there is, it turns out, a system, but it's rigged. Despair is a braver and more honest option, but no one can cling to it and survive: It enacts love and creation in reverse, ending in self-annihilation.

After that day on the highway in Wyoming, I flirted with both cynicism and despair. I took up cigarettes again and drank too much. I sat at bars as my father had done at Talley's Tap, and I fulminated. But at some level I understood that my calling out to God and his apparent lack of response could be proof of something other than nonexistence: his callousness. A part of me was inclined to say, *This is what you get for your trouble when you ask God for a favor.* That proposition, with its anger and sense of betrayal, presumes something rather than nothing. It presupposes that its object is real. It is the position of Job, and also that of Jesus on the cross when he asks why his father has forsaken him.

In my bitterness and sense of grievance I had, therefore, opened up a kind of dialogue after years of silence. It was sporadic to be sure, and had nothing to do with belief per se, never mind with doctrine or religion. My inclination was to adopt a kind of modified fatalism, made sweeter and more bearable by a specific engagement with the natural world. I spent a lot of time hiking during this period, as well as reading in the genre known as nature writing. It came to seem to me that Nature in its purity, its beauty, and even its apparent randomness and amorality gave the lie to the notion of a creation abandoned by its creator. Nature, I believed, must say something, must be a sign, an indication of something rather than nothing.

It was then that I went back to my grandfather's house. I was forty years old, and my grandfather had died the previous summer. His death—the death of the man who had been the closest I had come to having a father, and in relationship to whom I came closest to being a son—had been another among the losses that seemed in those days to define my life. My mother and her siblings had decided to sell the house, which was, of course, not the house of my childhood but the one he had built after the fire. Still, the woods and outbuildings remained, and perhaps there would be something on the property I would like to take as a keepsake.

When I arrived, the only thing I recognized from my childhood was the cabin where I had slept when I was old enough and where now no one had slept for years. I went in, pushing past the dense mob of spruce and pine that had then been mere shrubs and saplings, but that now, tall as me and taller, blocked the way and surrounded the cabin. Inside, the floor tipped like a ship in a gale and wallpaper dangled from the walls. Yet the smell was the same as it always had been: green Palmolive soap, damp sheets and chenille bedspreads, paper, dust, and scorched lampshades. The light was sparse, the windows blocked by the spruce trees outside.

Tacked to the wall was a map of the lake that must have been placed there before I was born, and the point of land where I was standing was visible upon it, though no larger than a mote. If there was a picture window in heaven overlooking this place, perhaps this was the view. Before it had first been hung, the map had been altered in a few respects: Someone had brushed the lake blue with watercolor and painted a beautiful Indian princess in the corner, her eyes and hair dark and shiny as coal. She had been my emblem of desire when desire first came to haunt my bones, after the wasps, before the fire, when I began to lie beneath the picture window; when I still believed, as perhaps my grandfather always did, that naïveté was the mark of innocence—of ourselves in what used to be called "the state of nature"—rather than of mere ignorance. But then it seemed to me also true that since we were in that way a part of nature—coequal with Nature rather than its offspring—then Nature could not itself be our true parent, our creator, our God. Nature was but a sign of something greater, not the thing itself. And so, in that moment, I found myself bereft of the closest thing to a god I had in those days been able to imagine.

On an impulse, I decided to take the map, along with some of my grandfather's papers and scrapbooks, home to where I live now, near a park that encircles a lake. The map seemed to be all that was left of the view I remembered here, a speck no larger than the black of the Indian princess's eye. I pulled out the thumbtacks, flyblown with rust, rolled up the map, opened the door, and pushed my way back out through the trees. They stood all around, thronging the cabin, like children waiting to be let in.

N. Scott Momaday

FROM *THE WAY TO RAINY MOUNTAIN*

Retreat and return mingle in N. Scott Momaday's memoir. Coming back to the Oklahoma knoll that is Rainy Mountain, he retreats from his assimilated North American lifestyle to the life of the Kiowas. His retreat is also a return—to his own childhood memories, to his grandmother, to her childhood, to three hundred years of Kiowa history, to the dawn of Creation itself. And this retreat and return is composed as largely of imagination as it is of place; it ends in a particular location—Rainy Mountain—but it begins as a pilgrimage to understand his birthright culture: "I wanted to see in reality what she had seen more perfectly in the mind's eye," says Momaday, as he travels fifteen hundred miles to the headwaters of the Kiowa nation.

> *This retreat and return is composed as largely of imagination as it is of place.*

Yet, his grandmother did not need to take that journey to replenish her spirit. At night, Momaday remembers, she would retreat to prayer, her voice raised "in a high and descending pitch, exhausting her breath to silence; then again and again" composing prayers out of the memory of suffering and the promise of hope. But each day she would return to the busy life of a wife and mother, extending her hospitality to "aged visitors" and aunts and uncles and cousins and—most especially, across the years—to one, small, thoughtful grandson.

FROM *THE WAY TO RAINY MOUNTAIN*

A single knoll rises out of the plain in Oklahoma, north and west of the Wichita Range. For my people, the Kiowas, it is an old landmark, and they gave it the name Rainy Mountain. The hardest weather in the world is there. Winter brings blizzards, hot tornadic winds arise in the spring, and in summer the prairie is an anvil's edge. The grass turns brittle and brown, and it cracks beneath your feet. There are green belts along the rivers and creeks, linear groves of hickory and pecan, willow and witch hazel. At a distance in July or August the steaming foliage seems almost to writhe in fire. Great green and yellow grasshoppers are everywhere in the tall grass, popping up like corn to sting the flesh, and tortoises crawl about on the red earth, going nowhere in the plenty of time. Loneliness is an aspect of the land. All things in the plain are isolate, there is no confusion of objects in the eye, but *one* hill *or one* tree or *one* man. To look upon that landscape in the early morning, with the sun at your back, is to lose the sense of proportion. Your imagination comes to life, and this, you think, is where Creation was begun.

I returned to Rainy Mountain in July. My grandmother had died in the spring, and I wanted to be at her grave. She had lived to be very old and at last infirm. Her only living daughter was with her when she died, and I was told that in death her face was that of a child.

I like to think of her as a child. When she was born, the Kiowas were living that last great moment of their history. For more than a hundred years they had controlled the open range from the Smoky Hill River to the Red, from the headwaters of the Canadian to the fork of the Arkansas and Cimarron. In alliance with the Comanches, they had ruled the whole of the southern Plains. War was their sacred business, and they were among the finest horsemen the world has ever known. But warfare for the Kiowas was preeminently a matter of disposition rather than of survival, and they never understood the grim, unrelenting advance of the U.S. Cavalry. When at last, divided and ill-provisioned, they were driven onto the Staked Plains in the cold rains of autumn, they fell into panic. In Palo Duro Canyon they abandoned their crucial stores to pillage and had nothing then but their lives. In order to save themselves, they surrendered to the soldiers at Fort Sill and were imprisoned in the old stone corral that now stands as a military museum. My grandmother was spared the humiliation of those high gray walls by eight or ten years, but she must have known from birth the affliction of defeat, the dark brooding of old warriors.

Her name was Aho, and she belonged to the last culture to evolve in North America. Her forebears came down from the high country in western Montana nearly three centuries ago. They were a mountain people, a mysterious tribe of hunters whose language has never been positively classified in any major group. In the late seventeenth century they began a long migration to the south and east. It was a journey toward the dawn, and it led to a golden age. Along the way the Kiowas were befriended by the Crows, who gave them the culture and religion of the Plains. They acquired horses, and their ancient nomadic spirit was suddenly free of the ground. They acquired Tai-me, the sacred Sun Dance doll, from that moment the object and symbol of their worship, and so shared in the divinity of the sun. Not least, they acquired the sense of destiny, therefore courage and pride. When they entered upon the southern Plains they had been transformed. No longer were they slaves to the simple necessity of survival; they were a lordly and dangerous society of fighters and thieves, hunters and priests of the sun. According to their origin myth, they entered the world through a hollow log. From one point of view, their migration was the fruit of an old prophecy, for indeed they emerged from a sunless world.

Although my grandmother lived out her long life in the shadow of Rainy Mountain, the immense landscape of the continental interior lay like memory in her blood. She could tell of the Crows, whom she had never seen, and of the Black Hills, where she had never been. I wanted to see in reality what she had seen more perfectly in the mind's eye, and traveled fifteen hundred miles to begin my pilgrimage.

Yellowstone, it seemed to me, was the top of the world, a region of deep lakes and dark timber, canyons and waterfalls. But, beautiful as it is, one might have the sense of confinement there. The skyline in all directions is close at hand, the high wall of the woods and deep cleavages of shade. There is a perfect freedom in the mountains, but it belongs to the eagle and the elk, the badger and the bear. The Kiowas reckoned their stature by the distance they could see, and they were bent and blind in the wilderness.

Descending eastward, the highland meadows are a stairway to the plain. In July the inland slope of the Rockies is luxuriant with flax and buckwheat, stonecrop and larkspur. The earth unfolds and the limit of the land recedes. Clusters of trees, and animals grazing far in the distance, cause the vision to reach away and wonder to build upon the mind. The sun follows a longer course in the day, and the sky is immense beyond all comparison. The great billowing clouds that sail upon it are shadows that move upon the grain like water, dividing light. Farther down, in the land of the Crows and Blackfeet, the plain is yellow. Sweet clover takes hold of the hills and bends upon itself to cover and seal the soil. There the Kiowas paused on their way; they had come to the place where they must change their lives. The sun is at home on the plains. Precisely there does it have the certain character of a god. When the Kiowas came to the land of the Crows, they could see the dark lees of the hills at dawn across the Bighorn River, the profusion of light on the grain shelves, the oldest deity ranging after the solstices. Not yet would they veer southward to the caldron of the land that lay below; they must wean their blood from the northern winter and hold the mountains a while longer in their view. They bore Tai-me in procession to the east.

A dark mist lay over the Black Hills, and the land was like iron. At the top of a ridge I caught sight of Devil's Tower upthrust against the gray sky as if in the birth of time the core of the earth had broken through its crust and the motion of the world was begun. There are things in nature that engender an awful quiet in the heart of man; Devil's Tower is one of them. Two centuries ago, because they could not do otherwise, the Kiowas made a legend at the base of the rock. My grandmother said:

Eight children were there at play, seven sisters and their brother. Suddenly the boy was struck dumb; he trembled and began to run upon his hands and feet. His fingers became claws, and his body was covered with fur. Directly there was a bear where the boy had been. The sisters were terrified; they ran, and the bear after them. They came to the stump of a great tree, and the tree spoke to them. It bade them climb upon it, and as they did so it began to rise into the air. The bear came to kill them, but they were just beyond its reach. It reared against the tree and scored the bark all around with its claws. The seven sisters were borne into the sky, and they became the stars of the Big Dipper.

From that moment, and so long as the legend lives, the Kiowas have kinsmen in the night sky. Whatever they were in the mountains, they could be no more. However tenuous their well-being, however much they had suffered and would suffer again, they had found a way out of the wilderness.

My grandmother had a reverence for the sun, a holy regard that now is all but gone out of mankind. There was a wariness in her, and an ancient awe. She was a Christian in her later years, but she had come a long way about, and she never forgot her birthright. As a child she had been to the Sun Dances; she had taken part in those annual rites, and by them she had learned the restoration of her people in the presence of Tai-me. She was about seven when the last Kiowa Sun Dance was held in 1887 on the Washita River above Rainy Mountain Creek. The buffalo were gone. In order to consummate the ancient sacrifice—to impale the head of a buffalo bull upon the medicine tree—a delegation of old men journeyed into Texas, there to beg and barter for an animal from the Goodnight herd. She was ten when the Kiowas came together for the last time as a living Sun Dance culture. They could find no buffalo; they had to hang an old hide from the sacred tree. Before the dance could begin, a company of soldiers rode out from Fort Sill under orders to disperse the tribe. Forbidden without cause the essential act of their faith, having seen the wild herds slaughtered and left to rot upon the ground, the Kiowas backed away forever from the medicine tree. That was July 20, 1890, at the great bend of the Washita. My grandmother was there. Without bitterness, and for as long as she lived, she bore a vision of deicide.

Now that I can have her only in memory, I see my grandmother in the several postures that were peculiar to her: standing at the wood stove on a winter morning and turning meat in a great iron skillet; sitting at the south window, bent above her beadwork, and afterwards, when her vision failed, looking down for a long time into the fold of her hands; going out upon a cane, very slowly as she did when the weight of age came upon her; praying. I remember her most often at prayer. She made long, rambling prayers out of suffering and hope, having seen many things. I was never sure that I had the right to hear, so exclusive were they of all mere custom and company. The last time I saw her she prayed standing by the side of her bed at night, naked to the waist, the light of a kerosene lamp moving upon her dark skin. Her long, black hair, always drawn and braided in the day, lay upon her shoulders and against her breasts like a shawl. I do not speak Kiowa, and I never understood her prayers, but there was something inherently sad in the sound, some merest hesitation upon the syllables of sorrow. She began in a high and descending pitch, exhausting her breath to silence; then again and again—and always the same intensity of effort, of something that is, and is not, like urgency in the human voice. Transported so in the dancing light among the shadows of her room, she seemed beyond the reach of time. But that was illusion; I think I knew then that I should not see her again.

Houses are like sentinels in the plain, old keepers of the weather watch. There, in a very little while, wood takes on the appearance of great age. All colors wear soon away in the wind and rain, and then the wood is burned gray and the grain appears and the nails turn red with rust. The windowpanes are black and opaque; you imagine there is nothing within, and indeed there are many ghosts, bones given up to the land. They stand here and there against the sky, and you approach them for a longer time than you expect. They belong in the distance; it is their domain.

Once there was a lot of sound in my grandmother's house, a lot of coming and going, feasting and talk. The summers there were full of excitement and reunion. The Kiowas are a summer people; they abide the cold and keep to themselves, but when the season turns and the land becomes warm and vital they cannot hold still; an old love of going returns upon them. The aged visitors who came to my grandmother's house when I was a child were made of lean and leather, and they bore themselves upright. They wore great black hats and bright ample shirts that shook in the wind. They rubbed fat upon their hair and wound their braids with strips of colored cloth. Some of them painted their faces and carried the scars of old and cherished enmities. They were an old council of warlords, come to remind and be reminded of who they were. Their wives and daughters served them well. The women might indulge themselves; gossip was at once the mark and compensation of their servitude. They made loud and elaborate talk among themselves, full of jest and gesture, fright and false alarm. They went abroad in fringed and flowered shawls, bright beadwork and German silver. They were at home in the kitchen, and they prepared meals that were banquets.

There were frequent prayer meetings, and great nocturnal feasts. When I was a child I played with my cousins outside, where the lamplight fell upon the ground and the singing of the old people rose up around us and carried away into the darkness. There were a lot of good things to eat, a lot of laughter and surprise. And afterwards, when the quiet returned, I lay down with my grandmother and could hear the frogs away by the river and feel the motion of the air.

Now there is a funeral silence in the rooms, the endless wake of some final word. The walls have closed in upon my grandmother's house. When I returned to it in mourning, I saw for the first time in my life how small it was. It was late at night, and there was a white moon, nearly full. I sat for a long time on the stone steps by the kitchen door. From there I could see out across the land; I could see the long row of trees by the creek, the low light upon the rolling plains, and the stars of the Big Dipper. Once I looked at the moon and caught sight of a strange thing. A cricket had perched upon the handrail, only a few inches away from me. My line of vision was such that the creature filled the moon like a fossil. It had gone there, I thought, to live and die, for there, of all places, was its small definition made whole and eternal. A warm wind rose up and purled like the longing within me.

The next morning I awoke at dawn and went out on the dirt road to Rainy Mountain. It was already hot, and the grasshoppers began to fill the air. Still, it was early in the morning, and the birds sang out of the shadows. The long yellow grass on the mountain shone in the bright light, and a scissortail hied above the land. There, where it ought to be, at the end of a long and legendary way, was my grandmother's grave. Here and there on the dark stones were ancestral names. Looking back once, I saw the mountain and came away.

Madeleine L'Engle

SELECTIONS FROM *THE SUMMER OF THE GREAT-GRANDMOTHER*

The summer after her mother turned ninety, Madeleine L'Engle brought her home for the last time. It was the L'Engle family tradition to spend summers together at Crosswicks, an old farmhouse outside New York City—four generations sharing a single home. Gracchi, Grandmadeleine, Josephine, Léna—the names and nicknames of great-grandmother, mother, daughter, grandchild stitched the family together as surely as did their love.

> *A* refuge is not a defense against death but the place where we prepare to meet it.

During this summer of dying, Crosswicks becomes a refuge. A refuge for the great-grandmother who fights her daughter's efforts to feed her but still takes pleasure in a small, warm cat and a small, warm great-granddaughter. A refuge for Madeleine, confused over the change in roles from daughter to caregiver and angry that she can no longer connect with the one person who has known her all her life. A refuge for young Léna, who knows simply that summer is the time for family love.

But even Crosswicks cannot hold out death—for, indeed, a refuge is not a defense against death but the place where we prepare to meet it. Nor is it, at the end, a place at all, but a Person in whose arms we securely rest and to whom we return at last, at home.

"It's all right," L'Engle tells her mother and then reflects: "I do this well aware of the enormity of the promise. There is a chill and empty feeling within me; nevertheless, there is something which impels me to put my arms around the Madeleine who is ninety and the Madeleine who has just turned three, and say, 'Don't be afraid. It's all right.'"

SELECTIONS FROM *THE SUMMER OF THE GREAT-GRANDMOTHER*

This is the summer of the great-grandmother, more her summer than any other summer. This is the summer after her ninetieth birthday, the summer of the swift descent.

Once, when I was around twelve, we took a twenty-mile toboggan ride down a Swiss mountainside. The men guiding the toboggan were experienced mountaineers; the accelerating speed was wildly exciting. Mother and I both clutched the sides of the toboggan as we careened around sharply banked curves. The guides could keep it on the hard-packed snow of the path, but they could not stop it in its descent. My mother's plunge into senility reminds me of that toboggan ride. When I look at the long green and gold days of this summer, the beautiful days are probably more beautiful, and the horrible days more horrible, than in actuality. But there's no denying that it's a summer of extremes.

I am tired, and numb. Mother's first two nights in Crosswicks I do not get any sleep, despite my fatigue. She needs more attention during the night than we had expected. The two girls who do night duty are young and completely inexperienced in nursing; Vicki has another year in high school; she was born during the years we lived in Crosswicks year round; it is difficult for me to realize that she is now a young woman, and a very capable young woman. Janet, too, I have known all her life; her father died when she was a baby, and her mother only a summer ago, and I wonder if she does not feel a certain irony in taking care of an old woman who has lived long past normal life expectancy. And I feel that the two girls need help, not physical help, simply my being there, awake and available if they need me.

After the first two wakeful nights it is clear to me how competent they are, and that I must get some rest.

It's a good thing to have all the props pulled out from under us occasionally. It gives us some sense of what is rock under our feet and what is sand. It stops us from taking anything for granted. It has also taught me a lot about living in the immediate moment. I am somehow managing to live one day, one hour at a time. I have to. Hugh is in Crosswicks for four days, and somehow or other I am able simply to be with him, without projecting into the future. When he goes back to New York he will be going to the neurologist.

Each evening after dinner I walk the dogs down the lane for a few minutes, to catch my breath and regain perspective. The girls prepare the great-grandmother for bed, and we learned the first night that this is done more easily if I am out of the house; if I am there she calls for me, and will not do anything for any of us.

This night, when I return, she has been put to bed, and the larger family—Hugh, Bion, Josephine, the girls, assorted friends and neighbors (Maria and Peter are not back from their honeymoon)—have gathered in the living room to play poker with ancient poker chips. Alan is out in the Tower writing. I'm not a poker player either, so I go in to say good night to Mother and sit with her for a while. Our quiet times together have always been in the morning, over coffee, and at night before bedtime. For a moment, a flash, she is there, is herself, and we laugh at Tyrrell lying on her back, all four legs spread out, tail wagging in this upside-down position. Thomas, the amber cat, is also on his back, lying beside the big dog, rear legs abandoned, forepaws folded prayerfully across his chest. Titus, the yellow puffball kitten, is in Mother's lap, purring.

Then the moment is gone. "Something's wrong," my mother says. "I don't know what it is, but something's wrong."

"It's all right, Mother. Nothing is wrong."

"It is, it is. Something's wrong. I want to go home." This has been a constant refrain since her arrival. "I want to go home. I want to go home."

"You *are* home, Mother. You're with your family, with all your children."

"I want to go home."

Yesterday Alan put his arms around me to give me comfort, and said, "Yes, she wants to go home, but she doesn't mean down South."

Her fear touches off an enormous wave of protectiveness in me, and I know no way to keep her terror at bay.

"I want to go home," she repeats.

I sit on the bed beside her, and hold her hand. She fumbles with the other hand for the bell we have rigged up for her. A summer ago she used it sparingly; this summer it seems that the raucous buzz goes off every few minutes. "Mother, you don't need to ring for the girls. I'm right here."

"Where are they?"

"In the living room."

"What are they doing?"

"Playing poker."

She reaches again for the bell.

"Don't call them, Mother. I'm right here." I am obviously a poor substitute. Why am I hurt? This is not my mother who is rejecting me, my mother who was always patient, tolerant, wise.

Then she turns toward me, reaches for me. "I'm scared. I'm scared."

I put my arms around her and hold her. I hold her as I held my children when they were small and afraid in the night; as this, summer, I hold my grandchildren. I hold her as she, once upon a time and long ago, held me. And I say the same words, the classic, maternal, instinctive words of reassurance. "Don't be afraid. I'm here. It's all right."

"Something's wrong. I'm scared. I'm scared."

I cradle her and repeat, "It's all right."

What's all right? What am I promising her? I'm scared too. I don't know what will happen when Hugh goes to the neurologist. I don't know what's going to happen with my mother this summer. I don't know what the message may be the next time the phone rings. What's all right? How can I say it?

But I do. I hold her close, and kiss her, and murmur, "It's all right, Mother. It's all right."

I mean these words. I do not understand them, but I mean them. Perhaps one day I will find out what I mean. They are implicit in everything I write. I caught a hint of them during that lecture, even as I was cautioning against false promises. They are behind everything, the cooking of meals, walking the dogs, talking with the girls. I may never find out with my intellectual self what I mean, but if I am given enough glimpses perhaps these will add up to enough so that my heart will understand. It does not; not yet.

The Psalmist cries out his anguish: My sight faileth for very trouble; Lord, I have called daily upon thee, I have stretched forth my hands unto thee. Dost thou show wonders among the dead? or shall the dead rise up again, and praise thee? Shall thy loving-kindness be showed in the grave? or thy faithfulness in destruction? Shall thy wondrous works be known in the dark? and thy righteousness in the land where all things are forgotten?

O God. O God.

To the ancient Hebrew the ultimate hell consisted in being forgotten, erased from the memory of family and tribe, from the memory of God. If God forgets you, it is as though you have never existed. You have no meaning in the ultimate scheme of things. Your life, your being, your *ousia*, is of no value whatsoever. You are a tale told by an idiot; forgotten; annihilated.

I will never forget my mother. I do not think that my children will forget their grandmother. Perhaps the little girls will not remember their great-grandmother with "the vivid image and the very scene" but they are not likely to forget that they knew her, and shared in her last summer. They may absorb some of the things we have told them about Gracchi, so that these stories become part of their *ousia*. But their children? And their children's children?

And what of Greatie? And Mado?

How many people have been born, lived rich, loving lives, laughed and wept, been part of creation, and are now forgotten, unremembered by anybody walking the earth today?

Our memories are, at best, so limited, so finite, that it is impossible for us to envisage an unlimited, infinite memory, the memory of God. It is something I want to believe in: that no atom of creation is ever forgotten by him; always is; cared for; developing; loved.

My memory of Mother, which is the fullest memory of anybody living, is only fragmentary. I would like to believe that the creator I call God still remembers all of my mother, knows and cares for the *ousia* of her, and is still teaching her, and helping her to grow into the self he created her to be, her integrated, whole, redeemed self.

A Gathering of Summer Poems

The solaces of a summer retreat are meant to be temporary. They are not for themselves but are restorative, meant to send us back outside. Summer is when we fit ourselves for the rigors of autumn, with its return to routines. And for winter, with its long and empty spaces. And for spring, with its resurrections.

Thus, in these poems, speakers recall summer when the days were long, and their memories bring warmth, even when the world turns colder and emptier. And speakers are heartened with new desires against haunted nights and sullen blood. And speakers learn to bear with understanding the lonelinesses of silence. In these ways, summer teaches us to retreat so that we may return.

> Summer is when we fit ourselves for the rigors of autumn, with its return to routines. And for winter, with its long and empty spaces. And for spring, with its resurrections.

Summer Magic

LESLIE PINCKNEY HILL

So many cares to vex the day,
    So many fears to haunt the night,
My heart was all but weaned away
    From every lure of old delight.
Then summer came, announced by June,
    With beauty, miracle and mirth.
She hung aloft the rounding moon,
    She poured her sunshine on the earth,
She drove the sap and broke the bud,
    She set the crimson rose afire.
She stirred again my sullen blood,
    And waked in me a new desire.
Before my cottage door she spread
    The softest carpet nature weaves,
And deftly arched above my head
    A canopy of shady leaves.
Her nights were dreams of jeweled skies,
    Her days were bowers rife with song,
And many a scheme did she devise
    To heal the hurt and soothe the wrong.
For on the hill or in the dell,
    Or where the brook went leaping by
Or where the fields would surge and swell
    With golden wheat or bearded rye,
I felt her heart against my own,
    I breathed the sweetness of her breath,
Till all the cark of time had flown,
    And I was lord of life and death.

Summer Days

WATHEN MARKS WILKS CALL

In summer, when the days were long,
We walk'd, two friends, in field and wood;
Our heart was light, our step was strong,
And life lay round us, fair as good,
In summer, when the days were long.

We stray'd from morn till evening came,
We gather'd flowers, and wove us crowns;
We walk'd mid poppies red as flame,
Or sat upon the yellow downs,
And always wish'd our life the same.

In summer, when the days were long,
We leap'd the hedgerow, cross'd the brook;
And still her voice flow'd forth in song,
Or else she read some graceful book,
In summer, when the days were long.

And then we sat beneath the trees,
With shadows lessening in the noon;
And in the sunlight and the breeze
We revell'd, many a glorious June,
While larks were singing o'er the leas.

In summer, when the days were long,
We pluck'd wild strawberries, ripe and red,
Or feasted, with no grace but song,
On golden nectar, snow-white bread,
In summer, when the days were long.

We lov'd, and yet we knew it not,
For loving seem'd like breathing then;
We found a heaven in every spot;
Saw angels, too, in all good men,
And dream'd of gods in grove and grot.

In summer, when the days are long,
Alone I wander, muse alone;
I see her not, but that old song
Under the fragrant wind is blown,
In summer, when the days are long.

Alone I wander in the wood,
But one fair spirit hears my sighs;
And half I see the crimson hood,
The radiant hair, the calm glad eyes,
That charm'd me in life's summer mood.

In summer, when the days are long,
I love her as I lov'd of old;
My heart is light, my step is strong,
For love brings back those hours of gold,
In summer, when the days are long.

Summer Night

KENNETH SLADE ALLING

Like a bell note shivered into fragments of fine sound:
The summer night. But silence and the stillness do
    astound
Me more than all this strange-go-round
Of multitudinously minted chords along the ground.

This is an edifice of silence, vast:
Into the chinks of silence sound will creep
A little while—and fall asleep,
Its strength being spent and past.

They say the crickets sing all night:
I know
They strike against the walls of silence,
Insistently, a futile blow.

Patricia Hampl

"Silence" from *Virgin Time*

Although we sometimes think of retreating to childhood and its simple pleasures during the summer, we often find ourselves retreating from childhood as well, from the casual cruelty of squashed bugs and dreams that haunt us into our adult lives. Yet, it is in childhood that we first experience the immensity of creation and ourselves as intimately intertwined in the "booming heart of the world." And it is in summer that we can hope to recapture something of that magic and majesty.

In this selection, Patricia Hampl takes us back to the summer when she was five years old and forward to a summer spent at a Franciscan monastery in the Pacific Northwest, where she tries to regain the reality she knew as a child.

Summer's spaciousness does invite us back to the "pleasure of being caught up in the arms of creation." In its retreat we learn again to pray, to sing, to be hushed, to throw ourselves with abandon into the arms of God. But here, too, we learn that "nothing can be taken for granted," and so we return to our work-a-day and imperfect world, to autumn and winter,

> *In its retreat we learn again to pray, to sing, to be hushed, to throw ourselves with abandon into the arms of God.*

not just with memories but with wisdom, with anticipation, and with renewed strength.

"Silence"

It happened before—or possibly just after—I drowned. The same trip any-
way, the summer I was five, when we went for two weeks to Lake
Kabetogama, far up in the Boundary Waters, near Canada. Strange, I think
of it that way—the summer I drowned—*instead of the obvious—when I*
almost drowned.

I am standing on the dry, bleached dock. Late in the afternoon, the sun
already laying the pine trees down in long black shadows. My mother has
been reading Charlotte's Web *to me all week, drawing out the story in*
slow, delectable segments. But just now she says I must wait: can't I see she
is talking to Bernice. This is the wife of Phil, who owns the greenhouse
where my father works. We have come here with them, though they have the
big house with the stone fireplace. We have the little cabin on stilts, farther
from the water. That doesn't matter, my father says. We're lucky to be here.

Mother and Bernice wear plaid shirts with big shoulders. They are
smoking and doing their nails, sitting on a bench, leaning against the gray
wood slats of the boathouse. Sally, Bernice's pretty blond daughter my age, is
pouring salt on leeches she has speared out of the water and laid on the
dock. She likes to see them curl up.

So do I, but not now. Earlier in the day, as we worked together on this
project, Sally had said suddenly, "My father owns your father's car. He owns
your house and everything you have. Because he's your dad's boss, and he can
fire him like that." She snapped her fingers, making a soft thumping sound.

"He cannot," I said.

"Can too," she said, and kept pouring out her pure white stream of salt.
It is possible she speaks truth. I walk past her now.

And continue down the long wooden sidewalk of the dock. Toward the
end, I see a small step built onto the side of the dock. People use it to get
into their boats. It is awash, satiny with green. A stringer is attached to the
dock, right by this step. I want to pull on the stringer to see the fish my
father has caught. Either I want to look at them or I want to hold them up

to show my mother, who should be giving me her attention. She does not go fishing. She reads to me until her voice goes hoarse, or she reads to herself, two-inch-thick historical novels, about Ireland if possible.

I lower myself, one foot and then the other, to the slimy step just below the dock. I remember seeing the red ovals of my Keds with their rind of white rubber. That happened.

Then, hardly having stepped onto the satin step, and not having touched the metal of the stringer, I am in the water. I am over my head. My eyes are open and everything is gold. I am level with the fish, who are alive but witless, linked like grapes in a cluster. There are more steps below the one I slipped from. Why are there steps into the lake? Who descends? For what purpose?

I realize I will die. I can't swim. Water is rushing around me. It is strong. I can't cry out. No one has seen me disappear. I have been swallowed, accepted, stolen. So easy to be gone.

I realize I must save myself. Although the water swirls and I am panicked and the fish are aloof, I have an overwhelming, heart-bursting sensation that I will live, that I will get out. Panicked—but not afraid. A strange buoyancy: I'm drowning, but I can think about it. *I have never experienced my mind as a thing distinct, as something capable of helping me. And now I realize it is not in my head; my mind resides in my breastbone; it surges with willpower.*

I reach out, I will the slick mossy step to accept my grasp. It refuses. I reach again and command with the authority of Poseidon. The step obeys.

And I am on the dock again, in air, dripping like a filled sponge, my red sweater gorgeous with water. I walk toward my mother. She is still sitting by the boathouse with Bernice, working now on her right hand, stroking the thumbnail with the brush. I come nearer; strands of water fall from me. I am from another dimension.

She sees me, jerks up; the little bottle of nail polish tips off the bench. Red spatters on the sand. She is running to me; Bernice jumps up, too, and instinctively runs to Sally. Just as instinctively, Sally clutches her blue Morton box. "You could have died," she says, and I hear the respect in her voice at last.

But even more than drowning, that other death, the happy one. The same summer at Kabetogama. It is my mother's birthday, late July. We are standing in the Hudson's Bay Store, across the border in Canada.

My hand is a small wad of moist dough in a dry, warm holder: her hand. Then the little red spade of her polished nail digs at a bolt of brown plaid wool next to us on a table with many other bolts, heaped like logs on top of each other. "Just feel that wool," she says. "That's challis." She lifts the edge of the fabric, flares it out in a dark ripple.

I take my hand out of its holder, reach up to touch the wool. Touch it. And die. Or leave my body. Or fly. Something wonderful is happening that has never happened before. What is it? But there is no question in it, no query. There is just this moment, and it is forever and everything is in it.

My hand, I know, is touching the bolt of brown wool. I am also touching the bone china cup my brother is holding across the store which he is buying for Mother's birthday. Dad has given us each a dollar. I am imprinted on the English downs of the cup's landscape. The floor of the Hudson's Bay store is made of broad wooden planks, scuffed raw of varnish. I am that, too. I am the dollar in my pocket. I am also air and small motes of dust caught in the light.

I have left my body and entered objects. I don't exist anymore. Or I exist everywhere. I no longer stop at my skin. It is the best thing that has ever happened. It is bliss.

Then it is over. I snap back. I am me, I am nothing. I mustn't move from this spot. This is a good spot, and if I don't budge maybe it will come back. Maybe I will die again. But they are calling me. My mother, who has moved to another counter. My brother, who says I can't buy a cup, he's already bought her a cup. My father, who points to a sugar and creamer set painted with cabbage roses: that's what I should use my dollar for.

There is no telling them—it would be a mistake to tell. I don't know why this is, but it is, I know. IT *doesn't want to be told.* IT *doesn't like words, and speaks no language.*

I must move, must remove my hand from the bolt of wool, must return to them. I belong to them and must leave with them. "Come on," my brother calls. "Do you want to be left on this side of the border?"

We are going out to the car. I am with them again. There's no explain-

ing the most important thing that has ever happened to me. But if I tried, I would put my hand back in her hand. I would say: You die, you fly. You don't stop inside, you go everywhere. It's heaven.

I stopped at the chapel before returning to my room, drawn to the big shadow of the place. The wall of window framing the basso profundo tree with its scraggle of pink rhododendron made an icon as eloquent as anything I'd stood before in Italy.

Some people speak of prayer as a need to surrender. All that swooning of the mystics, giving over to the Divine Lover. Bernini's St. Teresa in her ecstasy, still scandalizing the rationalists with the orgasmic joy of her prayer. But surrender doesn't *say* it—and even in silence, how I need a thing *said*. What is that impulse that has always been there, refuting logic and requiring song?

It must be the instinct for praise. A ferocious appetite for humility which we intuit is a proper recognition of our truth: We are not simply made, but embraced. Sing a new song to the Lord, for he has made you. Made you to sing. Surrender—surrender even your voice, enter this silence. And become song.

I have always had a powerful sense of something pulsing which I could not name but also could not deny: a dynamic existence beyond me, yet in me. Spirit it is called—and why not? The invisible essence that is everywhere, including within ourselves. It is the glorious impersonality of existence which throbs with the reality of this dream we call our life. It goes where it wills.

This rich experience of life is not personal, though it is interior. It is an aspect of what we know to be the Divine, to be God—who was called in Hebrew, the first language of our tradition, Yahweh. That is, Our Integrity. I wished to find this Integrity. That is why I took to the pilgrimage trails, why I came here to this silent place near the Lost Coast. On the hunt for Our Integrity. I lived with It as a child. It was not happiness: I have no idea what a happy childhood is—or an unhappy one. As a child, I often felt an oddity

inhabit me. It was related to silence, but it was not, as people sometimes speak of religion, a comfort. I was not aware of requiring
comfort. This sensation of oddity was pleasure, a spreading delight. I
lie on the bed in the flowery room my father has papered for me,
and I am enfolded in the booming heart of the world as the
chipped blue roller makes its way over the damp clay tennis court.
The doves mourn in the morning, and everything is mixed up, and
I can hear my mother saying I'm sleeping my life away and I smile.

Is that a happy childhood—the unfettered experience of the
strangeness of existence, the pleasure of being caught up in the arms
of creation? I stood under the cathedral elms on Linwood Avenue
and looked at my arm: Why an arm, why a nose? Why *this* life? It
was as if my personality were lodged just slightly askew in my body,
and in the inevitable wriggle I made to settle them in correct regis-
ter, I came upon these epiphanies of strangeness. And experienced
this sensation of strangeness as pleasure. Nothing could be taken for
granted, nothing was automatic. Yet everything—from my arm that
bent in the middle with its small knob of elbow, to the elm's great
umbrella of leaves on their splinted branches above me—everything, everything was part of one inseparable thing. It was—It. And
It really existed, outside me and inside me. These two facts came
together, like cymbals crashing on a downbeat: they hushed me,
they gave me that first exquisite taste of silence which was also a
draught of awe. Call it surrender. But I always understood it to be
song.

I walked back along the brook trail to my room, fell on the
narrow bed, and slept past Noon Prayer. Didn't hear Bob bustling
out, didn't hear the bell. Slept out the hours I'd lost in the cold
night, slept out the lethargy, slept beyond prayers and good intentions, slept away the life I'd brought on my back. Woke hours later,
the natural way: from hunger. And went up to dinner, finally arrived
at this hidden place ravenous, my appetite intact.

Back to the garden then. Where it all began.

Thomas, the gardener Brother, was a man of few words. He didn't actually make an announcement that he needed help in the garden, but somehow the message was conveyed. If you showed up at the gate, a flimsy thing made of grayed wood and chicken wire near the hut where he kept his tools and his rudimentary greenhouse, he was grateful and always had something that needed doing.

After breakfast, that's where I went. The chicken-wire fence that enclosed the garden plot was covered with climbing roses, and there were fruit trees here and there, old and knobbed as those worker trees often are. Thomas was already busy in his shed, transplanting seedlings. He was small, but one of those little men who seem bred so thoroughly of hard labor that the smallness comes always as a surprise. He seemed not small but built sensibly close to the earth, his element. He was wiry and had the face of an elderly angel. Most of the time, except in chapel, he wore a navy watchman's cap.

His hands, cracked and built on a bigger scale than his slight frame, were wonderful to look at. He was missing his ring finger on the right hand, but it wasn't disfiguring. It suited him, as if to have both hands whole would, in his case, have been the deformity. A couple of other fingers on that hand were covered with Band-Aids, suggesting that he was often banged up.

They were hands I knew. The hands of the growers in St. Paul years ago, in the summers I worked at my father's greenhouse. Sometimes I was delegated to spend a whole morning inching my way down one row of flats and up another, pinching back geraniums. Charlie Metz, the greenhouse foreman, was a big man, but with these same hands, cracked and much wounded. His yellowed nails seemed made of horn. Hands I would know anywhere. And here they were.

Charlie had allowed me to keep the flowers I clipped, and I left the geranium house with bunches of salmon-colored or engine-red flowers I needed a wheelbarrow to cart away. But when I attempted to cram them into my father's Ford at the end of the day, he frowned. "Take those to the dump," he said. They were a limp mess by then, but I fought their fate. "All right, make yourself a bouquet," he said, "but ditch the rest." As I rolled the wheelbarrow to the dump, he called after me, "Three, five, seven," which was his artistic reminder: Every bouquet should be composed of odd numbers. I never questioned the logic of this law. Its rightness was obvious and profound; there was a slight off-kilter quality to life, something perhaps missing but not something mourned for. This imbalance was life's way. In art it was necessary to acknowledge it: three, five, seven.

Now Thomas loaned me a pair of big rubber boots and gave me a tour of his fenced garden. It was a big area, divided like a diminutive neighborhood of several toy blocks, running along streets that intersected, allowing for a place to kneel or crouch down to work on the slightly raised beds.

My assignment was a bed of onions, hardly sprouted. I took the bucket Thomas handed me for the weeds, and two burlap seed sacks to kneel on as I worked my way down the onion street. I had the place to myself, and the day was fresh. "Early is best," Thomas said, looking up and around, as if inspecting the day and finding he could approve. He turned and went back to the shed.

I knelt on the seed sacks and disappeared for three hours. That's how it was. My mind went to the roots. I disentangled, with more patience than I knew I possessed, the fragile onions, which were hardly distinguishable from the weeds. Sometimes I yanked up a few onions by accident. Then I crammed the white wiggles of rootlets back in the crumbly soil madly, as if burying a secret. But even at such a frantic moment, I was gone, absorbed, not thinking. As if I had been gathered into the very psalm of the day, not singing, but song:

> *You keep your pledge with wonders …*

> *You care for the earth, give it water;*
> *you fill it with riches.*
> *Your river in heaven brims over*
> *to provide it grain.*

You provide for the earth;
you drench its furrows;
you level it, soften it with showers;
you bless its growth.
You crown the year with your goodness.
Abundance flows in your steps;
in the pastures of the wilderness it flows.

The hills are girded with joy,
the meadows covered with flocks,
the valleys are decked with wheat.
They shout for joy, yes, they sing.

When the bell rang for Noon Prayer, I put the seed sacks away in the shed and left the big boots by Thomas's door. I walked up the brook path to the chapel, took my place next to Cecile, and stood in the softened light of that vaulted chamber. It was all one thing. We passed the day's Word between us on the immaculate trays of chant, me still on my knees with the onions, one choir bowing, offering, to the other.

Psalm 91

Whoso dwelleth in the shelter of the Most High and abideth under the shadow of the Almighty shall say unto the Lord: O my hope and my stronghold, my God, in whom I will trust.

For he shall deliver thee from the snare of the hunter and from the noisome pestilence. He shall cover thee under his wings that thou mayest be safe under his feathers. His faithfulness and truth shall be thy shield and buckler.

Thou shalt not need to be afraid for any bugs by night, nor for any arrow that flyeth by day, nor for the pestilence that creepeth in the darknesse, nor for the sicknesse that destroyeth in the noonday.

A thousand shall fall beside thee and ten thousand at thy right hand, but it shall not come nigh thee. Yea with thine eyes shalt thou behold and see the reward of the ungodly.

For the Lord is thy hope; thou hast set thy house of defense very high. There shall no evil happen unto thee, neither shall any plague come nigh thy dwelling. For he shall give his angels charge over thee, to keep thee in all thy ways. They shall bear thee in their hands, that thou hurt not thy foot against a stone. Thou shalt tread upon the lion and adder, the young lion and the dragon shalt thou tread under thy feet.

"Because you have set your love upon me, I shall deliver you. I shall defend you, for you have known my name. When you call upon me, I shall hear you. Yea, I am with you in your trouble, from out of it I will deliver you and bring you to honor. With long life will I satisfy you and show you my salvation."

ACKNOWLDGMENTS

While it may be true that too many cooks spoil the broth, the same cannot be said of an anthology. We are grateful for the many writers whose works we have included here and for the many hands that have lightened our load. Leslie Harkema, James Schmidt, and Melissa Van Til cheerfully scanned pages of texts; Chrissie Schinktanz joined them in the tedious but oh-so-necessary task of proofreading. Kathy Struck and Kathy De Mey, librarians extraordinaire, tracked down out-of-print books and exotic journal articles. Our colleagues in the English department at Calvin College, Jim Vanden Bosch and Bill Vande Kopple, wrote pieces especially for this volume.

The recipes for Dandelion Wine, Mixed Greens and Walnuts, Spicy Herb Dip, and Eggplant Spread were originally published by Old Fashioned Living (www.oldfashionedliving.com); they are reprinted by the kind permission of Brenda Hyde. The recipe for African Squash and Yams is reprinted by permission of Jennifer A. Wickes and may also be found at www.oldfashionedliving.com.

Barry Moser's vegetable drawings were originally printed in Nancy Wilkes Bubel, *The Adventurous Gardener* (Boston: David R. Godine, 1979), and are used by permission of Barry Moser.

We can never say "thank you" too often to our spouses, Anne Elizabeth Schmidt and Doug Felch, who share all our summers—

indeed all our seasons—and enrich them with love, laughter, and good humor.

Tada Chimako: "Late Summer" from *Like Underground Water: The Poetry of Mid-Twentieth Century Japan,* translated by Naoshi Koriyama and Edward Lueders. Copyright © 1995 by Naoshi Koriyama and Edward Lueders. Used with the permission of Copper Canyon Press, P.O. Box 271, Port Townsend, WA 98368-0271, www.coppercanyonpress.org

Robert Clark*:* Selections from *My Grandfather's House: A Genealogy of Doubt and Faith.* Copyright © 1999 by the author and reprinted by permission of St. Martin's Press, LLC.

Barbara Crooker: "Ephemera" and "Peony" were first published in *Perspectives: A Journal of Reformed Thought.* Copyright © 2004. Reprinted by permission of the author.

William Henry Davies: "When on a Summer's Morn" from *Georgian Poetry, 1913–1915,* edited by E. H. Marsh. Copyright © 1916. Public Domain.

Frederick Douglass: "What to the Slave Is the Fourth of July?" from *My Bondage and My Freedom.* Copyright © 1857. Public Domain.

Paul Laurence Dunbar: "In Summer" from *Complete Poems of Paul Laurence Dunbar.* Copyright © 1913. Public Domain.

Gretel Ehrlich: "From a Sheepherder's Notebook: Three Days" from *The Solace of Open Spaces* by Gretel Ehrlich. Copyright © 1985. Used by permission of Viking Penguin, a division of Penguin Group (USA) Inc..

Patricia Hampl: "Silence" from *Virgin Time* by Patricia Hampl. Copyright © 1992. Reprinted by permission of Farrar, Straus and Giroux.

Leslie Pinckney Hill: "Summer Magic" from *The Book of American Negro Poetry*, chosen and edited by James Weldon Johnson. Copyright © 1922. Public Domain.

Gerard Manley Hopkins: "As kingfishers catch fire" from *Poems of Gerard Manley Hopkins.* Copyright © 1918. Public Domain.

Barbara Hurd: "Refugium" from *Stirring the Mud: On Swamps, Bogs, and Human Imagination* by Barbara Hurd. Copyright © 2001 by Barbara Hurd. Reprinted by permission of Beacon Press, Boston.

Richard Jefferies: "Meadow Thoughts" from *Selected English Essays*, chosen and arranged by W. Peacock. Copyright © 1903. Public Domain.

Sarah Orne Jewett: "The Backward View" from *The Country of the Pointed Firs* by Sarah Orne Jewett. Copyright © 1896. Public Domain.

Jamaica Kincaid: "The Circling Hand" from *Annie John* by Jamaica Kincaid. Copyright © 1985. Reprinted by permission of Farrar, Straus and Giroux.

Anne Lamott: "Altar" from *Traveling Mercies: Some Thoughts on Faith* by Anne Lamott. Copyright © 1999 by Anne Lamott. Used by permission of Pantheon Books, a division of Random House, Inc.

Madeleine L'Engle: Selections from *The Summer of the Great-Grandmother*. Copyright ©1974. Reprinted by permission of Farrar, Straus and Giroux.

Denise Levertov: "Living" from *Poems, 1960–1967*. Copyright © 1966 by Denise Levertov. Reprinted by permission of New Directions Publishing Corp.

Li-Bai: "In the Mountains on a Summer Day," from *More Translations from the Chinese*, edited and translated by Arthur Waley. Copyright © 1919. Public Domain.

Irving Yucheng Lo: "Summer" by Cheung Hsieh, translated by Irving Yucheng Lo from *Sunflower Splendor: Three Thousand Years of Chinese Poetry* edited by Wu-chi Lui and Irving Yucheng Lo. Copyright © 1975. Reprinted by permission of Irving Yucheng Lo.

Thomas Lynch: "The Oak Grove Imbroglio" from *Bodies in Motion and at Rest: On Metaphor and Mortality* by Thomas Lynch. Copyright © 2000 by Thomas Lynch. Used by permission of W. W. Norton & Company, Inc.

Dorothea Mackellar: "In a Southern Garden" from *The Oxford Book of Australasian Verse*, edited by Walter Murdoch. Copyright © 1918. Public Domain.

N. Scott Momaday: Introduction from *The Way to Rainy Mountain* by N. Scott Momaday. Copyright © 1969. Reprinted by permission of University of New Mexico Press.

Michael Pollan: "Weeds Are Us" from *Second Nature: A Gardener's Education*. Copyright © 1991 by Michael Pollan. Used by permission of Grove/Atlantic, Inc.

Lee Robinson: "The Garden," from *Hearsay* by Lee Robinson. Copyright © 2004. Reprinted by permission of the author.

Carl Sandburg: "Good-night," "Silver Wind," and "Summer Stars," from *Smoke and Steel* by Carl Sandburg. Copyright © 1920. "Village in Late Summer" from *Cornhuskers* by Carl Sandburg. Copyright © 1918. "Mask" and "On the Breakwater" from *Chicago Poems* by Carl Sandburg. Copyright © 1916. Public Domain.

Siegfried Sassoon: "Butterflies" and "Idyll" from *Picture-Show* by Siegfried Sassoon. Copyright © 1920. Public Domain.

Richard Selzer: "Toenails," from *Letters to a Young Doctor* by Richard Selzer. Copyright © 1987, 2001 by Richard Selzer. Reprinted by permission of George Borchardt, Inc., on behalf of the author.

Luci Shaw: "Raspberries" and "Summer road remembered" from *Polishing the Petoskey Stone* by Luci Shaw. Copyright © 1990. Reprinted by permission of the author.

Elinore Pruitt Stewart: "A Busy, Happy Summer" from *Letters of a Woman Homesteader*. Copyright © 1914. Public Domain.

Celia Thaxter: Selections from *Among the Isles of Shoals*. Copyright © 1873. Public Domain.

Barbara Tuchman: From *Practicing History* by Barbara Tuchman. Copyright © 1981 by Barbara W. Tuchman. Used by permission of Alfred A. Knopf, a division of Random House, Inc.

William Vande Kopple: "Bright Hope." Copyright © 2004. Reprinted by permission of the author.

Ronna N. Welsh: "Camp Food." Copyright © 1999. Reprinted by permission of the author.

Walt Whitman: Selections from *Specimen Days* from *Complete Prose Works* by Walt Whitman. Copyright © 1892. Public Domain.

NOTES

Preface

"Sumer is Icumen In" is a thirteen-century lyric. It is printed on a plaque that today is hung on the ruins of Reading Abbey; the original manuscript is housed in the British Library. The Middle English lyric, whose accompanying music survives, is found in virtually all anthologies of medieval lyrics; this translation is by the editors, and mirrors common transcriptions. Li-Bai's "In the Mountains on a Summer Day" is collected and translated by Arthur Waley in *More Translations from the Chinese* (New York: Alfred A. Knopf, 1919), 29. William Shakespeare's sonnet #12 was first published in Thomas Thorpe's 1609 edition of *Shakespeare's Sonnets*; this version is modernized by the editors. William Henry Davies's poem "When on a Summer's Morn" may be found in *Georgian Poetry, 1913–1915*, edited by Edward Hall Marsh (London: The Poetry Bookshop, 1915), 68.

Part One

Introduction: Hobbinoll's speech comes from the first eight lines of Edmund Spenser's "June," from *The Shepheardes Calender* (London: Hugh Singleton, 1579), folio 23.

The prayers that begin each section were written by James Vanden Bosch and are original to this volume.

The opening scene from *Dandelion Wine* was written by Ray Bradbury (New York: Doubleday, 1957). This selection is taken from the Avon edition, pages 1–3.

Ronna N. Welsh's "Camp Food" was first published in *The Austin Chronicle*, vol. 18, issue 45 (9 July 1999).

Scott Cairns's "Accepting Blood" was first published in *The Theology of Doubt* (Cleveland OH: Cleveland State University Poetry Center, 1985); "Yellow" was first published in *The Translation of Babel* (Athens: University of Georgia Press, 1990). Both poems are taken from Scott Cairns, *Philokalia: new and selected poems* (Lincoln, NE: Zoo Press, 2002), 55; 71.

The selections from Jamaica Kincaid's "The Circling Hand" come from the second chapter of *Annie John* (New York: Farrar, Straus, and Giroux), 13–19.

G. K. Chesterton's "A Piece of Chalk" first appeared in the *Daily News* and was later published in *Tremendous Trifles* (New York: Dodd, Mead, and Co., 1913), 8–16.

Richard Jefferies's "Meadow Thoughts" was first included in *The Life in the Fields* (Chatto and Windus, 1884) and was reprinted in *Selected English Essays,* chosen and arranged by W. Peacock, from which this selection is taken (London: Oxford University Press, 1903), 524–529.

T'ao Ch'ien's "Reading *The Book of Hills and Seas*" is translated by Arthur Waley and is included in his *One Hundred and Seventy Chinese Poems* (London: Constable and Col., 1918), 59. This translation is slightly altered by the editors.

Anne Lamott's "Altar" is from *Traveling Mercies: Some Thoughts on Faith* (New York: Pantheon, 1999), 266–272.

Psalm 99 (100) is taken from the first complete Bible printed in English, Miles Coverdale's edition published in 1535; spelling is modernized by the editors. The Coverdale version follows the Latin Vulgate and the Greek Septuagint in its numbering of the Psalms (here 99); Protestant Bible and Hebrew numbering is in parentheses.

Part Two

Introduction: *Laddie: A True Blue Story* by Gene Stratton-Porter was published by Grosset and Dunlap in 1913; the poem is cited on page 408. The quotation from Lauren F. Winner is taken from her book *Mudhouse Sabbath* (Brewster, MA: Paraclete Press, 2003), 15. Alice Meynell's reflections come from "The Colour of Life" in *The Colour of Life and Other Essays on Things Seen and Heard* (London: John Lane, 1896), 4–5. Po Chüi's "Lazy

Man's Song" is collected and translated by Arthur Waley in *More Transla-tions from the Chinese* (New York: Alfred A. Knopf, 1919), 51.

The prayers that begin each section were written by James Vanden Bosch and are original to this volume.

Cheung Hsieh's *"Summer"* is translated by Irving Yucheng Lo and is part of *A Four-season Song on the Hardships and Joys of Farming Life*. This song cycle is collected in *Sunflower Splendor: Three Thousand Years of Chinese Poetry* edited by Wu-chi Lui and Irving Yucheng Lo and (Bloomington: Indiana University Press, 1975), 488–489. Paul Laurence Dunbar's "In Summer" was collected in the *Complete Poems of Paul Laurence Dunbar* (New York: Dodd and Mead, 1913), 144–145.

Elinore Pruitt Stewart first published her homesteading letters in *The Atlantic Monthly*. "A Busy, Happy Summer" is taken from *Letters of a Woman Homesteader*, edited by Elinore Pruitt Stewart (Boston and New York: Houghton Mifflin, 1914), 15–21.

Gretel Ehrlich's "From a Sheepherder's Notebook: Three Days" is taken from *The Solace of Open Spaces* (New York: Penguin, 1985), 54–61.

Sherman Alexie's poem "The Summer of Black Widows" is also the title of his collection, *The Summer of Black Widows* (New York: Hanging Loose Press, 1996), 12–13.

Michael Pollan's "Weeds Are Us" is chapter six of *Second Nature: A Gardener's Education* (New York: Grove Press, 1991), 98–101, 102–105, 116.

Barbara Crooker's "Peony" was first published in *Perspectives: A Journal of Reformed Thought* (June/July 2004), 20. Lee Robinson's "The Garden" was first published in *Yemassee* (University of South Carolina) and may be found in her collection of poems, *Hearsay* (New York: Fordham University Press, 2004), 16. Dorothea Mackellar's "In a Southern Garden" is included in *The Oxford Book of Australasian Verse*, chosen by Walter Murdoch (London: Humphrey Milford, Oxford University Press, 1918), 279–80.

Richard Selzer's "Toenails" is from his *Letters to a Young Doctor* (Orlando: Harcourt and Brace, 1982), 64–69.

Psalm 64 (65), verses 5–13, is adapted from Miles Coverdale's 1535 edition of the English Bible. The Coverdale version follows the Latin Vul-gate and the Greek Septuagint in its numbering of the Psalms; Protestant Bible and Hebrew numbering is in parentheses.

Part Three

Introduction: John Milton's "L'Allegro" is a companion piece to his cele-bration of Melancholy, "Il Penseroso"; both were first published in his collected *Poems of Mr. John Milton both English and Latin* (London: Ruth Raworth for Humphrey Moseley, 1645). The quoted lines are ll. 63–68, 95–98, 117–118, and 125–130. "River Village" by Du Fu was translated by Tony Barnstone and Chou Ping and is included in *Literatures of Asia, Africa, and Latin America* (Upper Saddle Ridge, NJ: Prentice Hall, 1999), 265. The descriptions of New Portland, Maine, and Lebanon, New Hampshire, are taken from John Hayward's *New England Gazetteer* (Concord, NH: Israel S. Boyd and William White, 1939) [Unpaged].

The prayers that begin each section were written by James Vanden Bosch and are original to this volume.

Thomas Lynch's "The Oak Grove Imbroglio" is taken from *Bodies in Motion and at Rest: On Metaphor and Mortality* (New York: W. W. Norton, 2000), 237–243.

"Bright Hope" by William Vande Kopple is original to this volume.

Carl Sandburg's "Mask" and "On the Breakwater" were published in *Chicago Poems* (New York: Henry Holt and Company, 1916), 125; 124. His "Village in Late Summer" was first published in *Cornhuskers* (New York: Henry Holt and Company, 1918), 20. His "Silver Wind," "Summer Stars," and "Good-night" were first published in *Smoke and Steel* (New York: Harcourt, Brace and Howe, 1920), 117, 120, 61.

The Declaration of Independence is transcribed from the document held by the United States National Archives: http://www.archives.gov/national_archives_experience/charters/declaration_transcript.html

Frederick Douglass's "What to the Slave Is the Fourth of July?" was first delivered on July 5, 1852, at a meeting sponsored by the Rochester Ladies' Anti-Slavery Society. It was published as a pamphlet and then reprinted in *My Bondage and My Freedom* by Frederick Douglass, with an introduction by Dr. James M'Cune Smith (New York and Auburn: Miller, Orton, & Co., 1857), 441–445.

Barbara Tuchman's "On Our Birthday—America as Idea" was first published on July 12, 1976, in *Newsweek* magazine as a bicentennial salute. It is taken here from *Practicing History* by Barbara Tuchman (New York: Alfred A. Knopf, 1981), 304–306.

"Summer" by Donald Hall is taken from *Seasons at Eagle Pond* (New York: Ticknor & Fields, 1987), 43–65.

Psalm 132 (133) is adapted from Miles Coverdale's 1535 edition of the English Bible. The Coverdale version follows the Latin Vulgate and the Greek Septuagint in its numbering of the Psalms; Protestant Bible and Hebrew numbering is in parentheses.

Part Four

Introduction: The quotation from Joseph Wood Krutch is from "August," in *The Twelve Seasons: A Perpetual Calendar for the Country* (New York: William Morrow, 1949), 65, 67. Andrew Marvell's "To His Coy Mistress" was first printed posthumously by his wife, Mary, in *Miscellaneous Poems by Andrew Marvell* (London: Robert Boulter, 1681), 20–21. The adaptation of the biblical psalm is from Psalm 8:4. The Vedic hymn to the dawn is taken from Viscount Amberley, *An Analysis of Religious Belief* (New York: D. M. Bennett, 1877), 435. The quotation from John Donne is taken from a sermon preached on August 25, 1622; it is here printed from *The Oxford Authors: John Donne*, ed. John Carey (Oxford: Oxford University Press, 1990), 314–315. "As kingfishers catch fire" by Gerard Manley Hopkins was published posthumously in *Poems of Gerard Manley Hopkins* (London: Humphrey Milford, 1918), 54. The quotation from the "Preacher" is taken from Ecclesiastes 3:11.

The prayers that begin each section were written by James Vanden Bosch and are original to this volume.

Luci Shaw's poems "Raspberries" and "Summer road remembered" were first published in *The Reformed Journal* and were reprinted in *Polishing the Petoskey Stone* (Wheaton, IL: Harold Shaw, 1990), 21, 241.

Walt Whitman's *Specimen Days* was published in *Complete Prose Works* (Philadelphia: David McKay, 1892), 81, 83, 87, 102, 112–113.

"Butterflies" and "Idyll" by Siegfried Sassoon are collected in his book, *Picture-Show* (New York: E. P. Dutton, 1920), 33, 37. Denise Levertov's "Living" was published in *Poems, 1960–1967* (New York: New Directions, 1983), 240. Barbara Crooker's "Ephemera" was first published in *Perspectives: A Journal of Reformed Thought* (June/July 2004), 20. Tada Chimako's "Late Summer" is translated by Naoshi Koriyama and Edward Lueders and included in their collection *Like Underground Water: The Poetry of Mid-Twentieth Century Japan* (Port Townsend, WA: Copper Canyon Press, 1995), 160. "Sun" by Ibn Abi I-Haytham is translated by Willis Barnstone and included in the collection *Literature of Asia, Africa, and Latin America*, edited by Willis Barnstone and Tony Barnstone (Upper Saddle Ridge, NJ: Prentice Hall, 1999), 1050–1051.

Celia Thaxter's *Among the Isles of Shoals* was first published in 1873 by J. R. Osgood and Company of Boston. The selections reprinted here are taken from the 1901 edition (Boston: Houghton, Mifflin, 1901), 123–132.

Psalm 103 (104), verses 1, 10–24, 27–28, is adapted from Miles Coverdale's 1535 edition of the English Bible. The Coverdale version follows the Latin Vulgate and the Greek Septuagint in its numbering of the Psalms; Protestant Bible and Hebrew numbering is in parentheses.

Part Five

Introduction: The story of Jacob's wrestling with the angel is found in Genesis 32:22–32. Toru Dutt published only one volume of verse, *A Sheaf Gleaned in French Fields*, before she died in 1877 at the age of twenty-one. These four lines are taken from "Miscellaneous Poems by Toru Dutt" in Epiphanius Wilson, ed., *Hindu Literature*, revised edition (New York: P. F. Collier & Son, 1900). The excerpt from Mary Sidney Herbert's paraphrase of Psalm 51 is taken from the first printed edition of the psalm poems she wrote with her brother, Sir Philip Sidney: *The Psalmes of David*, ed. S. W. Singer (London: Chiswick Press, 1823), 90. The phrase "a certain holy vacation" is found in Alexander Nowell's *A Catechisme*, translated by Thomas Norton (London: John Day, 1571), 31; the words of the prophet are from Isaiah 58:13. The citation from Nan Fink is from *Stranger in the Midst* (New York: Basic Books, 1997) as quoted in Lauren F. Winner, *Mudhouse Sabbath* (Brewster, MA: Paraclete Press, 2003), 1. "As imperceptibly as grief" is the first line of a poem by Emily Dickinson and may be found in *Poems by Emily Dickinson*, edited by two of her friends, T. W. Higginson and Mabel Loomis Todd, second series (Boston: Roberts Brothers, 1892), 168.

The prayers that begin each section were written by James Vanden Bosch and are original to this volume.

Barbara Hurd's "Refugium" is Chapter 6 from *Stirring the Mud: On Swamps, Bogs, and Human Imagination* (Boston and New York: Houghton Mifflin, 2003), 45–49; 54–57; 60–63.

Charles C. Abbott's "A Fence-rail Fancy" is taken from *In Nature's Realm* (Trenton, NJ: Albert Brandt, 1900), 182–190.

Sarah Orne Jewett's "The Backward View" was first published as Chapter 21 of *The Country of the Pointed Firs* (Boston and New York: Houghton Mifflin, 1896), 207–208.

The selections from Robert Clark come from his *My Grandfather's House: A Genealogy of Doubt and Faith* (New York: Picador, 1999), 250–262.

The selections are taken from the Introduction to N. Scott Momaday's *The Way to Rainy Mountain* (Albuquerque: The University of New Mexico Press, 1969), 5–12.

The selections from Madeleine L'Engle come from her book *The Summer of the Great-Grandmother* (New York: Farrar, Straus and Giroux, 1974), 73; 3; 17–20; 234–235.

Leslie Pinckney Hill's "Summer Magic" was included by James Weldon Johnson in his *The Book of American Negro Poetry* (New York: Harcourt, Brace and Company, 1922), 104. Wathen Marks Wilks Call's "Summer Days" was collected in *A Victorian Anthology, 1837–1895*, edited by Edmund Clarence Stedman (Boston and New York: Houghton Mifflin, 1906), 152-153. Kenneth Slade Alling's "Summer Night" was first published in *The Measure* (October 1921) and was reprinted in the *Anthology of Magazine Verse for 1922 and Yearbook of American Poetry*, edited by William Stanley Braithwaite (Boston: Small, Maynard, and Co., 1923), 3.

Patricia Hampl's "Silence" is taken from *Virgin Time* (New York: Farrar, Straus and Giroux, 1992), 185–188; 201–203; 209–212.

Psalm 90 (91) is adapted from Miles Coverdale's 1535 edition of the English Bible. The Coverdale version follows the Latin Vulgate and the Greek Septuagint in its numbering of the Psalms; Protestant Bible and Hebrew numbering is in parentheses.

Global Spiritual Perspectives

Spiritual Perspectives on America's Role as Superpower
by the Editors at SkyLight Paths

Are we the world's good neighbor or a global bully? Explores broader issues surrounding the use of American power around the world, including in Iraq and the Middle East. From a spiritual perspective, what are America's responsibilities as the only remaining superpower? Contributors:

Dr. Beatrice Bruteau • Rev. Dr. Joan Brown Campbell • Tony Campolo • Rev. Forrest Church • Lama Surya Das • Matthew Fox • Kabir Helminski • Thich Nhat Hanh • Eboo Patel • Abbot M. Basil Pennington, ocso • Dennis Prager • Rosemary Radford Ruether • Wayne Teasdale • Rev. William McD. Tully • Rabbi Arthur Waskow • John Wilson

5½ x 8½, 256 pp, Quality PB, ISBN 1-893361-81-0 **$16.95**

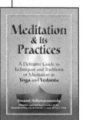

Spiritual Perspectives on Globalization, 2nd Edition
Making Sense of Economic and Cultural Upheaval
by Ira Rifkin; Foreword by Dr. David Little, Harvard Divinity School

What is globalization? What are spiritually minded people saying and doing about it? This lucid introduction surveys the religious landscape, explaining in clear and nonjudgmental language the beliefs that motivate spiritual leaders, activists, theologians, academics, and others involved on all sides of the issue. This edition includes a new Afterword and Discussion Guide designed for group use.

5½ x 8½, 256 pp, Quality PB, ISBN 1-59473-045-8 **$16.99**

Hinduism / Vedanta

Meditation & Its Practices: A Definitive Guide to Techniques and Traditions of Meditation in Yoga and Vedanta
by Swami Adiswarananda

The complete sourcebook for exploring Hinduism's two most time-honored traditions of meditation. Drawing on both classic and contemporary sources, this comprehensive sourcebook outlines the scientific, psychological, and spiritual elements of Yoga and Vedanta meditation.

6 x 9, 504 pp, HC, ISBN 1-893361-83-7 **$34.95**

Sri Sarada Devi: Her Teachings and Conversations
Translated and with Notes by Swami Nikhilananda
Edited and with an Introduction by Swami Adiswarananda

Brings to life the Holy Mother's teachings on human affliction, self-control, and peace in ways both personal and profound, and illuminates her role as the power, scripture, joy, and guiding spirit of the Ramakrishna Order.

6 x 9, 288 pp, HC, ISBN 1-59473-070-9 **$29.99**

The Vedanta Way to Peace and Happiness
by Swami Adiswarananda

Using language that is accessible to people of all faiths and backgrounds, this book introduces the timeless teachings of Vedanta—divinity of the individual soul, unity of all existence, and oneness with the Divine—ancient wisdom as relevant to human happiness today as it was thousands of years ago.

6 x 9, 240 pp, HC, ISBN 1-59473-034-2 **$29.99**

Or phone, mail or e-mail to: SKYLIGHT PATHS Publishing
An imprint of Turner Publishing Company
4507 Charlotte Avenue • Suite 100 • Nashville, Tennessee 37209
Tel: (615) 255-2665 • www.skylightpaths.com
Prices subject to change.

Children's Spirituality—Board Books

How Did the Animals Help God? (A Board Book)
by Nancy Sohn Swartz, Full-color illus. by Melanie Hall
Abridged from Nancy Sohn Swartz's *In Our Image*, God asks all of nature to offer gifts to humankind—with a promise that they will care for creation in return.
5 x 5, 24 pp, Board Book, Full-color illus., ISBN 1-59473-044-X **$7.99** *For ages 0–4*

Where Is God? (A Board Book)
by Lawrence and Karen Kushner; Full-color illus. by Dawn W. Majewski
A gentle way for young children to explore how God is with us every day, in every way. Abridged from *Because Nothing Looks Like God* by Lawrence and Karen Kushner. 5 x 5, 24 pp, Board, Full-color illus., ISBN 1-893361-17-9 **$7.95** *For ages 0–4*

What Does God Look Like? (A Board Book)
by Lawrence and Karen Kushner; Full-color illus. by Dawn W. Majewski
A simple way for young children to explore the ways that we "see" God. Abridged from *Because Nothing Looks Like God* by Lawrence and Karen Kushner.
5 x 5, 24 pp, Board, Full-color illus., ISBN 1-893361-23-3 **$7.95** *For ages 0–4*

How Does God Make Things Happen? (A Board Book)
by Lawrence and Karen Kushner; Full-color illus. by Dawn W. Majewski
A charming invitation for young children to explore how God makes things happen in our world. Abridged from *Because Nothing Looks Like God* by Lawrence and Karen Kushner. 5 x 5, 24 pp, Board, Full-color illus., ISBN 1-893361-24-1 **$7.95** *For ages 0–4*

What Is God's Name? (A Board Book)
by Sandy Eisenberg Sasso; Full-color illus. by Phoebe Stone
Everyone and everything in the world has a name. What is God's name? Abridged from the award-winning *In God's Name* by Sandy Eisenberg Sasso.
5 x 5, 24 pp, Board, Full-color illus., ISBN 1-893361-10-1 **$7.99** *For ages 0–4*

What You Will See Inside ...

This important new series of books is designed to show children ages 6–10 the Who, What, When, Where, Why and How of traditional houses of worship, liturgical celebrations, and rituals of different world faiths, empowering them to respect and understand their own religious traditions—and those of their friends and neighbors.

What You Will See Inside a Catholic Church
by Reverend Michael Keane; Foreword by Robert J. Keeley, Ed.D.
Full-color photographs by Aaron Pepis
A colorful, fun-to-read introduction to the traditions of Catholic worship and faith. Visually explains the common use of the altar, processional cross, baptismal font, votive candles, and more. 8½ x 10½, 32 pp, HC, ISBN 1-893361-54-3 **$17.95**

Also available in Spanish: **Lo que se puede ver dentro de una iglesia católica**
8½ x 10½, 32 pp, Full-color photos, HC, ISBN 1-893361-66-7 **$16.95**

What You Will See Inside a Mosque
by Aisha Karen Khan; Photographs by Aaron Pepis
Featuring full-page pictures and concise descriptions of what is happening, the objects used, the spiritual leaders and laypeople who have specific roles, and the spiritual intent of the believers. Demystifies the celebrations and ceremonies of Islam throughout the year.
8½ x 10½, 32 pp, Full-color photos, HC, ISBN 1-893361-60-8 **$16.95**

What You Will See Inside a Synagogue
by Rabbi Lawrence A. Hoffman and Dr. Ron Wolfson; Full-color photos by Bill Aron
A colorful, fun-to-read introduction that explains the ways and whys of Jewish worship and religious life. Full-page photos; concise but informative descriptions of the objects used, the clergy and laypeople who have specific roles, and much more.
8½ x 10½, 32 pp, Full-color photos, HC, ISBN 1-59473-012-1 **$17.99**

Children's Spiritual Biography

Ten Amazing People
And How They Changed the World
by Maura D. Shaw; Foreword by Dr. Robert Coles
Full-color illus. by Stephen Marchesi

For ages 7 & up

Black Elk • Dorothy Day • Malcolm X • Mahatma Gandhi • Martin Luther King, Jr. • Mother Teresa • Janusz Korczak • Desmond Tutu • Thich Nhat Hanh • Albert Schweitzer

This vivid, inspirational, and authoritative book will open new possibilities for children by telling the stories of how ten of the past century's greatest leaders changed the world in important ways.

8½ x 11, 48 pp, HC, Full-color illus., ISBN 1-893361-47-0 **$17.95** *For ages 7 & up*

Spiritual Biographies for Young People—For ages 7 and up

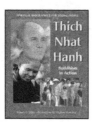 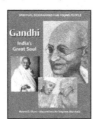 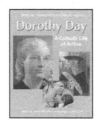 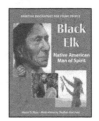

Black Elk: Native American Man of Spirit
by Maura D. Shaw; Full-color illus. by Stephen Marchesi
Through historically accurate illustrations and photos, inspiring age-appropriate activities, and Black Elk's own words, this colorful biography introduces children to a remarkable person who ensured that the traditions and beliefs of his people would not be forgotten.
6¾ x 8¾, 32 pp, HC, Full-color illus., ISBN 1-59473-043-1 **$12.99**

Dorothy Day: A Catholic Life of Action
by Maura D. Shaw; Full-color illus. by Stephen Marchesi
Introduces children to one of the most inspiring women of the twentieth century, a down-to-earth spiritual leader who saw the presence of God in every person she met. Includes practical activities, a timeline, and a list of important words to know.
6¾ x 8¾, 32 pp, HC, Full-color illus., ISBN 1-59473-011-3 **$12.99**

Gandhi: India's Great Soul
by Maura D. Shaw; Full-color illus. by Stephen Marchesi
There are a number of biographies of Gandhi written for young readers, but this is the only one that balances a simple text with illustrations, photographs, and activities that encourage children and adults to talk about how to make changes happen without violence. Introduces children to important concepts of freedom, equality, and justice among people of all backgrounds and religions.
6¾ x 8¾, 32 pp, HC, Full-color illus., ISBN 1-893361-91-8 **$12.95**

Thich Nhat Hanh: Buddhism in Action
by Maura D. Shaw; Full-color illus. by Stephen Marchesi
Warm illustrations, photos, age-appropriate activities, and Thich Nhat Hanh's own poems introduce a great man to children in a way they can understand and enjoy. Includes a list of important Buddhist words to know.
6¾ x 8¾, 32 pp, HC, Full-color illus., ISBN 1-893361-87-X **$12.95**

Midrash Fiction

Daughters of the Desert: Tales of Remarkable Women from Christian, Jewish, and Muslim Traditions   *by Claire Rudolf Murphy, Meghan Nuttall Sayres, Mary Cronk Farrell, Sarah Conover, and Betsy Wharton*
Breathes new life into the old tales of our female ancestors in faith. Uses traditional scriptural passages as starting points, then with vivid detail fills in historical context and place. Chapters reveal the voices of Sarah, Hagar, Huldah, Esther, Salome, Mary Magdalene, Lydia, Khadija, Fatima, and many more. Historical fiction ideal for readers of all ages.
5½ x 8¼, 192 pp, Quality PB, ISBN 1-59473-106-3 **$14.99**; HC, ISBN 1-893361-72-1 **$19.95**

The Triumph of Eve & Other Subversive Bible Tales
by Matt Biers-Ariel
Many people were taught and remember only a one-dimensional Bible. These engaging retellings are the antidote to this—they're witty, often hilarious, always profound, and invite you to grapple with questions and issues that are often hidden in the original text.
5½ x 8¼, 192 pp, HC, ISBN 1-59473-040-7 **$19.99**

Religious Etiquette / Reference

How to Be a Perfect Stranger, 3rd Edition: The Essential Religious Etiquette Handbook   *Edited by Stuart M. Matlins and Arthur J. Magida*
The indispensable guidebook to help the well-meaning guest when visiting other people's religious ceremonies. A straightforward guide to the rituals and celebrations of the major religions and denominations in the United States and Canada from the perspective of an interested guest of any other faith, based on information obtained from authorities of each religion. Belongs in every living room, library, and office. Covers:
African American Methodist Churches • Assemblies of God • Baha'i • Baptist • Buddhist • Christian Church (Disciples of Christ) • Christian Science (Church of Christ, Scientist) • Churches of Christ • Episcopalian and Anglican • Hindu • Islam • Jehovah's Witnesses • Jewish • Lutheran • Mennonite/Amish • Methodist • Mormon (Church of Jesus Christ of Latter-day Saints) • Native American/First Nations • Orthodox Churches • Pentecostal Church of God • Presbyterian • Quaker (Religious Society of Friends) • Reformed Church in America/Canada • Roman Catholic • Seventh-day Adventist • Sikh • Unitarian Universalist • United Church of Canada • United Church of Christ
6 x 9, 432 pp, Quality PB, ISBN 1-893361-67-5 **$19.95**

The Perfect Stranger's Guide to Funerals and Grieving Practices: A Guide to Etiquette in Other People's Religious Ceremonies   *Edited by Stuart M. Matlins*
6 x 9, 240 pp, Quality PB, ISBN 1-893361-20-9 **$16.95**

The Perfect Stranger's Guide to Wedding Ceremonies: A Guide to Etiquette in Other People's Religious Ceremonies   *Edited by Stuart M. Matlins*
6 x 9, 208 pp, Quality PB, ISBN 1-893361-19-5 **$16.95**

Sacred Texts—SkyLight Illuminations Series
Andrew Harvey, series editor

Offers today's spiritual seeker an enjoyable entry into the great classic texts of the world's spiritual traditions. Each classic is presented in an accessible translation, with facing pages of guided commentary from experts, giving you the keys you need to understand the history, context, and meaning of the text. This series enables readers of all backgrounds to experience and understand classic spiritual texts directly, and to make them a part of their lives. Andrew Harvey writes the foreword to each volume, an insightful, personal introduction to each classic.

Bhagavad Gita
Annotated & Explained
Translation by Shri Purohit Swami; Annotation by Kendra Crossen Burroughs

"The very best Gita for first-time readers." —Ken Wilber. Millions of people turn daily to India's most beloved holy book, whose universal appeal has made it popular with non-Hindus and Hindus alike. This edition introduces you to the characters, explains references and philosophical terms, shares the interpretations of famous spiritual leaders and scholars, and more.
5½ x 8½, 192 pp, Quality PB, ISBN 1-893361-28-4 **$16.95**

Dhammapada
Annotated & Explained
Translation by Max Müller and revised by Jack Maguire; Annotation by Jack Maguire

The Dhammapada—believed to have been spoken by the Buddha himself over 2,500 years ago—contain most of Buddhism's central teachings. This timeless text concisely and inspirationally portrays the route a person travels as he or she advances toward enlightenment and describes the fundamental role of mental conditioning in making us who we are.
5½ x 8½, 160 pp, b/w photographs, Quality PB, ISBN 1-893361-42-X **$14.95**

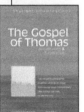

The Gospel of Thomas
Annotated & Explained
Translation and annotation by Stevan Davies

Discovered in 1945, this collection of aphoristic sayings sheds new light on the origins of Christianity and the intriguing figure of Jesus, portraying the Kingdom of God as a present fact about the world, rather than a future promise or future threat.
5½ x 8½, 192 pp, Quality PB, ISBN 1-893361-45-4 **$16.95**

Hasidic Tales
Annotated & Explained
Translation and annotation by Rabbi Rami Shapiro

Introduces the legendary tales of the impassioned Hasidic rabbis, which demonstrate the spiritual power of unabashed joy, offer lessons for leading a holy life, and remind us that the Divine can be found in the everyday.
5½ x 8½, 240 pp, Quality PB, ISBN 1-893361-86-1 **$16.95**

The Hebrew Prophets
Selections Annotated & Explained
Translation and annotation by Rabbi Rami Shapiro

Focuses on the central themes covered by all the Hebrew prophets: moving from ignorance to wisdom, injustice to justice, cruelty to compassion, and despair to joy, and challenges us to engage in justice, kindness, and humility in every aspect of our lives.
5½ x 8½, 224 pp, Quality PB, ISBN 1-59473-037-7 **$16.99**

Sacred Texts—SkyLight Illuminations Series

Andrew Harvey, series editor

The Hidden Gospel of Matthew: Annotated & Explained
Translation and annotation by Ron Miller
Takes you deep into the text cherished around the world to discover the words and events that have the strongest connection to the historical Jesus. Reveals the underlying story of Matthew, a story that transcends the traditional theme of an atoning death and focuses instead on Jesus's radical call for personal transformation and social change.
5½ x 8½, 272 pp, Quality PB, ISBN 1-59473-038-5 **$16.99**

The Secret Book of John
The Gnostic Gospel—Annotated & Explained
Translation and annotation by Stevan Davies
Introduces the most significant and influential text of the ancient Gnostic religion. This central myth of Gnosticism tells the story of how God fell from perfect Oneness to imprisonment in the material world, and how by knowing our divine nature and our divine origins—that we are one with God—we reverse God's descent and find our salvation.
5½ x 8½, 208 pp, Quality PB, ISBN 1-59473-082-2 **$16.99**

Rumi and Islam: Selections from His Stories, Poems, and
Discourses—Annotated & Explained
Translation and annotation by Ibrahim Gamard
Offers a new way of thinking about Rumi's poetry. Focuses on Rumi's place within the Sufi tradition of Islam, providing insight into the mystical side of the religion—one that has love of God at its core and sublime wisdom teachings as its pathways.
5½ x 8½, 240 pp, Quality PB, ISBN 1-59473-002-4 **$15.99**

Selections from the Gospel of Sri Ramakrishna
Annotated & Explained
Translation by Swami Nikhilananda; Annotation by Kendra Crossen Burroughs
The words of India's greatest example of God-consciousness and mystical ecstasy in recent history. Introduces the fascinating world of the Indian mystic and the universal appeal of his message that has inspired millions of devotees for more than a century.
5½ x 8½, 240 pp, b/w photographs, Quality PB, ISBN 1-893361-46-2 **$16.95**

The Way of a Pilgrim: Annotated & Explained
Translation and annotation by Gleb Pokrovsky
This classic of Russian spirituality is the delightful account of one man who sets out to learn the prayer of the heart—also known as the "Jesus prayer"—and how the practice transforms his life.
5½ x 8½, 160 pp, Illus., Quality PB, ISBN 1-893361-31-4 **$14.95**

Zohar: Annotated & Explained
Translation and annotation by Daniel C. Matt
The best-selling author of *The Essential Kabbalah* brings together in one place the most important teachings of the Zohar, the canonical text of Jewish mystical tradition. Guides you step by step through the midrash, mystical fantasy, and Hebrew scripture that make up the Zohar, explaining the inner meanings in facing-page commentary.
5½ x 8½, 176 pp, Quality PB, ISBN 1-893361-51-9 **$15.99**

Kabbalah from Jewish Lights Publishing

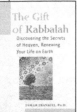

Ehyeh: A Kabbalah for Tomorrow *by Dr. Arthur Green*
6 x 9, 224 pp, Quality PB, ISBN 1-58023-213-2 **$16.99**; HC, ISBN 1-58023-125-X **$21.95**

The Enneagram and Kabbalah: Reading Your Soul *by Rabbi Howard A. Addison*
6 x 9, 176 pp, Quality PB, ISBN 1-58023-001-6 **$15.95**

Finding Joy: A Practical Spiritual Guide to Happiness *by Dannel I. Schwartz with Mark Hass*
6 x 9, 192 pp, Quality PB, ISBN 1-58023-009-1 **$14.95**; HC, ISBN 1-879045-53-2 **$19.95**

The Gift of Kabbalah: Discovering the Secrets of Heaven, Renewing Your Life on Earth
by Tamar Frankiel, Ph.D.
6 x 9, 256 pp, Quality PB, ISBN 1-58023-141-1 **$16.95**; HC, ISBN 1-58023-108-X **$21.95**

Zohar: Annotated & Explained
Translation and annotation by Dr. Daniel C. Matt. Foreword by Andrew Harvey
5½ x 8½, 160 pp, Quality PB, ISBN 1-893361-51-9 **$15.99**

Meditation / Prayer

Prayers to an Evolutionary God
by William Cleary; Afterword by Diarmuid O'Murchu

How is it possible to pray when God is dislocated from heaven, dispersed all around us, and more of a creative force than an all-knowing father? Inspired by the spiritual and scientific teachings of Diarmuid O'Murchu and Teilhard de Chardin, Cleary reveals that religion and science can be combined to create an expanding view of the universe—an evolutionary faith.
6 x 9, 208 pp, HC, ISBN 1-59473-006-7 **$21.99**

The Song of Songs: A Spiritual Commentary
by M. Basil Pennington, OCSO; Illustrations by Phillip Ratner

Join M. Basil Pennington as he ruminates on the Bible's most challenging mystical text. You will follow a path into the Songs that weaves through his inspired words and the evocative drawings of Jewish artist Phillip Ratner—a path that reveals your own humanity and leads to the deepest delight of your soul.
6 x 9, 160 pp, HC, 14 b/w illus., ISBN 1-59473-004-0 **$19.99**

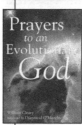

Women of Color Pray: Voices of Strength, Faith, Healing,
Hope, and Courage   *Edited and with Introductions by Christal M. Jackson*

Through these prayers, poetry, lyrics, meditations and affirmations, you will share in the strong and undeniable connection women of color share with God. It will challenge you to explore new ways of prayerful expression.
5 x 7¼, 240 pp, Quality PB, ISBN 1-59473-077-6 **$15.99**

The Art of Public Prayer, 2nd Edition: Not for Clergy Only
by Lawrence A. Hoffman   6 x 9, 288 pp, Quality PB, ISBN 1-893361-06-3 **$18.95**

Finding Grace at the Center: The Beginning of Centering Prayer
by M. Basil Pennington, ocso, Thomas Keating, ocso, and Thomas E. Clarke, SJ
5 x 7¼, 112 pp, HC, ISBN 1-893361-69-1 **$14.95**

A Heart of Stillness: A Complete Guide to Learning the Art of Meditation
by David A. Cooper   5½ x 8½, 272 pp, Quality PB, ISBN 1-893361-03-9 **$16.95**

Meditation without Gurus: A Guide to the Heart of Practice
by Clark Strand   5½ x 8½, 192 pp, Quality PB, ISBN 1-893361-93-4 **$16.95**

Praying with Our Hands: Twenty-One Practices of Embodied Prayer from the
World's Spiritual Traditions   *by Jon M. Sweeney; Photographs by Jennifer J. Wilson; Foreword by Mother Tessa Bielecki; Afterword by Taitetsu Unno, PhD*
8 x 8, 96 pp, 22 duotone photographs, Quality PB, ISBN 1-893361-16-0 **$16.95**

Silence, Simplicity & Solitude: A Complete Guide to Spiritual Retreat at Home
by David A. Cooper   5½ x 8½, 336 pp, Quality PB, ISBN 1-893361-04-7 **$16.95**

Three Gates to Meditation Practice: A Personal Journey into Sufism, Buddhism,
and Judaism   *by David A. Cooper*   5½ x 8½, 240 pp, Quality PB, ISBN 1-893361-22-5 **$16.95**

Women Pray: Voices through the Ages, from Many Faiths, Cultures, and Traditions
Edited and with introductions by Monica Furlong
5 x 7¼, 256 pp, Quality PB, ISBN 1-59473-071-7 **$15.99**;
Deluxe HC with ribbon marker, ISBN 1-893361-25-X **$19.95**

Spiritual Practice

Divining the Body
Reclaim the Holiness of Your Physical Self   *by Jan Phillips*
A practical and inspiring guidebook for connecting the body and soul in spiritual practice. Leads you into a milieu of reverence, mystery, and delight, helping you discover a redeemed sense of self.
8 x 8, 256 pp, Quality PB, ISBN 1-59473-080-6 **$16.99**

Finding Time for the Timeless
Spirituality in the Workweek   *by John McQuiston II*
Simple, refreshing stories that provide you with examples of how you can refocus and enrich your daily life using prayer or meditation, ritual, and other forms of spiritual practice.   5½ x 6½, 208 pp, HC, ISBN 1-59473-035-0 **$17.99**

The Gospel of Thomas: A Guidebook for Spiritual Practice
by Ron Miller; Translations by Stevan Davies
An innovative guide to bring a new spiritual classic into daily life. Offers a way to translate the wisdom of the Gospel of Thomas into daily practice, manifesting in your life the same consciousness revealed in Jesus of Nazareth. Written for readers of all religious backgrounds, this guidebook will help you to apply Jesus's wisdom to your own life and to the world around you.
6 x 9, 160 pp, Quality PB, ISBN 1-59473-047-4 **$14.99**

The Knitting Way: A Guide to Spiritual Self-Discovery
by Linda Skolnik and Janice MacDaniels
Through sharing stories, hands-on explorations, and daily cultivation, Skolnik and MacDaniels help you see beyond the surface of a simple craft in order to discover ways in which nuances of knitting can apply to the larger scheme of life and spirituality. Includes original knitting patterns.
7 x 9, 240 pp, Quality PB, ISBN 1-59473-079-2 **$16.99**

Earth, Water, Fire, and Air: Essential Ways of Connecting to Spirit
by Cait Johnson   6 x 9, 224 pp, HC, ISBN 1-893361-65-9 **$19.95**

Forty Days to Begin a Spiritual Life
Today's Most Inspiring Teachers Help You on Your Way
Edited by Maura Shaw and the Editors at SkyLight Paths; Foreword by Dan Wakefield
7 x 9, 144 pp, Quality PB, ISBN 1-893361-48-9 **$16.95**

Labyrinths from the Outside In
Walking to Spiritual Insight—A Beginner's Guide
by Donna Schaper and Carole Ann Camp
6 x 9, 208 pp, b/w illus. and photographs, Quality PB, ISBN 1-893361-18-7 **$16.95**

Practicing the Sacred Art of Listening: A Guide to Enrich Your Relationships
and Kindle Your Spiritual Life—The Listening Center Workshop
by Kay Lindahl   8 x 8, 176 pp, Quality PB, ISBN 1-893361-85-3 **$16.95**

The Sacred Art of Bowing: Preparing to Practice
by Andi Young   5½ x 8½, 128 pp, b/w illus., Quality PB, ISBN 1-893361-82-9 **$14.95**

The Sacred Art of Chant: Preparing to Practice
by Ana Hernandez   5½ x 8½, 192 pp, Quality PB, ISBN 1-59473-036-9 **$15.99**

The Sacred Art of Fasting: Preparing to Practice
by Thomas Ryan, CSP   5½ x 8½, 192 pp, Quality PB, ISBN 1-59473-078-4 **$15.99**

The Sacred Art of Listening: Forty Reflections for Cultivating a Spiritual Practice
by Kay Lindahl; Illustrations by Amy Schnapper
8 x 8, 160 pp, Illus., Quality PB, ISBN 1-893361-44-6 **$16.99**

Sacred Speech: A Practical Guide for Keeping Spirit in Your Speech
by Rev. Donna Schaper   6 x 9, 176 pp, Quality PB, ISBN 1-59473-068-7 **$15.99**;
HC, ISBN 1-893361-74-8 **$21.95**

Spiritual Poetry—The Mystic Poets

Experience these mystic poets as you never have before. Each beautiful, compact book includes: A brief introduction to the poet's time and place; a summary of the major themes of the poet's mysticism and religious tradition; essential selections from the poet's most important works; and an appreciative preface by a contemporary spiritual writer.

 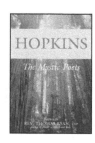  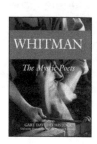

Hafiz: The Mystic Poets
Preface by Ibrahim Gamard
Hafiz is known throughout the world as Persia's greatest poet, with sales of his poems in Iran today only surpassed by those of the Qur'an itself. His probing and joyful verse speaks to people from all backgrounds who long to taste and feel divine love and experience harmony with all living things.
5 x 7¼, 144 pp, HC, ISBN 1-59473-009-1 **$16.99**

Hopkins: The Mystic Poets
Preface by Rev. Thomas Ryan, CSP
Gerard Manley Hopkins, Christian mystical poet, is beloved for his use of fresh language and startling metaphors to describe the world around him. Although his verse is lovely, beneath the surface lies a searching soul, wrestling with and yearning for God.
5 x 7¼, 112 pp, HC, ISBN 1-59473-010-5 **$16.99**

Tagore: The Mystic Poets
Preface by Swami Adiswarananda
Rabindranath Tagore is often considered the "Shakespeare" of modern India. A great mystic, Tagore was the teacher of W. B. Yeats and Robert Frost, the close friend of Albert Einstein and Mahatma Gandhi, and the winner of the Nobel Prize for Literature. This beautiful sampling of Tagore's two most important works, *The Gardener* and *Gitanjali,* offers a glimpse into his spiritual vision that has inspired people around the world.
5 x 7¼, 144 pp, HC, ISBN 1-59473-008-3 **$16.99**

Whitman: The Mystic Poets
Preface by Gary David Comstock
Walt Whitman was the most innovative and influential poet of the nineteenth century. This beautiful sampling of Whitman's most important poetry from *Leaves of Grass*, and selections from his prose writings, offers a glimpse into the spiritual side of his most radical themes—love for country, love for others, and love of Self.
5 x 7¼, 192 pp, HC, ISBN 1-59473-041-5 **$16.99**

Spiritual Biography—SkyLight Lives

SkyLight Lives reintroduces the lives and works of key spiritual figures of our time—people who by their teaching or example have challenged our assumptions about spirituality and have caused us to look at it in new ways.

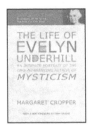   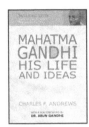

The Life of Evelyn Underhill
An Intimate Portrait of the Groundbreaking Author of *Mysticism*
by Margaret Cropper; Foreword by Dana Greene
Evelyn Underhill was a passionate writer and teacher who wrote elegantly on mysticism, worship, and devotional life. This is the story of how she made her way toward spiritual maturity, from her early days of agnosticism to the years when her influence was felt throughout the world.
6 x 9, 288 pp, 5 b/w photos, Quality PB, ISBN 1-893361-70-5 **$18.95**

Mahatma Gandhi: His Life and Ideas
by Charles F. Andrews; Foreword by Dr. Arun Gandhi
Examines from a contemporary Christian activist's point of view the religious ideas and political dynamics that influenced the birth of the peaceful resistance movement, the primary tool that Gandhi and the people of his homeland would use to gain India its freedom from British rule.
6 x 9, 336 pp, 5 b/w photos, Quality PB, ISBN 1-893361-89-6 **$18.95**

Simone Weil: A Modern Pilgrimage
by Robert Coles
The extraordinary life of the spiritual philosopher who's been called both saint and madwoman. Robert Coles' intriguing study of Weil is an insightful portrait of the beloved and controversial thinker whose life and writings influenced many (from T. S. Eliot to Adrienne Rich to Albert Camus), and continue to inspire seekers everywhere.
6 x 9, 208 pp, Quality PB, ISBN 1-893361-34-9 **$16.95**

Zen Effects: The Life of Alan Watts
by Monica Furlong
Through his widely popular books and lectures, Alan Watts (1915–1973) did more to introduce Eastern philosophy and religion to Western minds than any figure before or since. Here is the first and only full-length biography of one of the most charismatic spiritual leaders of the twentieth century.
6 x 9, 264 pp, Quality PB, ISBN 1-893361-32-2 **$16.95**

More Spiritual Biography

Bede Griffiths: An Introduction to His Interspiritual Thought
by Wayne Teasdale 6 x 9, 288 pp, Quality PB, ISBN 1-893361-77-2 **$18.95**

Inspired Lives: Exploring the Role of Faith and Spirituality in the Lives of Extraordinary People
by Joanna Laufer and Kenneth S. Lewis 6 x 9, 256 pp, Quality PB, ISBN 1-893361-33-0 **$16.95**

Spiritual Innovators: Seventy-Five Extraordinary People Who Changed the World in
the Past Century *Edited by Ira Rifkin and the Editors at SkyLight Paths; Foreword by Robert Coles*
6 x 9, 304 pp, b/w photographs, Quality PB, ISBN 1-893361-50-0 **$16.95**; HC, ISBN 1-893361-43-8 **$24.95**

White Fire: A Portrait of Women Spiritual Leaders in America
by Rabbi Malka Drucker; Photographs by Gay Block
7 x 10, 320 pp, 30+ b/w photos, HC, ISBN 1-893361-64-0 **$24.95**

Spirituality

Prayer for People Who Think Too Much
A Guide to Everyday, Anywhere Prayer from the World's Faith Traditions   *by Mitch Finley*
5½ x 8½, 224 pp, Quality PB, ISBN 1-893361-21-7 **$16.95**; HC, ISBN 1-893361-00-4 **$21.95**

The Shaman's Quest: Journeys in an Ancient Spiritual Practice
by Nevill Drury; with a Basic Introduction to Shamanism by Tom Cowan
5½ x 8½, 208 pp, Quality PB, ISBN 1-893361-68-3 **$16.95**

Show Me Your Way: The Complete Guide to Exploring Interfaith Spiritual Direction
by Howard A. Addison   5½ x 8½, 240 pp, Quality PB, ISBN 1-893361-41-1 **$16.95**;
HC, ISBN 1-893361-12-8 **$21.95**

Spirituality 101: The Indispensable Guide to Keeping—or Finding—Your Spiritual Life
on Campus   *by Harriet L. Schwartz, with contributions from college students at nearly thirty cam-*
puses across the United States   6 x 9, 272 pp, Quality PB, ISBN 1-59473-000-8 **$16.99**

Spiritually Incorrect: Finding God in All the Wrong Places
by Dan Wakefield; Illus. by Marian DelVecchio
5½ x 8½, 192 pp, b/w illus., HC, ISBN 1-893361-88-8 **$21.95**

Spiritual Manifestos: Visions for Renewed Religious Life in America from Young
Spiritual Leaders of Many Faiths   *Edited by Niles Elliot Goldstein; Preface by Martin E. Marty*
6 x 9, 256 pp, HC, ISBN 1-893361-09-8 **$21.95**

A Walk with Four Spiritual Guides: Krishna, Buddha, Jesus, and Ramakrishna
by Andrew Harvey   5½ x 8½, 192 pp, 10 b/w photos & illus., HC, ISBN 1-893361-73-X **$21.95**

What Matters: Spiritual Nourishment for Head and Heart
by Frederick Franck   5 x 7¼, 144 pp, 50+ b/w illus., HC, ISBN 1-59473-013-X **$16.99**

Who Is My God?, 2nd Edition
An Innovative Guide to Finding Your Spiritual Identity
Created by the Editors at SkyLight Paths   6 x 9, 160 pp, Quality PB, ISBN 1-59473-014-8 **$15.99**

Spirituality—A Week Inside

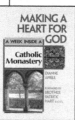

Come and Sit: A Week Inside Meditation Centers
by Marcia Z. Nelson; Foreword by Wayne Teasdale
The insider's guide to meditation in a variety of different spiritual traditions.
Traveling through Buddhist, Hindu, Christian, Jewish, and Sufi traditions, this essential guide takes you to different meditation centers to meet the teachers and students
and learn about the practices, demystifying the meditation experience.
6 x 9, 224 pp, b/w photographs, Quality PB, ISBN 1-893361-35-7 **$16.95**

Lighting the Lamp of Wisdom: A Week Inside a Yoga Ashram
by John Ittner; Foreword by Dr. David Frawley
This insider's guide to Hindu spiritual life takes you into a typical week of retreat inside
a yoga ashram to demystify the experience and show you what to expect from your own
visit. Includes a discussion of worship services, meditation and yoga classes, chanting
and music, work practice, and more.   6 x 9, 192 pp, b/w photographs, Quality PB, ISBN 1-
893361-52-7 **$15.95**; HC, ISBN 1-893361-37-3 **$24.95**

Making a Heart for God: A Week Inside a Catholic Monastery
by Dianne Aprile; Foreword by Brother Patrick Hart, ocso
This essential guide to experiencing life in a Catholic monastery takes you to the
Abbey of Gethsemani—the Trappist monastery in Kentucky that was home to
author Thomas Merton—to explore the details. "More balanced and informative
than the popular *The Cloister Walk* by Kathleen Norris." —*Choice: Current
Reviews for Academic Libraries*   6 x 9, 224 pp, b/w photographs, Quality PB, ISBN 1-893361-
49-7 **$16.95**; HC, ISBN 1-893361-14-4 **$21.95**

Waking Up: A Week Inside a Zen Monastery
by Jack Maguire; Foreword by John Daido Loori, Roshi
An essential guide to what it's like to spend a week inside a Zen Buddhist monastery.
6 x 9, 224 pp, b/w photographs, Quality PB, ISBN 1-893361-55-1 **$16.95**;
HC, ISBN 1-893361-13-6 **$21.95**

Spirituality

Autumn: A Spiritual Biography of the Season
Edited by Gary Schmidt and Susan M. Felch; Illustrations by Mary Azarian

Autumn is a season of fruition and harvest, of thanksgiving and celebration of abundance and goodness of the earth. But it is also a season that starkly and realistically encourages us to see the limitations of our time. Warm and poignant pieces by Wendell Berry, David James Duncan, Robert Frost, A. Bartlett Giamatti, Kimiko Hahn, P. D. James, Julian of Norwich, Garret Keizer, Tracy Kidder, Anne Lamott, May Sarton, and many others rejoice in autumn as a time of preparation and reflection. 6 x 9, 320 pp, 5 b/w illus., HC, ISBN 1-59473-005-9 **$22.99**

Awakening the Spirit, Inspiring the Soul
30 Stories of Interspiritual Discovery in the Community of Faiths
Edited by Brother Wayne Teasdale and Martha Howard, MD; Foreword by Joan Borysenko, PhD

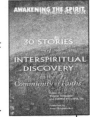

Thirty original spiritual mini-biographies that showcase the varied ways that people come to faith—and what that means—in today's multi-religious world. 6 x 9, 224 pp, HC, ISBN 1-59473-039-3 **$21.99**

Winter: A Spiritual Biography of the Season
Edited by Gary Schmidt and Susan M. Felch; Illustrations by Barry Moser

Delves into the varied feelings that winter conjures in us, calling up both the barrenness and the beauty of the natural world in wintertime. Includes selections by Will Campbell, Rachel Carson, Annie Dillard, Donald Hall, Ron Hansen, Jane Kenyon, Jamaica Kincaid, Barry Lopez, Kathleen Norris, John Updike, E. B. White, and many others. "This outstanding anthology features top-flight nature and spirituality writers on the fierce, inexorable season of winter.... Remarkably lively and warm, despite the icy subject." —*Publishers Weekly* Starred Review 6 x 9, 288 pp, 6 b/w illus., Deluxe PB w/flaps, ISBN 1-893361-92-6 **$18.95**; HC, ISBN 1-893361-53-5 **$21.95**

The Alphabet of Paradise: An A–Z of Spirituality for Everyday Life
by Howard Cooper 5 x 7¾, 224 pp, Quality PB, ISBN 1-893361-80-2 **$16.95**

Creating a Spiritual Retirement: A Guide to the Unseen Possibilities in Our Lives
by Molly Srode 6 x 9, 208 pp, b/w photos, Quality PB, ISBN 1-59473-050-42 **$14.99**; HC, ISBN 1-893361-75-6 **$19.95**

The Geography of Faith: Underground Conversations on Religious, Political and Social Change
by Daniel Berrigan and Robert Coles; Updated introduction and afterword by the authors 6 x 9, 224 pp, Quality PB, ISBN 1-893361-40-3 **$16.95**

God Lives in Glass: Reflections of God for Adults through the Eyes of Children
by Robert J. Landy, PhD; Foreword by Sandy Eisenberg Sasso 7 x 6, 64 pp, HC, Full-color illus., ISBN 1-893361-30-6 **$12.95**

God Within: Our Spiritual Future—As Told by Today's New Adults
Edited by Jon M. Sweeney and the Editors at SkyLight Paths 6 x 9, 176 pp, Quality PB, ISBN 1-893361-15-2 **$14.95**

Jewish Spirituality: A Brief Introduction for Christians
by Lawrence Kushner 5½ x 8½, 112 pp, Quality PB, ISBN 1-58023-150-0 **$12.95** (a Jewish Lights book)

A Jewish Understanding of the New Testament
by Rabbi Samuel Sandmel; New preface by Rabbi David Sandmel 5½ x 8½, 384 pp, Quality PB, ISBN 1-59473-048-2 **$19.99**

Journeys of Simplicity: Traveling Light with Thomas Merton, Basho, Edward Abbey, Annie Dillard & Others
by Philip Harnden 5 x 7¼, 128 pp, HC, ISBN 1-893361-76-4 **$16.95**

Keeping Spiritual Balance As We Grow Older: More than 65 Creative Ways to Use Purpose, Prayer, and the Power of Spirit to Build a Meaningful Retirement
by Molly and Bernie Srode 8 x 8, 224 pp, Quality PB, ISBN 1-59473-042-3 **$16.99**

The Monks of Mount Athos: A Western Monk's Extraordinary Spiritual Journey on Eastern Holy Ground
by M. Basil Pennington, ocso; Foreword by Archimandrite Dionysios 6 x 9, 256 pp, 10+ b/w line drawings, Quality PB, ISBN 1-893361-78-0 **$18.95**

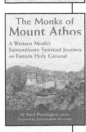

One God Clapping: The Spiritual Path of a Zen Rabbi
by Alan Lew with Sherril Jaffe 5½ x 8½, 336 pp, Quality PB, ISBN 1-58023-115-2 **$16.95** (a Jewish Lights book)

About SKYLIGHT PATHS Publishing

SkyLight Paths Publishing is creating a place where people of different spiritual traditions come together for challenge and inspiration, a place where we can help each other understand the mystery that lies at the heart of our existence.

Through spirituality, our religious beliefs are increasingly becoming a part of our lives—rather than *apart* from our lives. While many of us may be more interested than ever in spiritual growth, we may be less firmly planted in traditional religion. Yet, we do want to deepen our relationship to the sacred, to learn from our own as well as from other faith traditions, and to practice in new ways.

SkyLight Paths sees both believers and seekers as a community that increasingly transcends traditional boundaries of religion and denomination—people wanting to learn from each other, *walking together, finding the way.*

For your information and convenience, at the back of this book we have provided a list of other SkyLight Paths books you might find interesting and useful. They cover the following subjects:

Buddhism / Zen	Gnosticism	Mysticism
Catholicism	Hinduism /	Poetry
Children's Books	Vedanta	Prayer
Christianity	Inspiration	Religious Etiquette
Comparative	Islam / Sufism	Retirement
Religion	Judaism / Kabbalah /	Spiritual Biography
Current Events	Enneagram	Spiritual Direction
Earth-Based	Meditation	Spirituality
Spirituality	Midrash Fiction	Women's Interest
Global Spiritual	Monasticism	Worship
Perspectives		

9 781683 365778